"An excellent description of perfectionism and its self-sabotaging disadvantages. Presents many efficient and effective cognitive-behavioral methods for dealing with and minimizing this affliction. Quite practical and thorough—but nicely flexible and unperfectionistic!"

—Albert Ellis, Ph.D., President, Albert Ellis Institute, New York City; author of *A Guide to Rational Living*

"All of us know someone who is a perfectionist and most of us have joked about it at one time or another. For some it can be a useful trait that ensures some organization in a disorganized world. But for those individuals coping with too much perfectionism, it can be a curse that takes the pleasure out of life and in some cases can lead to severe anxiety disorders. Now two leading mental health practitioners and clinical scientists provide up to date, scientifically validated skills for overcoming perfectionism and regaining control of one's life. This long overdue book should relieve much suffering and enhance functioning for the millions of individuals dealing with excessive perfectionism."

—David H. Barlow, Ph.D., Professor of Psychology and Director of Center for Anxiety and Related Disorders, Boston University

"*When Perfect Isn't Good Enough* surpasses any of the other books on perfectionism in quality and scope. Drs. Antony and Swinson have synthesized what we know about perfectionism and used it to create the first well-integrated approach to reduce the suffering caused by it. The chapters clearly define perfectionism and provide concrete steps to master this demon. Final chapters focus on how perfectionism can manifest itself in other disorders, demonstrating how pernicious this phenomenon can be—and why such a book is so essential. This book will be invaluable to people suffering with perfectionism and to the therapists trying to help them."

—Randy O. Frost, Ph.D., Professor of Psychology, Smith College

"*When Perfect Isn't Good Enough* is an excellent source for people looking to adjust their standards and expectations, and by so doing, increase the joy in their lives. It is easy to read, filled with solid advice, and based on the best scientific research. Unlike most other self-help books, the many exercises suggested by the authors provide the reader with the tools to put these words into action. Drs. Antony and Swinson have produced a thorough and systematic manual to lead the perfectionist out of the misery of depression, anger, worry and social anxiety, and into the promised land of realistic self-evaluation, self-esteem and positive interpersonal relations. Bravo!"

—Richard Heimberg, Ph.D., Adult Anxiety Clinic, Department of Psychology, Temple University

When Perfect *Isn't* Good Enough

Strategies for Coping with Perfectionism

Martin M. Antony, Ph.D.,
& Richard P. Swinson, M.D.

New Harbinger Publications

Distributed in Canada by Raincoast Books.

Copyright © 1998 by Martin M. Antony, Ph.D. and Richard P. Swinson, M.D.
New Harbinger Publications, Inc.
5674 Shattuck Avenue
Oakland, CA 94609

Cover design by Lightbourne Images.
Edited by Angela Watrous.
Text design by Michele Waters.

Library of Congress Catalog Card Number: 98-66704
ISBN 1-57224-124-1 Paperback

New Harbinger Publications' Web site address: www.newharbinger.com

06   05   04

20   19   18   17   16   15   14   13   12   11

For Cynthia
　　—MMA

For Carolyn
　　—RPS

Contents

Part III
Working with Specific Problems and Perfectionism

Acknowledgments

The authors wish to thank the following people for reading various chapters and making detailed comments and suggestions: Terri Baker, Kirsten Blokland, Cynthia Crawford, Karyn Hood, Michelle Laliberté, Andrea Liss, Neil Pilkington, Christine Purdon, Laura Rocca, Deborah Roth, and Alex Shendelman. Also, we are grateful to the staff at New Harbinger Publications for their invitation to write this book and their support and help throughout the process of bringing the project to completion.

Introduction

The Purpose of This Book

When we first began to develop this book, we struggled to decide on the scope of the book. It was difficult to choose exactly which aspects of perfectionism to discuss, because the term "perfectionist" can be applied to many different types of people. Consider the following three examples:

> People who worked with director James Cameron on the blockbuster film *Titanic* often described him in interviews as being a perfectionist. They told stories of how he often lost his temper when things didn't go his way. In fact, Cameron's apparent temper, stemming from his insistence that his film crew meet his high standards, was the subject of many stories in the media around the time of the film's release.

> In her 1994 biography, *Movement Never Lies: An Autobiography*, Canadian ballet dancer Karen Kain described herself as a perfectionist. Although she had established herself as one of the most respected dancers in the world, she occasionally had bouts of depression, stemming from self-imposed standards that she felt she rarely met.

> The character Felix Unger from *The Odd Couple* (played by Tony Randall on television and Jack Lemmon on film) was considered by many people to be a perfectionist. This character insisted that everything be neat, clean, and tidy—greatly annoying his not-so-tidy housemate. When the apartment was the least bit messy, Felix became very anxious.

All three of these people might be described as perfectionists. However, they are very different in the way they express their perfectionism. In the first case, perfectionism is associated with anger; in the second case, perfectionism is associated with depression; in the third case, perfectionism is associated with anxiety, inflexibility, and a lack of spontaneity. Despite these differences, the people in each of these examples share an important quality. In each case, the person appears to have set standards or expectations for themselves or others that either cannot be met or can only be met at a great cost.

Perfectionism is often associated with certain psychological problems, including excessive anger, depression, social anxiety, body image problems, obsessive-compulsive behaviors, and worry. Although this is a book about perfectionism, it seemed inappropriate to consider writing a book on the topic without also addressing these other issues, which are so often associated with perfectionism. At the same time, it was impossible to write a book that could provide enough detail to help readers overcome any and all of these problems.

Therefore, in writing this book, we chose to focus on methods of dealing with perfectionistic thoughts and behaviors in general, as well as perfectionistic thoughts and behaviors that are associated with specific psychological problems. Part I of this book discusses general aspects of perfectionism, including the nature and impact of perfectionism and the role of thoughts and behaviors in maintaining perfectionism. Part II provides specific instructions on how to conduct a self-assessment of your perfectionism and how to use specific strategies to overcome perfectionistic thinking and related behaviors. Part III discusses the association between perfectionism and specific clinical syndromes (e.g., depression, social anxiety, etc.). These chapters will be helpful if you suffer from some of these psychological problems, as well as if you just experience mild or occasional symptoms that are associated with these problems. See Further Readings at the end of the book if you want more in-depth information about various topics covered in this book.

How to Use This Book

We recommend that you read all of the chapters in Parts I and II. In Part III, you may wish to select chapters that are most relevant to you and read them thoroughly. It can also be helpful to read the other chapters, as you may recognize issues that you were not aware you had.

Many of the chapters include exercises designed to change perfectionistic beliefs and behaviors. On its own, just *reading* this book is unlikely to lead to a dramatic reduction in your perfectionistic thoughts and behaviors. To see real changes, it will be important to actually use the strategies described. This book isn't a replacement for obtaining help from a qualified mental health professional, and you may wish to seek professional help for your perfectionism and associated problems. The chapters in Part III describe treatments that have been effective for the particular clinical problems that are sometimes related to perfectionism. In addition, chapter 6 includes ideas regarding how to find additional help if necessary.

How Not to Use This Book

A warning: Don't try to do everything in this book *perfectly*. We describe many more techniques, strategies, and ideas than you could possibly use effectively. It is best to choose a relatively small number of techniques and practice them until you can use them well. If you try to do everything that this book suggests, you probably won't benefit much from any of the strategies. Instead, pick and choose techniques that seem most relevant to your problem.

However, many of the strategies described in this book require repeated practice to be beneficial. If you find that a particular method is not working for you, you will need to decide whether to continue practicing that technique or to move on to another strategy. If a particular suggestion is not working for you, try not to react like a perfectionist. You don't need to become angry or depressed if it takes time to make noticeable changes. Giving yourself permission to fall short of meeting your high expectations while trying to overcome your perfectionism is a good first step toward learning to have more flexible and realistic expectations.

Part I

Understanding Perfectionism

Chapter 1

The Nature of Perfectionism

Most people are continually bombarded with demands to improve their performance. From the time you are born, you must endure being evaluated and corrected by different people in your lives. When you first learn to talk, your parents correct your pronunciation. When you are young, you are taught by others how to walk, dress yourself, hold your fork properly, refrain from putting your elbows on the table, wash behind your ears, and make your bed.

As you grow up, your behavior continues to be evaluated, criticized, corrected, and rewarded. In school and at home, you learn very quickly that in order to attain the approval of others, you must achieve specific standards. When you make mistakes, there are often practical negative consequences. For example, as a child, if your grades fell below a particular level, you may have been criticized by your teachers, parents, and friends. Sometimes, privileges (i.e., permission to talk on the telephone, go out with friends, or receive an allowance) are taken away until the level of performance is back where it should be.

The frequent demands to meet and surpass established standards continue into adulthood. Many companies and organizations expect employees to make continued efforts to improve the quality of their performance by accomplishing more in less time. Sales people might be expected to break the previous years' sales records. Companies continually strive to be more successful than their competitors.

In addition to pressures from the outside, many people feel pressure from within to succeed or perform at a certain level. When cooking a meal for friends, it feels good to have your guests enjoy their meal. When trying to maintain a level of physical fitness, you may feel a sense of personal satisfaction when you have reached some new goal, such as being able to run a mile in less time.

The desire to improve your performance or to meet high standards is not the same as being perfectionistic. It is this very desire to meet certain goals that often helps you perform effectively in your environment. For example, students who don't care about their performance in school probably don't study as hard and are likely to perform more poorly than students who have high personal standards. If this pattern of performance becomes habitual, there are generally consequences. Their grades are lower, and they may not be accepted into their preferred college or university. People at the top of their field, such as elite athletes, must also set high standards to achieve what they do. Without standards, people generally achieve less.

Definitions of Perfectionism

So, what is perfectionism, and how does it differ from a healthy desire to achieve high standards? As a starting point, let's consider a dictionary definition. The tenth edition of Merriam Webster's Collegiate Dictionary (1996) defines perfectionism as "a disposition to regard anything short of perfection as unacceptable." In contrast, professionals who study perfectionism tend to define the term in more detail. For example, in his article in *Psychology Today*, psychiatrist David Burns (1980b) defined perfectionists as people "whose standards are high beyond reach or reason" and "who strain compulsively and unremittingly toward impossible goals and who measure their own worth entirely in terms of productivity and accomplishment." Burns pointed out that for these individuals, the drive to do well can actually impair performance.

Multidimensional Definitions of Perfectionism

Recently, psychologists have begun to define perfectionism as a multidimensional concept. In other words, they have begun to view perfectionism as consisting of several different components or aspects. Canadian psychologists Paul Hewitt and Gordon Flett have published a number of papers (Hewitt and Flett 1990; 1991a, 1991b) based on their view that there are three main types of perfectionism:

self-oriented perfectionism, other-oriented perfectionism, and socially prescribed perfectionism.

Psychologist Randy Frost and his colleagues (Frost and Martin 1990; Frost et al. 1990) have also been influential with respect to increasing the understanding of the multidimensional aspects of perfectionism. However, unlike Hewitt and Flett, Frost and colleagues have six different dimensions in their definition of perfectionism: excessive concern over mistakes, high personal standards, doubts about actions, need for organization, high parental expectations, and excessive parental criticism.

Hewitt & Flett's Perfectionsism

Self-Oriented Perfectionism This is a tendency to have standards for yourself that are unrealistically high and impossible to attain. These standards are self-imposed and tend to be associated with self-criticism and an inability to accept your own mistakes and faults. When "self-oriented" perfectionism is combined with negative life events or perceived failure, it can lead to difficulties with depression.

Other-Oriented Perfectionism This is a tendency to demand that others meet your unrealistically high standards. People who are "other-oriented" perfectionists are often unable to delegate tasks to others, for fear of being disappointed by a less than perfect performance of the job. Other-oriented perfectionists may also have problems with excessive anger, relationship stress, and other difficulties related to their high expectations of others.

Socially Prescribed Perfectionism "Socially prescribed" perfectionists have an exaggerated belief that others have expectations of them that are impossible to meet. Furthermore, people who are socially prescribed perfectionists believe that in order to gain approval from others, these high standards must be met. Unlike self-oriented perfectionism, in which expectations are self-imposed, in socially prescribed perfectionism, the high standards are believed to be imposed by others. Socially prescribed perfectionism can lead to feelings of anger (at people who are perceived to have unrealistically high standards), depression (if high standards are not met), or social anxiety (fear of being judged by other people).

Frost and Colleagues' Perfectionism

Excessive Concern over Mistakes This is a tendency to believe that it is extremely important not to make mistakes and that making mistakes is the same as failure. Research in our own clinic and in other centers suggests that being excessively concerned about making mistakes is associated with elevated social anxiety and worry about being judged by other people (Antony et al. 1998; Juster et al. 1996). This dimension of perfectionism overlaps somewhat with what Hewitt and Flett described as "self-oriented perfectionism."

High Personal Standards This dimension reflects a tendency to set high expectations and standards for yourself and to believe that not meeting these standards is associated with being a second-rate person. Like excessive concern over mistakes, high personal standards is related to what Hewitt and Flett called "self-oriented perfectionism."

Doubts about Actions Doubting your actions in a perfectionist sense involves an exaggerated feeling that you have not completed tasks correctly. People who experience these doubts may take longer to get their work done and may feel a need to check things over and over or to repeat actions. Excessive doubts about actions are sometimes found in people who suffer from obsessive-compulsive disorder, a problem that is discussed in detail in later chapters. Like excessive concern over mistakes and high personal standards, doubts about actions are best thoughts of as a component of what Hewitt and Flett called "self-oriented perfectionism."

Need for Organization This is a tendency to be overly fussy and concerned about neatness, order, and organization. Although it is helpful to have good organizational skills, people who are overly concerned about organization can spend so much time organizing and maintaining order that they don't get other important things done. Also, when people are very rigid and inflexible about how things are done, it can lead to problems with other people who might have different ways of doing things.

High Parental Expectations This dimension is probably more useful as an explanation of the origins of perfectionism, rather than as a dimension of perfectionism per se. This dimension overlaps somewhat with what Hewitt and Flett call "socially prescribed perfectionism." For people who feel pressure from others to perform perfectly, parents can often be one source of this external pressure. People who are shy and socially anxious tend to report that their parents had overly high expectations of them.

High Parental Criticism

When parents are perceived as being overly critical when mistakes are made, it can lead to perfectionistic tendencies. Excessive parental criticism is very much related to high parental expectations, and the two often go hand in hand. You can imagine that parents who have unrealistic expectations may also be overly critical when their standards are not met. Like high parental expectations, parental criticism has been shown to be associated with social anxiety and worry about negative evaluation from others.

In summary, there are several different ways in which perfectionism is defined. Some researchers define perfectionism as a single concept or dimension. Others view perfectionism as consisting of several related dimensions. Regardless of which view is taken, most definitions appear to share several features that can be summarized as follows:

- People who are perfectionistic tend to have standards and expectations that are very difficult or impossible to meet.

- Although having high standards is often helpful, perfectionism is associated with having standards that are so high that they actually interfere with performance.

- Perfectionism is often associated with other problems, such as anxiety and depression.

Appropriately High Standards versus Perfectionistic Beliefs

Most people have strong opinions about how they should perform and about how certain things should be done. Although some standards are helpful, others standards may not be beneficial. Unfortunately, it is often difficult for each person to assess the accuracy of their own beliefs regarding standards, partly because most people assume that their beliefs are correct. For example, a person who has to speak in front of groups may have the belief: "It is important to do an excellent job." Is this a perfectionistic belief or just an appropriate belief that leads to improved performance in public speaking situations?

The appropriateness of a belief about standards for performance depends on several factors: the excessiveness of the standard (e.g., can this goal be met?), the accuracy of the belief (e.g., is it true that this standard must be met?), the costs and benefits of imposing the standard (e.g., does it help me to have the belief or standard?), and the flexibility of the standard or belief (e.g., am I able to adjust my standards and change my beliefs when necessary?).

Consider an example. Most people believe that it is important to wash regularly and to keep clean. Is this a perfectionistic belief or realistic high standard? Well, for most people, the standards for cleanliness are defined in a way that can be met with little effort, and, for most people, keeping clean has more benefits than costs. For example, with minimal effort, keeping clean makes it more likely that others will want to spend time with you. Finally, most people are also able to be flexible regarding their standards for cleanliness. Surgeons may raise the standard and wash their hands more carefully before doing surgery, while people who are camping in the wilderness may lower their standards and tolerate being less clean.

In contrast, an individual who has perfectionistic thoughts regarding cleanliness may have excessive beliefs that are inaccurate, inflexible, and cause more harm than good. For example, in our clinic, we see some individuals with obsessive-compulsive disorder who wash their hands hundreds of times each day, to the point where their hands are red and sore from scrubbing. This repetitive washing may be triggered by perfectionistic beliefs about avoiding contamination from germs, toxins, and other substances. However, this level of washing doesn't reduce the risk of becoming ill (compared to a more moderate amount of washing), and the person might actually be more at risk for infections (from cracking skin on their hands, etc.). For these individuals, the excessive frequency of washing often takes up hours each day and can interfere with all aspects of functioning, including work and social relationships.

This may seem like an extreme example of perfectionistic behavior. For more subtle perfectionistic beliefs and behaviors, it may be difficult to decide whether the reactions are excessive, but the same principles apply. You must first determine whether the beliefs and standards are excessive, accurate, helpful, and flexible. We will return to the issue of how to determine whether beliefs are excessively perfectionistic in later chapters.

The main point to consider here is that the more inflexible your beliefs are and the more situations in which you have inflexible opinions, the more likely you are to run into problems. This is particularly true in situations where your beliefs are arbitrary and subjective, rather than based on facts or hard evidence. For example, the belief that one should not drink and drive is consistent with statistics showing that more than half of automobile accidents involve alcohol. On the other hand, an inflexible belief that people should only listen to classical music and that all other types of music are inferior might cause problems if you are surrounded by other people who are not classical music lovers.

Perfectionism as a Personality Trait

One way of understanding perfectionism is to think of it as an example of a personality trait. Personality traits are stable characteristics that make people who they are. The term "stable" implies that personality traits affect your behavior across situations and over time. For years, psychologists have debated about the exact number of basic personality traits. Earlier, researchers tended to view personality as being comprised of many different personality traits. The exact number of traits differed from theory to theory, although in some cases, the number of traits specified was in the hundreds. These traits included such dimensions as perfectionism, happiness, honesty, aggressiveness, anxiety, creativity, ambition, and just about any other dimension imaginable.

More recently, many psychologists have come to believe that there are relatively few basic personality dimensions on which personality should be measured. One view of personality dimensions that has been supported by extensive research is that proposed by Robert McCrae and Paul Costa (1986, 1990), called the "Big Five Theory." According to this view, there are five main dimensions on which personality can be measured: neuroticism (the extent to which people are insecure and anxious versus the extent to which they are calm and secure), extraversion (the extent to which people are sociable and talkative versus the extent to which they are quiet and reserved), openness (the extent to which people are curious and imaginative versus the extent to which they are conventional and unimaginative), agreeableness (the extent to which people are good natured and trusting versus the extent to which they are rude, suspicious, and irritable), and conscientiousness (the extent to which people are organized, reliable, and scrupulous versus the extent to which they are unreliable and careless).

According to researchers who adhere to personality theories such as the Big Five model, the specific ways in which people fall on the five basic personality dimensions determine the precise personality composition that makes each person unique. This is similar to the way in which three primary colors (red, blue, and yellow) can be combined in different ways to produce all the different colors that we see.

A number of the big five dimensions may contribute to perfectionistic behavior. Excessive conscientiousness can lead a person to be overly concerned with organization, order, cleanliness, and following rules. Neuroticism may contribute to the anxiety and poor self-esteem that is sometimes seen in perfectionists. Not being open can make it difficult for perfectionistic individuals to view situations in new and flexible ways. Perfectionistic individuals who aren't very agreeable may also be harder on others who do not meet their high standards.

In addition to which dimensions make up the basic building blocks of personality, psychologists have also debated about the role of individuals versus their situations in determining their behavior. Some researchers have argued that stable personality traits determine people's behavior across a broad range of situations. Others have argued that personality traits are relatively unimportant and that people behave differently across situations. For example, people who are shy and withdrawn at work may be very comfortable when socializing with their friends.

Some investigators emphasize the ways in which stable traits interact with specific situations to produce a person's behavior. In other words, they believe that behavior is the result of a complex interaction of personality traits and the situations in which people find themselves. This is the approach that we will be taking in this book; although your perfectionistic beliefs and behaviors may cause problems across a range of situations and activities, the particular situation in which you find yourself probably affects the extent to which your perfectionism is an issue.

Areas Prone to Perfectionism

Perfectionism can affect a broad range of situations and activities. Below are some of the common areas in life in which unreasonably high standards can lead to problems.

Performance at Work or School

Some people tend to be particularly perfectionistic in their work, setting overly strict standards for their own performance or for the performance of their co-workers. For example, a construction worker who is very concerned about having every measure perfect may spend too much time measuring and re-measuring, only to find that jobs are never completed on time. Similarly, supervisors who have very strict standards regarding the time their staff should arrive at work may frequently become angry and frustrated when employees arrive for work a few minutes late. Finally, a student who believes that any grade that is less than an A is unacceptable may feel depressed for a week or more after receiving a B on a test or a paper.

Neatness and Aesthetics

People who are perfectionistic when it comes to neatness and cleaning often spend so much time cleaning that little time is left for other activities. Sometimes people can have very rigid beliefs about what looks good and may have difficulty allowing someone else to see things differently. Perfectionism can interfere with a person's ability to get along with roommates or partners who do not meet these standards for cleanliness or aesthetics. For example, individuals who believe that the house should be vacuumed twice daily may have difficulty convincing their housemates to share equally in the labor, especially if the housemates believe that vacuuming once every week or so is enough. Felix Unger, from *The Odd Couple*, is an example of an individual who is excessively perfectionistic with respect to cleanliness.

Organization and Ordering

Perfectionism can be associated with a need to have things organized or ordered in a particular way. For example, people who are perfectionistic in this way may feel a need to have all their clothes folded and stored in a particular order (e.g., according to color). Another individual who is overly concerned with organization may spend hours each day making and revising lists of things that need to be done.

Writing

Writing can be difficult for some people who are perfectionistic. For example, individuals who fear making mistakes when writing often take a long time to fill out forms, write letters, and complete other written work. Students who are perfectionistic sometimes have difficulty completing their papers on time, taking much more time than needed to get it written. Perfectionism can also lead to procrastination, so that the paper is not started early enough to get it done on time.

Speaking

People who have perfectionistic standards regarding speaking are often very self-conscious about how they speak and often worry about mispronouncing words or saying things incorrectly. Some perfectionists have overly rigid standards for others and feel compelled to correct other people when they perceive that a mistake has been made, no matter how trivial.

Physical Appearance

For some individuals, perfectionism is an issue particularly in the area of physical appearance. For example, eating disorders are associated with extremely perfectionistic standards about weight and body image (e.g., the belief that, "If I weigh above ninety pounds, I am fat"). Even people without eating disorders may hold these beliefs, to some degree. These perfectionistic beliefs may also exist for other aspects of one's appearance. For example, some men are overly concerned about hair loss, holding the belief that losing one's hair necessarily makes a person unattractive. Other people are perfectionistic about their clothing. For example, one person who was seen in our clinic spent hours getting dressed in the morning. She tended to try on many different outfits, searching for the one that looked "just right." As a result of this behavior, she was rarely on time for work.

People can also hold perfectionistic beliefs regarding the appearance of other individuals. Throughout the successful run of the television show *Seinfeld*, the character of Jerry Seinfeld was never able to find a perfect partner with whom to settle down. Many of the women he dated had something "wrong" with them from his perspective, including hands that were too big, a voice that was too low, and a laugh that he perceived as unattractive. If his standards had been more flexible, Jerry might have found the "right" partner before the show finally ended in the spring of 1998.

Health and Personal Cleanliness

Sometimes health can be the focus of perfectionistic behavior. Some people become very rigid about what they do, for fear of compromising their health. This may include being very particular about foods eaten (e.g., never eating anything containing fat), compulsively exercising, or avoiding computer screens and other devices that give off radiation. Health-obsessed perfectionists may visit doctors frequently to check out unusual symptoms or to have unnecessary medical tests administered. Perfectionism can also cause some people to wash themselves excessively or to avoid touching anything that might be viewed as contaminated (e.g., toilet seats, money, people's hands, etc.).

The Origins of Your Perfectionism

Where does perfectionism come from? Is it learned through your experiences? Is it genetically inherited, like eye or hair color? Very little research has been done in this area, so a definitive answer will have to await further study. Nevertheless, we can speculate regarding the causes of perfectionism based on what we know about the origins of other personality styles. It appears that both psychological factors (e.g., learning) and biological factors (e.g., genetics) probably contribute to the development of particular personality traits. This view has been supported by various studies examining the role of genetics and learning in the development of personality traits in general, and in the development of specific psychological problems, like depression and anxiety (Nurnberger and Cooper 1992; Kendler et al. 1992; Skre et al. 1993; Bouchard et al. 1990; Tellegen et al. 1988).

It is possible that biological and psychological factors both contribute to perfectionism in the same way as they do in other personality styles and in emotional difficulties that are often associated with perfectionism. For example, it is possible that the experience of being repeatedly criticized for making mistakes might lead to perfectionistic beliefs and behaviors in a person who is genetically predisposed or at risk for having excessively high standards.

Biological Influences

Over the past decade or two, numerous research studies have shown that genetics plays a role in the development of personality styles. One way scientists have been able to study this is by researching pairs of identical twins who have either been raised together or raised apart. Because identical twins are genetically identical, this method has allowed researchers to estimate separately the degree to which genetics and environment each contribute to various personality traits. Although there appear to be some differences across specific traits, on average, the contribution of genetics to personality seems to be about 40 percent, with the remaining 60 percent being due to other factors, such as learning and experience (Plomin, Chipuer, and Loehlin 1990).

If genetics does play a role in causing perfectionism, does that mean that perfectionism cannot be changed? Not at all. Genetics affects just about every aspect of who you are, including physical fitness, academic ability, depression, anxiety, and even your interests and hobbies. Yet exercise can have an enormous effect on fitness level. Likewise, specific types of psychological therapies can help people to overcome problems with anxiety and depression. So, while there may be a biological component to your perfectionism, you can still change the way you think or behave.

Psychological Influences

While it is impossible to know for sure why you are more perfectionistic than certain other people, it can be helpful to examine possible learning experiences that may have contributed to the problem. Identifying relevant learning experiences may help you gain insight into the problem. Several possible ways in which perfectionism can be learned include reward and reinforcement, punishment, modeling, and information and instruction. We will now consider each of these in turn. As each method of learning is reviewed, try to think back on your own experiences to identify whether these ways of learning have contributed to your own perfectionism.

Reward and Reinforcement

As discussed earlier, having high standards is often rewarded by society. For example, society reinforces your working hard at school. Doing well in high school generally leads to higher grades, praise from teachers and parents, and admission to better colleges and universities. Society also rewards physical attractiveness. Looking your best by dressing nicely and staying clean can result in others finding you more attractive, which can, in turn, improve your chances of attracting a romantic partner and finding certain types of work.

You may frequently hear stories of successful artists (i.e., actors, painters, and film directors) who are difficult to work with because they are perfectionists. Perhaps their perfectionism has been rewarded or reinforced by their success. Being rewarded for perfectionistic behavior may lead to the belief that if one isn't perfectionistic, one's work will be compromised and the final product will be inferior.

Exercise 1.1

How Reward and Reinforcement Have
Contributed to Your Perfectionism

Are there ways in which you have been rewarded for being a perfectionist? Try to recall situations from your past as well as from your current life. Think back to when you were in school—were you rewarded for being a perfectionist (e.g., did you do better in school when you set higher standards for yourself)? Think about your work—did you ever have a supervisor who was especially appreciative of the care and high standards that went into your job? What about when you were growing up at home—did your parents ever reward you with praise, gifts, or special privileges when you engaged in perfectionistic behavior? What about in your current life—do friends or family reinforce your perfectionistic behavior in subtle ways? As you recall ways in which you might have been rewarded or reinforced for perfectionistic behavior, record them in the spaces provided.

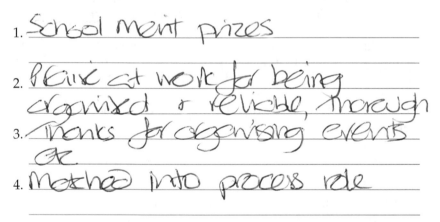

1. School merit prizes

2. Praise at work for being organised + reliable, thorough

3. Thanks for organising events etc.

4. Matched into process role

Punishment

A second type of learning experience that can affect an individual's behavior is punishment. Punishment involves receiving some sort of negative consequence following an unwanted behavior. The overall effect of punishment is often to decrease the frequency of the unwanted behavior. For example, a store clerk who often unintentionally gives customers too much change might be asked by the manager to make up the difference with their own money (the punishment) when the cash register is short at the end of a shift (the behavior). After having this happen a couple of times, the clerk is likely to learn to be more careful when giving out change and should make mistakes less frequently.

Is it possible that you have been punished at times for making mistakes or for behaving "imperfectly"? If so, this may have contributed to your perception that it is important for certain things to be done perfectly. Consider some examples of how criticism from others (a form of punishment) can contribute to perfectionism. A child who is often criticized for doing things improperly (e.g., making a mess at the bathroom sink, not making the bed properly, mispronouncing words) may learn that it is always important to do things correctly. A teacher who is very critical when children make mistakes in their schoolwork could instill an extreme desire to be perfect in children who are overly sensitive to criticism. Finally, individuals who are in a relationship with a person who is never pleased with their partner's behavior (e.g., clothing, hair style, cooking, etc.), can develop a belief that it is very important to meet certain standards in order to please others.

Criticism is only one form of punishment. Other forms of punishment may include receiving low grades on a test, being laughed at by one's peers, losing money, getting reprimanded at work, developing an illness (e.g., after eating food that has gone bad), or failing to be hired for a new job. In fact, any type of negative consequence that follows a behavior can be considered punishment. If individuals are punished excessively for making even small mistakes, they may be more likely to develop the rigid belief that it is very important not to make mistakes.

Exercise 1.2
How Punishment Has Contributed to Your Perfectionism

Can you recall times when you behaved in a particular way and were punished for your behavior? Did this tend to happen a lot when you were growing up? What about in your current life? Consider past and present situations at home, at school, and with friends. If you have frequently been punished for making mistakes, do some of these experiences appear to be responsible for triggering perfectionistic attitudes?

1. _Rows from Dad_
   eg for lying

2. *Criticism at work - email re*
employee)

3. *Punish myself for getting*
things wrong es cooking/baking

4. _____

Modeling

Observing the behavior of other people and attempting to do things similarly, also known as modeling, is an important way in which you learn how to behave yourself. Researchers have shown that people can develop specific fears by observing others who are afraid in particular situations (e.g., around snakes, in high places, etc.) (Antony and Barlow 1997). In the same way, teenagers who smoke cigarettes, drink alcohol, or use drugs may initially learn these behaviors from watching their peers use these substances. Finally, some researchers have demonstrated that there is a relationship between watching violence on television and engaging in violent behavior, and that observing violent behavior can lead to more violence (Friedrich-Coter and Huston 1986; Wood et al. 1991). All of these are examples of modeling.

If people can learn certain behaviors by observing the behavior of others, it is possible that perfectionistic behaviors can develop in the same way. Many people who describe themselves as overly perfectionistic report that they grew up around others who were overly perfectionistic. As a result, there were opportunities to develop perfectionistic beliefs and behaviors by observing other family members, especially parents and older siblings.

Exercise 1.3
How Modeling Has Contributed to Your Perfectionism

Did you grow up with other people who might be considered overly perfectionistic? If so, is it possible that modeling or observational learning contributed to your own perfectionistic attitudes? Can you think of ways in which your family members or other important people in your life are overly perfectionistic?

1. Mum & Dad - house, garage, garden very neat & tidy
2. Dad critical of others' mistakes
3. Mum critical of other people
4.

Information and Instruction

A fourth way in which people learn particular styles of behavior is through exposure to information through the media, talking to other people, or any other source of information. A good example of how information can contribute to exaggerated beliefs is the development and maintenance of flying phobias. Whenever there is a major airline crash, the media covers the story relentlessly. In addition to making the front page of every newspaper, the story is often covered in detail at the start of every television and radio newscast. At times, the coverage can continue for days, weeks, or even months, as investigations into the cause of the crash continue and new information becomes available. However, although it is always tragic when an airplane crashes, it is also a relatively rare occurrence. You hear about plane crashes every few months, but what you don't hear about is all the planes that take off and land safely. In fact, a recent estimate (reported on CNN) of the number of people who fly on airplanes per year in North America was 1.2 billion. Estimates of the number of planes that take off and land safely for every one plane that crashes are in the neighborhood of ten million. Clearly, flying is not dangerous in comparison to many of the things that everyone does each day (e.g., driving, walking on icy streets, smoking). Nevertheless, many people who fear flying report that the coverage of plane crashes in the media contributes to their fear. This is a clear example of how information, and the distortion of that information, can have a huge impact on a person's beliefs and behavior.

How can information contribute to perfectionism? Consider the following case example. One individual who was seen in our clinic reported intense anxiety over completing her college term papers perfectly. She wanted to be accepted into graduate school, so it was very important that her grades be high. She worked endlessly on each paper and had prepared many rough drafts for each one. However, she was not quite able to complete her work and hand in the papers, for fear that they would not be good enough. While exploring the origins of her perfectionistic behavior, it became clear that the client's parents may have had something to do with it. She was an only child and her parents had very high expectations for her. From a very young age, the client's parents had told her that they expected her to attend medical school at a top university and to eventually win the Nobel prize in medicine. No other career paths were possible for her. The client was not even sure whether she wanted to attend medical school, but she didn't see herself as having any choice. Her parents were supporting her financially and had made their expectations clear since she was a child. In addition, the client truly believed that anything less than near-perfect performance in school was unacceptable. Of course, the price she was paying for this belief was not being able to complete her papers and not doing well in her courses.

Another patient from our clinic reported that her perfectionistic beliefs about physical attractiveness were related to constantly being bombarded by extremely attractive people in advertising, movies, and magazines and catalogues. This particular individual had very perfectionistic beliefs about the importance of being thin, having perfect hair, and dressing immaculately. Not only were her beliefs unrealistic, but they were also unhealthy, leading her to maintain a weight level lower than that recommended for her height and frame. Apparently, for this individual, constantly being confronted with models and actors that she perceived as looking "perfect" provided her with an unreachable and unrealistic standard. Not surprisingly, eating disorders such as anorexia nervosa are particularly common among models, dancers, and other professions where there is intense pressure to be thin.

Exercise 1.4
How Exposure to Information Has Contributed to Your Perfectionism

Being told repeatedly by parents, teachers, or partners, or even by society in general, that it is important that things are done in a particular way, or that it is essential that mistakes are not made, can contribute to perfectionism. Can you think of ways in which you were exposed to certain types of information or instruction that contributed to your perfectionistic beliefs and behaviors?

1. Boss an overcare very critical, controlling
2. employee work had to be perfect
3. SA return perfect
4. _____

Why Isn't Everyone Perfectionistic?

The four types of learning experiences—reward and reinforcement, punishment, modeling, and information and instruction—are common to most people. Most people are occasionally rewarded for having high standards, punished at times for making mistakes, exposed to others who are perfectionistic, and instructed to strive for high standards and to try not to make mistakes. If these types of experiences are universal and are in part responsible for causing perfectionistic behavior, why isn't everyone overly perfectionistic? The answer to that question is complex.

Human behavior is caused by many different factors—not just learning experiences. Consider the development of a dog phobia. Research by Dr. Peter Di Nardo and his colleagues (1988) has shown that about 50 percent of people who fear dogs report that they have been bitten by a dog in the past. In many of these individuals, the experience of having been bitten by the dog contributed to the fear. However, about 50 percent of people without dog phobias also reported having been bitten by dogs. So, although being bitten by a dog led to phobias in some people, it appears that many people did not develop fear after being bitten. So, the interesting question is: Why do some people develop fears following a negative learning experience, whereas other people do not? The same question can be asked regarding fears of flying. Although information in the media regarding plane crashes may contribute to fears of flying for some individuals, it is clearly not a problem for others. Most people are able to fly comfortably, even after reading about a horrific plane crash. Again, the question to ask is: Why do some people develop fears of flying upon repeated exposure to information about plane crashes, whereas others do not?

More importantly, in terms of this book, you might ask: Why do some people develop perfectionistic beliefs and behaviors following relevant learning experiences, whereas other people do not? We still don't have the answer to this question. Although we know that learning experiences affect different people in different ways, we do not know why this is the case or how to predict the effects of a given experience on any one person. It is possible that some people are more vulnerable to responding to these experiences in negative ways. In the case of perfectionism, some people are less vulnerable to learning perfectionistic habits; perhaps this is because of their genetic makeup, or perhaps it is due to a history of additional learning experiences that counteract the effects of experiences that might otherwise have triggered perfectionistic beliefs. In any case, it seems clear that learning experiences are only partly responsible for perfectionistic attitudes. Furthermore, for some individuals, the role of specific learning experiences may be quite minimal.

What If You Can't Recall Any Specific Learning Experiences?

It's not a problem if you can't recall any specific experiences that may have contributed to your perfectionistic beliefs or behaviors. Although some people find it helpful to have an understanding of where their perfectionism may have come from, this understanding is not necessary in changing perfectionistic ways of thinking and doing things. In fact, the factors that may have initially caused you to become perfectionistic in certain situations may not be the same factors that maintain current perfectionistic thinking.

Who Is to Blame for Your Perfectionism?

Throughout this section, we have described negative experiences that may have contributed to your perfectionism. In many cases, the examples and illustrations may seem to imply that criticism from others (e.g., parents, teachers, etc.) plays a role. However, we are not suggesting that these other people are to blame for your problem. Nor are we suggesting that you are to blame for your perfectionism.

Although your patterns of thinking and behaving, as well as the way others have behaved around you, may have contributed to the development of excessively high standards, there are many factors that interact to form a person's personality. In fact, it is preferable to completely sidestep the issue of who is to blame (because you will never know for sure exactly how the problem came to be) and focus instead on what can be done to change the problem.

Chapter 2

The Impact of Perfectionism

How Perfectionism Affects Your Life

Perfectionism is a problem when it leads to unhappiness or interferes with functioning. Having excessively high standards can affect almost any area of life, including health, diet, work, relationships, and interests. In this section, we focus on some of the main areas that are often impaired by perfectionism: work and school, relationships, and recreation.

Work, Home, and School

Many people define themselves, at least in part, by the work they do. Therefore, it is generally important to them to do a good job. A salesperson generally experiences a sense of satisfaction after making a large sale. Similarly, a student usually feels good after receiving an outstanding grade on an exam or assignment. You may enjoy doing some spring cleaning each year. However, perfectionism may get in the way of your performance at work, home, or school. Even if your performance is not affected directly, perfectionism may still reduce your ability to enjoy your work or may influence the ways in which you treat others at work.

For example, a high school history teacher who was overly concerned about doing an outstanding job when the principal was observing his class was so focused on how he was coming across that he was unable to focus on the content of the class. As a result, he actually made more mistakes than he might have if he was willing to settle for doing an "average" job on that particular day.

One person who was seen in our clinic was so concerned about doing well at her job as a government clerk that she felt very uncomfortable doing just about anything else. Although her workload was not especially heavy, she tended to avoid co-workers who wanted to talk during work hours, and she avoided taking breaks (including lunch). She was also the first person to arrive at work and the last person to leave. Although it was her intention to make a good impression at work, her behavior had the effect of alienating her co-workers, including her supervisor. In her case, excessively high standards for herself affected the impression that she made on others at work.

Another person who was seen in our clinic was overly perfectionistic about keeping the house clean, although you would never know it by looking at his house, which was extremely dirty and filled with clutter. He had grown up with parents who were extremely neat and tidy and expected the same of their children. His mother did not work outside of the home, and as far back as he could remember, she spent all of her day cleaning and re-cleaning the home. When he had moved into his own apartment after starting college, he had also cleaned excessively. Every room had to be spotless, and everything had to be put away properly at all times. After a few months, he began falling behind in his school work because of the time he spent cleaning. One day, after realizing that he could never keep the house clean enough to meet his standards, he stopped cleaning almost entirely. When he first came to our clinic, he hadn't done any cleaning for over six months; he feared that if he started, he would be unable to stop.

In our clinic, we worked with a hospital administrator who had very high standards for her staff. She was completely intolerant of anyone arriving late for work, making small mistakes, or completing their work after a deadline—with no exceptions. She tended to respond to these behaviors with anger and had a reputation for being overly critical when completing performance evaluations of her staff. As a result, her staff stayed away from her as much as possible. They neither trusted her nor liked her especially. Staff turnover was significantly higher in her department, in comparison to similar departments in other hospitals. Her staff were unmotivated in their work because they knew that the supervisor could not be satisfied, no matter how well they performed.

Another client, a student, was terrified of getting anything less than an A on his midterm history exam. He started studying two weeks before the exam. He put everything else aside, including friends, family, sleep, and even food. He ate irregularly and stayed up all night studying for three nights before the exam. Although he knew the material well, he was very tired the day of the exam. He drank several cups of coffee to stay alert, but the caffeine only made him more anxious. Although he passed the exam, he did more poorly than he would have if he had studied a bit less and had enough sleep.

Exercise 2.1
The Effects of Perfectionism in Your Career or Studies

Are there ways in which perfectionism affects your work? Are you sometimes so focused on doing well that you actually perform more poorly? Does your perfectionism affect your enjoyment of work or school? Does it affect the people who work with you? Do small tasks take too long because you spend too much time trying to do them perfectly? As you recall ways in which perfectionistic behavior detracts from your work or school life, record them in the spaces provided.

1. _____

   _____

2. _____

   _____

3. _____

   _____

4. _____

   _____

Relationships, Friendships, and Family Life

For many people, relationships have an all-important role in maintaining their sense of well-being. Important relationships may include those with romantic partners, friends, family members, co-workers, and even acquaintances and strangers. Perfectionism can have an enormous impact on relationships, sometimes even contributing to the end of a relationship.

Sometimes people who are perfectionistic are intolerant of people who do things differently than they do. This may be especially problematic in close relationships with family members or partners, and it can lead to any number of consequences. For example, if you are perfectionistic toward the people in your family, they may learn that the best way to please you is to not tell you things. They may assume (perhaps correctly) that what you don't know won't hurt *them*. An inability to communicate honestly in a relationship can compromise the quality of the relationship.

Perfectionistic standards for others may also lead to arguments and frequent disagreements from those around you, who may believe that you are being unreasonable or have expectations that are impossible to meet. If you continually criticize others who wash dishes differently than you do, choose to drive in a different lane than you would, or enjoy different types of movies than you do, people are likely to become angry or hurt about the criticism.

Perfectionistic standards toward others can also affect the self-esteem and sense of worth of those around you. If your children are constantly led to believe that they are not living up to your expectations, they may feel worse about themselves and may even stop trying in school or other activities in which they are involved. Perfectionistic standards can also contribute to anxiety problems in those who are close to you. For example, research has shown that people who are very anxious or uncomfortable in social situations often report that their parents had excessively high standards for them when they were growing up (Antony et al. 1998).

Being overly perfectionistic toward *oneself* can also lead to problems in relationships and friendships. For example, complaining excessively whenever you get less than an A on an exam may be insulting to friends who have to struggle to get a B or C. They might wonder what you think of them when they get less than an A.

People who have excessively high standards for themselves may also have problems with social anxiety that impairs their ability to make friends easily and develop close relationships. They may be overly concerned that others also have high standards and are likely to be critical. By avoiding contact with others, they never get to learn that others may be less critical than expected. Therefore, for people who are anxious in social situations, avoidance helps to maintain perfectionistic beliefs about the self. The relationship between perfectionism and social anxiety is discussed in more detail later in this chapter, as well as in chapter 11.

Exercise 2.2
The Effects of Perfectionism in Your Relationships

Does perfectionism affect your relationships? Do friends or family members complain about your need to do things perfectly? Does your perfectionism cause you to keep other people waiting? Do people feel as though others can't live up to your strict standards? As you recall ways in which perfectionistic behavior affects your relationships with other people, record them in the spaces provided.

1. _____

   _____

2. _____

   _____

3. _____

   _____

4. _____

   _____

Leisure and Recreation

Does perfectionism sometimes make it difficult for you to enjoy yourself? An executive who was assessed in our clinic complained that it was difficult for him to have fun. Upon further questioning, he reported that when he tried to have fun, his perfectionism got in the way. Leisure activities usually ended up feeling like work. One year, he decided to learn to play the guitar, thinking that it would help to relax him. He enrolled in private lessons with one of the best-known (and most expensive) teachers in the city and made a commitment to practice playing for two hours each evening. He set an alarm to ring after two hours and would not take a break until the whole time had elapsed. He never missed a practice, even on days when he worked evenings and didn't arrive home until quite late. After three weeks, he felt very discouraged because he was not enjoying practicing guitar and didn't like the way his playing sounded (he expected to sound more like a professional than he did—even though he had only been playing for a few weeks). He quit playing a few days later and never picked up the guitar again. This experience was typical for him. In fact, he had tried to learn a number of musical instruments over the years and always gave up after not meeting his own high standards.

Another person reported that his high standards made it very difficult to enjoy playing sports. Although he thought he *should* be involved in a sport, his perfectionism typically led him to take the game too seriously. For example, when playing baseball with friends, he tended to become very angry when a teammate dropped the ball or made some other mistake that cost the team a run. Usually, at the end of a game that didn't go well, he would leave feeling frustrated about losing and guilty for becoming angry with his friends. Although he got involved with baseball to get his mind off other stresses like work, the game itself ended up being another source of stress.

As seen in all of these examples, perfectionism can affect a person's ability to enjoy leisure activities and recreation. However, it can also make it almost impossible for some people to even get involved in these activities. For people who have very high standards in other areas (such as work), it may be very difficult to make the time to do something enjoyable that is not work related. If this is a problem for you, you may find that you spend almost no time getting involved in hobbies, sports, pleasure reading, or other forms of recreation.

Exercise 2.3
The Effects of Perfectionism in Your Leisure Time

Does perfectionism affect your ability to enjoy leisure time? Is it hard for you to take a break from work or other obligations? When you're engaged in some hobby or sport, does it feel like work? Do you feel compelled to do things perfectly, even when you are trying to relax and enjoy yourself? As you recall ways in which perfectionistic behavior affects your ability to have fun, record them on the spaces provided.

1. _____

   _____

2. _____

   _____

3. _____

_____

4. _____

_____

Perfectionism and Psychological Functioning

Depression

A number of studies have found that perfectionism is a feature of depression (Hewitt and Flett 1991b, 1993). Depressed mood can vary in intensity from the normal periods of sadness that everyone experiences on occasion to a much more severe level of depression (i.e., clinical depression) that interferes with functioning. The course of depression also varies from individual to individual. For some people, depressed mood may last a few hours or a day at a time. Other people may experience depression for longer periods of time. For people who suffer from *major depressive disorder*, depression must last at least two weeks, most of the day, almost every day.

On average, episodes of major depression last several months and can sometimes be quite impairing. In addition to depressed mood, symptoms of major depression may include lack of interest in one's normal activities, overeating or loss of appetite, changes in sleep, feeling restless and agitated (or very slowed down), feeling worthless or guilty, poor concentration or difficulty making decisions, feeling tired, or thoughts about death or suicide. People who suffer from major depressive disorder may find it difficult to socialize with others, to be productive at work, or to keep on top of housework.

Another form of clinical depression is called *dysthymic disorder*. This is generally viewed as a less intense but more chronic form of depression. Unlike major depressive disorder, which typically consists of discrete episodes lasting weeks or months, in dysthymic disorder, depressed mood is present most days for at least two years (and often a lot longer). However, the intensity of the depression is much less than the typical episode of major depression. Dysthymic disorder is associated with such symptoms as changes in appetite, increased sleep or insomnia, low energy, low self-esteem, poor concentration, difficulty making decisions, and feelings of hopelessness.

Clinical forms of depression appear to be related to a variety of factors. Biological factors that seem to play a role include genetics (depression appears to run in families, especially in family members who are more similar genetically—e.g., identical twins), changes in levels of chemicals in the brain called neurotransmitters (e.g., serotonin and norepinephrine), and changes in hormonal levels (e.g., variation in the phase of the menstrual cycle as well as hormonal changes associated with pregnancy and childbirth seem to affect depressed mood for some individuals). Other biological factors such as sleep, the amount of available sunlight, and diet can also play a role in depression for some individuals.

Psychological factors in depression include a person's learning history (e.g., growing up in a home where you are frequently told you are inadequate or worthless), history of uncontrollable stressful life events (e.g., death of a close friend or family member, loss of job), and negative thinking patterns (e.g., "things never seem to work out right"). Often, depressed individuals are more likely than people who are not depressed to remember negative things that have happened in the past and to interpret events in a negative way. For example, after failing an exam a person who is prone to depression may remember all the other tests that haven't gone well and may interpret the failure as evidence that he or she is worthless, stupid, or incompetent—thereby contributing to the depressed mood.

Perfectionistic thoughts and behaviors are often important in the maintenance of depression. People who are perfectionistic often set very high standards for themselves in their work, interpersonal relationships, or other areas. If these standards are continually not met, such an individual may start to feel inadequate, disappointed, or even hopeless or worthless. If depression is a problem for you, it might feel like there is something wrong with you that interferes with your ability to reach your goals and meet your expectations. However, the truth may be that the goals are unrealistic or that you place too much importance on reaching them. Finding ways to increase flexibility and become more willing to make mistakes and risk being average can help to decrease feelings of depression.

With respect to treatment, both biological treatments (i.e., medications) and psychological treatments (especially therapies that focus on changing negative thoughts, decreasing negative behavior patterns, and improving the quality of interpersonal relationships) have been shown to be useful. If you believe that you suffer from significant problems with depression, you should consider seeing your family doctor or a mental health professional for an evaluation. Strategies for coping with perfectionism as it relates to depression are discussed in detail in chapter 9.

Anger

Like sadness and fear, anger is a normal emotion that sometimes occurs when we are prevented (often by another individual)
from achieving some goal or are faced with some threat. For example,
a person who undeservingly receives a poor performance appraisal at
work might become angry at his or her supervisor. Anger has the
function of motivating a person to correct the situation (e.g., by confronting the supervisor and requesting that the performance appraisal
be changed) or to meet the threat head on. However, like other emotions, anger can lead to problems when it occurs too frequently, too
intensely, or in situations where it is not warranted.

Although most people experience excessive anger from time to
time, there are a number of psychological problems in which anger is
often a feature. Depression is sometimes associated with anger and
irritability, as is bipolar disorder (a problem in which people experience periods of feeling very low or depressed, as well as periods of
feeling very high or manic). Generalized anxiety disorder (a problem
in which a person worries frequently about many different things)
can also be associated with irritability. Additionally, people who
abuse alcohol or other drugs may find it difficult to control their temper when they are intoxicated or at other times. In fact, anger and irritability can be heightened by a whole range of different psychological
problems that people sometimes have, though anger, in and of itself,
can cause difficulties, even if there is no specific, definable psychological disorder present.

Like depression, a tendency to experience excessive anger
probably stems from a complex interaction between biological and
psychological processes. Genetic factors, as well as other biological
variables (neurotransmitters, hormones, etc.), all affect a tendency to
be angry. Learning probably plays a role (e.g., observing other people
who tend to behave angrily) and cognitive factors such as beliefs,
interpretations, and expectations also appear to be very important.

For example, inflexible beliefs about the way things "should be"
can easily lead to disappointment and anger when expectations are
not met. Therefore, people who are perfectionistic are often more
prone to have difficulties with anger, frustration, and irritability,
compared to individuals who are less perfectionistic. Because perfectionistic standards are often unattainable, rigid, and inflexible, they
often are not met. As a result, you may be very frustrated if your hair
is not cut exactly the way you expected or your children leave a book
or toy in the wrong place. Perfectionism can also lead other people to
become angry if you tend to correct them over and over again. Trying
too hard to make others see things or do things your way can lead to

bickering and arguments. One strategy for decreasing anger and irritability is learning to change unreasonable expectations of yourself and others.

Social and Performance Anxiety

By social anxiety, we are referring to anxiety, fear, or discomfort around other people. Typical social situations that are often feared by people include those involving interaction with others (e.g., talking to strangers, having friends over for dinner, going to parties, being assertive) as well as performance situations in which others might be focused on your behavior (e.g., public speaking, talking in a meeting, exercising in front of others, etc.). Other terms that are sometimes used to describe different types of social anxiety include "shyness," and "stage fright." When social anxiety is so intense that it begins to interfere with a person's life (e.g., by making it difficult to complete important tasks at work, to make friends, etc.), it may lead to an anxiety disorder called social phobia. Social phobia can involve intense fear of as little as one situation, or it can involve anxiety in many different social and performance situations.

When confronted with a feared situation, people who are socially anxious may experience a whole range of symptoms that may include racing heart, breathlessness, dizziness, and other symptoms of arousal. The most frightening of these symptoms are often those that might be noticed by other people, including blushing, sweating, shaking, and losing one's train of thought. People who are anxious in social situations often are particularly nervous that others will find them to be strange, incompetent, stupid, or unattractive. They may be fearful of saying the wrong thing or of seeming overly anxious.

From a psychological perspective, people with social phobia tend to believe that others are likely to judge them negatively. Also, studies from our center and elsewhere have shown that perfectionism is common among people who are socially anxious (Antony et al. 1998; Juster et al. 1996). In particular, social anxiety is associated with a tendency to be overly concerned about making mistakes, perhaps because they may lead to criticism by others. Often, people with social phobia have much higher standards for themselves than they do for others. For example, they may hold such beliefs as, "I should be liked by everyone," "I should never make mistakes," or "I should never allow my anxiety to show." Sometimes, however, people with social phobia also report having excessively high standards for other people.

A number of studies have shown that people who are socially anxious tend to describe their parents as having excessively high expectations and being overly critical when mistakes were made (in comparison to people who experience little or no social anxiety) (Antony et al. 1998; Juster et al. 1996). It is possible that high expectations and frequent criticism contribute to the perfectionism that is often seen in social phobia. Of course, it is also possible that people with social phobia are more sensitive to criticism from their parents and are therefore more likely to remember being criticized as children. Chapter 11 is devoted to the topic of social anxiety and its relationship with perfectionism.

Worry

Are you or any of your family members a worrywart? Excessive worry can be both unpleasant and unproductive. By worry, we are referring to a tendency to dwell on negative things that might happen in the future. Examples include thoughts about failing an exam, missing a flight, losing one's luggage, having harm come to your loved ones, or upsetting your supervisor. Excessive worry is out of proportion to the situation. For example, it would be natural to experience intense worry about a parent who was just diagnosed with cancer. However, most people would agree that worrying to the same degree about a relative who has a common cold is excessive.

Often, worry is very helpful, in that it helps you plan for the future. If people didn't worry at all, no one would bother studying for an exam or making it to work on time when they wanted to sleep in. Some anxiety and worry is essential in getting things done. However, when worry occurs too often or too intensely, it can begin to interfere with a person's sleep, concentration, and enjoyment of life. When worry becomes especially problematic, it may meet criteria for generalized anxiety disorder (GAD).

GAD is a problem in which an individual worries excessively about a number of different things (e.g., work, school, finances, relationships, family, etc.), on most days, over a long period of time. People with GAD often have difficulty turning off the worry and often have a number of associated symptoms, such as irritability, sleeplessness, fatigue, muscle tension, problems concentrating, and feeling on edge. People who worry too much often describe it as a chronic problem that began in childhood or early adulthood. People with GAD tend to worry about minor things, such as getting to places on time and completing household chores.

People who worry excessively tend to be more physically aroused (e.g., faster heart beat, faster breathing, etc.) than people who don't worry especially. Worry also tends to be associated with an increased sensitivity to threat in general. Some psychologists believe that worry may actually be a strategy that some people use to avoid facing difficult problems and negative emotions directly. In this case, problems tend not to get solved and worry continues to be a problem.

There are ways in which perfectionism may play a role in excessive worry. When very high standards are set for yourself or for others, there is always a risk of those standards not being met, which can lead to worry. For example, if you believe that your children should be performing at the highest level in all of their activities, including school, sports, piano practice, and anything else they may be involved in, you may always be worried that their performance may slip in one of these areas. You may also worry excessively about your abilities as a parent if your child does poorly in some area. For more information on the relationship between worry and perfectionism, as well as strategies for overcoming problems with generalized anxiety and worry, see chapter 12.

Obsessive-Compulsive Behavior

Up to 80 percent of people in the general population experience obsessions and compulsions from time to time. Obsessions are unwanted thoughts, images, or urges that occur repeatedly, despite efforts to resist them. Examples may include thoughts about being contaminated by germs; images of hurting other people, even though you have no desire to hurt anyone; and recurrent doubts about whether tasks have been completed correctly. Compulsions are repetitive behaviors that occur in response to obsessions or according to rigidly applied rules. Compulsions typically decrease the discomfort and anxiety created by the obsessions or are used to prevent some dreaded event. For example, people who have obsessions about cleanliness and germs may engage in compulsive rituals involving cleaning and washing. People with obsessive doubts about their actions may check their work excessively, to the point of not getting anything done.

Obsessive-compulsive disorder (OCD) is a problem in which people experience obsessions and compulsions frequently and there is impairment in functioning as a result. For example, whereas many people may feel compelled to check their appliances once or twice before leaving the house, an individual with OCD may check many times over the course of an hour or more. In the 1997 film *As Good as it Gets,* Jack Nicholson portrayed a man who suffers from OCD. In the film, his character had a fear of contamination (he would only eat with wrapped plastic utensils) and engaged in compulsive washing rituals. He also tended to be quite rigid about a range of activities. He insisted on eating at the same table each time he visited his favorite restaurant and would only be served by a particular server. Also, he could not step on sidewalk cracks and had to complete the same tasks each day, in the same order. Although Jack Nicholson's character had other problems that were not related to OCD (e.g., a tendency to offend everyone who interacted with him), the film did a nice job demonstrating some of the features of the disorder.

An individual who was seen in our clinic had obsessions about making mistakes when talking to other people, and he engaged in compulsions involving repeating sentences and asking for reassurance that he was understood correctly. For example, he feared that he might give someone incorrect directions or that some detail might be misunderstood when he told his co-workers about what he did on the weekend. As a result, he often avoided talking to people in case he said something wrong, and he usually repeated everything he said to other people to be sure that he was not misunderstood. Occasionally, he even tape recorded conversations over the telephone and even in person so he could check them later for possible misunderstandings.

Like the other problems discussed in this chapter, there is evidence that both biological and psychological factors contribute to OCD. Genetics appears to play a role. In addition, there is evidence that the neurotransmitter serotonin may be important in the development of the problem. From a psychological perspective, learning may play a role for some individuals. In addition, the types of beliefs and behaviors engaged in by individuals with OCD probably help to maintain the problem. For example, whereas most people have unpleasant intrusive thoughts from time to time, people with OCD are much more afraid of these thoughts compared to the average person. They may feel overly responsible for preventing negative things from happening. People with OCD are also more likely than others to suppress or to resist having their unpleasant intrusive thoughts. Unfortunately, one consequence of trying to resist unpleasant thoughts is that they tend to come back more strongly later.

Perfectionism plays a role in OCD, in that compulsive behaviors often need to be repeated over and over until they "feel right." Also, the order in which activities are completed is sometimes inflexible. For example, for some people who compulsively wash, the order in which various parts of the body are washed is very important. People with OCD may also doubt whether they have completed tasks or said things to others correctly, even though their definition of "correct" may be very different from that of another person.

In addition to OCD, there is a related problem called obsessive-compulsive-personality disorder (OCPD). OCPD is a dysfunctional personality style in which an individual is extremely perfectionistic and inflexible and is preoccupied with being orderly and organized. People with this problem tend to be so preoccupied with rules, lists, details, order, and organization that they actually get very little done. They tend to be overly devoted to work and productivity, leaving little time for recreation. Because of rigid views regarding how things should be done, people with OCPD typically have difficulty letting others do things for them. In many ways, the criteria for OCPD correspond directly with the defining factors of perfectionism.

Although OCD and OCPD have similar names, they differ in a number of important ways. In OCD, compulsive behaviors are designed to decrease anxiety created by very specific obsessions (e.g., washing in response to thoughts about contamination; checking in response to thoughts about losing things). In contrast, OCPD reflects a general personality style that cuts across many different activities and situations. Furthermore, OCPD is generally not considered to be anxiety based and the people with this problem may be unaware that their perfectionistic thoughts and behaviors are excessive. Chapter 13 discusses the relationship between perfectionism and obsessive-compulsive behavior in more detail.

Body Image Problems and Eating Disorders

Another domain in which some people are perfectionistic is their physical appearance. Especially in North American and Western European cultures, there has been an increasing emphasis on being thin, particularly regarding women. Consider some of the trends over the past few decades. A number of researchers have shown that models (e.g., Miss America contestants, *Playboy* centerfolds) have become consistently thinner from the late 1950s through the late 1980s (Garner et al. 1980; Wiseman et al. 1992). In fact, 69 percent of recent *Playboy* centerfolds and 60 percent of Miss America contestants had body weights at least 15 percent below that expected for their age and height—thin enough to meet the weight criterion for anorexia nervosa. Throughout the 1980s, there was also a significant increase in magazine articles on diet and exercise (Wiseman et al. 1992).

The standards for thinness reflected by the media are becoming increasingly impossible to meet. One study found that the average Miss America contestant exercised fourteen hours per week, with some exercising as much as thirty-five hours per week (Trebbe 1979). In another study (Dwyer et al. 1969), more than 80 percent of female high school seniors reported a desire to be thinner and almost a third were dieting. There has also been a steady increase in the number of individuals suffering from eating disorders. Perfectionism tends to be a feature of disordered eating, particularly for people suffering from anorexia nervosa and bulimia nervosa.

Anorexia nervosa is an eating disorder in which an individual engages in self-starvation in order to maintain a very low body weight (at least 15 percent below a minimally normal weight for a person's age and height). In addition, there is an intense fear of becoming fat and often a denial that one is underweight. In addition to having unhealthy standards for what one's weight should be, people with anorexia nervosa may be perfectionistic in other areas as well. Bulimia nervosa is an eating disorder in which the individual engages in frequent episodes of binge eating (that is, eating large amounts of food in a very short time and feeling a lack of control over eating). In addition, the individual uses various strategies to "undo" the effects of having overeaten, including self-induced vomiting, laxative abuse, the use of diuretics, or excessive exercise. Like anorexia nervosa, bulimia nervosa is associated with a tendency to put too much of an emphasis on body shape and weight when evaluating oneself.

People with eating disorders often have very rigid and inflexible rules about eating and food. We once saw two individuals with eating disorders who ended up having an argument about which part of their bread had more calories. One person insisted that the crust had more calories and would only eat the inside of the bread. The other person believed the inside of the bread was more fattening and would only eat the crust. Of course, both the inside and outside of a loaf of bread have similar amounts of fat, yet both women were very resistant to changing their views. Both had very strict views about what foods could be eaten and which were to be avoided. This rigidity is a characteristic of perfectionism.

Sometimes, individuals can have perfectionistic beliefs focused on some aspect of physical appearance other than weight. Such people may become very focused on a particular body part that they view as imperfect. For example, a person may become overly concerned with his or her hair, spending hours per day styling it and even cutting it so that it is perfect. Some men may become overly focused on losing their hair, imagining their hair loss to be extremely unattractive. Others may be unhappy with their nose, or the shape of their legs or other body part. Although many people are occasionally unhappy with some aspect of the way they look (the cosmetic surgery industry depends on this!), some people may be so preoccupied with some aspect of their appearance that they have trouble thinking about anything else. Typically, they imagine themselves to be extremely ugly, even though most people would disagree. When this imagined ugliness begins to interfere with functioning, it may meet criteria for a condition known as body dysmorphic disorder. Like the eating disorders, body dysmorphic disorder is associated with extremely rigid and perfectionistic thinking regarding physical appearance. Chapter 14 discusses further the relationship between perfectionism and problems related to body image.

Chapter 3 ———————

Perfectionism and Thoughts

———————

Research from around the world has consistently found a relationship between people's emotions and their beliefs, thoughts, expectations, and interpretations. Negative styles of thinking seem to be related to experiences of anxiety, anger, and sadness. Perfectionism, which is often part of these emotional states, is often associated with these negative styles of thinking. In this chapter, we will explain the styles of thinking; in later chapters, we will discuss how changing these styles of thinking can have a dramatic effect on the tendency to engage in perfectionistic behaviors.

How Beliefs Affect Emotions

Exercise 3.1 ———————
The Link between Your Beliefs and Emotions

Imagine that you have arranged to have a close friend pick you up at home and drive you to dinner at a restaurant where you had already made a reservation for 7:00 P.M. Because you live about fifteen minutes from the restaurant, your friend was scheduled to pick you up at 6:45 P.M. Imagine that your clock says 6:45, and your friend has not yet arrived. How might you feel at this point? What emotion do you think you might be experiencing, if any? What thoughts would be running through your head?

Emotions at 6:45 P.M.:

_____

Thoughts at 6:45 P.M.:

_____

Imagine that you continue to wait for your friend for another twenty minutes. It's 7:05, you are late for your reservation, and your friend has still not arrived. What emotion would you be feeling at this point? What thoughts might be going through your head?

Emotions at 7:05 P.M.:

_____

Thoughts at 7:05 P.M.:

_____

Imagine that another forty minutes go by. It's now 7:45, and you are very hungry. Still no friend at your door. You phone your friend's home and there is no answer. What would you be feeling and thinking now? Would your feelings or thoughts have changed from earlier?

Emotions at 7:45 P.M.:

_____

Thoughts at 7:45 P.M.:

_____

Imagine that three minutes later, your friend shows up covered in grease from having to change a flat tire on the highway, which, as it turns out, is the reason your friend was late. Your friend apologizes for the delay and clearly seems quite frazzled about the whole situation. You agree to stay home and order in food. How would you be feeling now that your friend has arrived? Would your feelings or thoughts be different than they were ten minutes earlier?

Emotions when friend arrives:

_____

Thoughts when friend arrives:

_____

Interpretation and Emotions

When working with people who experience problems with anxiety, depression, and related difficulties, we often ask them to imagine scenarios such as this one to help illustrate the relationship between thoughts and emotions. Although the scenario we describe is often the same, the responses we get from people to these questions differ dramatically from person to person. Some individuals tell us that they would be unlikely to react negatively to their friend's lateness. Rather, they might simply have a small snack to tide them over and keep busy with various chores around the house until the friend shows up. Other individuals tell us that they would become increasingly angry with the friend as they waited. These feelings might be associated with thoughts that the friend was behaving in a manner that was uncaring or inconsiderate. This behavior might be seen as contradicting a particular value or attitude, such as the belief that "people should not be late." When the friend arrives and it becomes clear that the delay was beyond his or her control, these feelings of anger might be replaced by feelings of guilt for assuming the worst about the friend.

Other people tell us that they would probably feel very worried if their friend hadn't arrived on time. As the evening progressed, they would be having increasingly frequent thoughts that something terrible had happened to their friend. When the friend finally arrives, these feelings of anxiety and worry might be replaced by feelings of relief.

Still other people tell us that they would feel sad if their friend did not show up on time. They might believe that the friend doesn't care enough about them to show up on time, and as a result, they might question their own self-worth as they waited for the friend. As with people who respond to this scenario with anxiety and worry, individuals who predict that they would feel sad often report that they would likely feel relieved when the person finally showed up and the reason for the friend's lateness became clear.

This scenario illustrates how the same situation can lead to a full range of emotions depending on an individual's interpretation of the events. Despite all the possible interpretations of this scenario, the actual situation is the same in all cases: A friend is late for dinner because of a flat tire. Yet, the reaction of the person waiting for the friend may be anger, anxiety, sadness, or any range of emotions, depending on how the situation is interpreted.

The key idea here is that, in general, people do not respond to *events* in their lives, but rather to their *interpretations* of events. The same event can lead to very different reactions from different people, depending on the meaning attached to the event. It is your beliefs, thoughts, interpretations, predictions, assumptions, and other cognitive patterns that determine how you react to situations and events.

People who are perfectionistic tend to have specific patterns of beliefs that help to maintain their perfectionism. For example, someone who tends to be perfectionistic might believe that there is only one correct way to wash the dishes. Most people believe that they know how to wash the dishes properly, but if you actually take the time to watch how different people wash dishes, it quickly becomes apparent that there are many different ways to get the job done—all of which work pretty well. For example, some people fill the sink with water and let the dishes soak. Other people let the water run continuously and wash each dish separately under the tap. People may use various kinds of scrubbers and sponges, or they may use only their hands. Some people insist on a particular brand of soap, whereas other people will use any kind of dish soap and still others may not use any soap at all. Some people will only use very hot water to ensure that all germs are killed; others prefer to use warm or cold water. Some people don't even bother with water and just wipe off the dishes. Some people wash their dishes right after they are used, and others let them sit for a few hours, days, or weeks before washing them.

You get the idea—there are many different ways to wash dishes. If a person adheres too rigidly to beliefs about how tasks should be completed, he or she is likely to run into problems with other people who also have strong opinions about how things should be done. Perfectionism can affect your interpretations (e.g., "That's the wrong way to wash dishes") which, in turn, affects your emotions (e.g., "Now I'm irritated").

Automatic and Unconscious Perfectionistic Thoughts

People are often unaware of the thoughts and interpretations that lead to their intense reactions to situations. Often, these thoughts occur so quickly and automatically that they are outside of your conscious awareness. This isn't surprising, when you think about it. There are many situations in which you process information outside of your awareness. When you walk, you don't have to think, "right foot . . . left foot . . . right foot . . . left foot." You are able to walk automatically. If there is a pole in the way, you automatically walk around it (although, admittedly, one of us has a tendency to bump into poles when distracted). In fact, a minute later, you might forget that there was a pole to be walked around.

In situations that are very familiar, such as walking, you are able to process information with limited cognitive resources or attention. In fact, you even process information while you sleep. For example, people are more likely to wake up to the sound of their own name than to other sounds. Many parents with new babies report that they are more likely to wake up to the sound of their own babies crying than to other sounds.

Given that people often process information outside of their awareness, many of their beliefs that are associated with perfectionistic thinking may be hard for each individual to identify. With practice, identifying perfectionistic beliefs will become easier. One way of doing this is to notice situations in which you experience a negative emotion such as anxiety, sadness, anger, frustration, or a feeling that something is not "right." Once the emotion has been identified and labeled, it is sometimes easier to identify the thoughts and interpretations that might be contributing to the negative feeling. There may even be contradictory beliefs leading to a mixture of emotions. For example, if a supervisor feels frustrated because an employee is not doing a job "properly," the supervisor might notice frustration-producing thoughts such as, "It is very important that my employees do the job my way." At the same time, the supervisor may still recognize on some level that there are different ways of doing the job and that it might be okay to have employees do the job their own way.

Before you can learn to change perfectionistic patterns of thinking, it is important to identify these thoughts, interpretations, and beliefs. Using a cognitive monitoring form, such as the one in exercise 3.2, can help you monitor such thoughts. The next time you find yourself feeling inadequate because you think you haven't performed well enough on a task or are frustrated by the behavior of someone around you, try completing this form. After reading the sample on the next page, use the first column of the blank form on the following page to record the situation that triggers your perfectionistic thoughts or brings these thoughts to your awareness. In the second column, record the emotion that you are experiencing (e.g., fear, anxiety, anger, sadness, frustration, etc.). Also, record the intensity of the emotion using a scale ranging from 0–100, where 0 means nonexistent and 100 equals emotion as intense as you can imagine. Finally, in the third column, record your perfectionistic beliefs and thoughts. By stepping back and observing your reactions in situations, perfectionistic thoughts are likely to become more evident.

Exercise 3.2
How to Identify Your Perfectionistic Thoughts, Beliefs, and Interpretations

Situation	Emotion and Intensity (0–100)	Perfectionistic Thoughts, Beliefs, and Interpretations
I keep writing and rewriting each sentence in this letter to my boss.	Frustrated (70) Anxious (50)	If I don't get each sentence just right, my boss will think I am stupid and incompetent. If I continue to rewrite this letter, eventually I will get it right. There is a right way and a wrong way to word things.
My wife arrived home from work one hour late and had not called me.	Angry (90) Worried (70)	I am never late, and neither should other people be late. If my wife continues to be late for things, she will never get anywhere in life.
I gained two pounds last week.	Depressed (80)	It is important that my weight does not fluctuate. I am less attractive now. I am going to continue to gain weight.
My roommate left his coat on my favorite chair.	Anger (50)	My roommate is inconsiderate. The smell of smoke from my roommate's coat will get all over my chair.

Situation	Emotion and Intensity (0–100)	Perfectionistic Thoughts, Beliefs, and Interpretations

Trying to Confirm Perfectionistic Beliefs

Everyone likes to be correct. Therefore, people tend to surround themselves with experiences that confirm their beliefs. In other words, people seek information in a biased way, in order to support their assumptions, interpretations, and thoughts. They try to spend time with people who think the way they do. If they are politically active, they may go to rallies for their own side—to hear what they already believe. If they are active in their religion, they may seek out experiences that bolster their religious beliefs (e.g., attending services at a church or some other place of worship) rather than seeking out experiences that challenge their beliefs.

Unfortunately, this tendency to seek out information that confirms one's beliefs can sometimes get people into trouble. For example, an individual who has a fear of flying is likely to pay extra attention to stories in the media about airline crashes, compared to the attention paid to all the airplanes that take off and land safely. People who are feeling depressed are more likely to remember all the mistakes that they have made, rather than their past successes. People who are socially anxious and believe that others are judging them negatively are more likely to interpret ambiguous social information (e.g., being given a negative look from another person) as confirming their feelings of inadequacy.

People who are particularly perfectionistic are in danger of paying more attention to events that confirm their perfectionistic beliefs than to information that contradicts these beliefs. For example, students who are afraid to hand in term papers without checking them over excessively might remember stories they have heard about students who handed in exams without checking them over and happened to forget to answer an entire page of questions. They might ignore the fact that there are also many people who hand things in after rechecking their work once, twice, or not at all—without any negative consequences.

Perfectionistic Styles of Thinking

People do not think like computers. Computers use complex mathematical formulas to process information and solve problems. In contrast, people often interpret their environments using what psychologists call *heuristics*. A heuristic is a rule that people use to make a decision or interpret an event. For example, if an individual sees an unleashed dog while walking on the sidewalk, he or she might rely on various stereotypes that he or she has of various dog breeds to help guide his or her decision of whether to cross the road and get away from the dog. If the dog is from a large breed known for biting, the individual might be more likely to avoid the dog than if it's a smaller breed that is unlikely to do any serious damage. This rule of thumb (i.e., "avoid big unleashed dogs that have a reputation for biting, but not dogs that are not known for biting") is an example of a heuristic. Following this rule may improve one's chances of not being bitten. However, it is not always going to lead to a correct decision. Many large dogs with reputations for biting are perfectly safe, and many small dogs can bite. Heuristics are quick ways of interpreting the environment and making decisions; they often lead to correct decisions, which is why the human mind continues to rely on these strategies for processing information.

However, sometimes people process information incorrectly or in ways that are biased. Psychologists sometimes refer to styles of thinking as *cognitive distortions*, particularly when they are biased in a negative direction. Proponents of cognitive therapy (Beck et al. 1979; Burns 1980a) have identified a number of cognitive distortions that make people more likely to experience feelings of anxiety, depression, anger, and other negative emotional states.

Albert Ellis, a well-known psychologist who developed a form of treatment called rational-emotive therapy [recently renamed rational-emotive behavior therapy (Ellis 1993)], was also instrumental in pointing out how unrealistic thoughts and standards (e.g., "should" statements) help to create negative emotions (Ellis 1962; Ellis and Dryden 1987).

In this section, we will highlight some of these cognitive distortions and other styles of thinking that are especially relevant to perfectionistic thinking. Note that these categories of negative thinking styles are not necessarily as distinct as they might seem on the surface. They overlap considerably and a particular perfectionistic thought may be described by several of these items.

All-or-Nothing Thinking and Excessively High Standards

All-or-nothing thinking (also known as black-and-white thinking, categorical thinking, or polarized thinking) is a tendency to see things as either right or wrong, without recognizing that situations are often complex and that there are often many points on the continuum between the extremes of "right" and "wrong." This is one of the most common cognitive distortions among people who are perfectionistic. This style of thinking is often associated with feelings of depression, anxiety, and anger, depending on the focus of the thoughts. Thoughts focused on the behavior of others (e.g., "People can do things my way or the wrong way") are often associated with anger, whereas all-or-nothing thoughts focused on one's own behavior are more often associated with feelings of anxiety, depression, or inadequacy.

All-or-nothing thinking may also be thought of as having excessively high standards. People who are perfectionistic often have standards, either for themselves or for others, that are unrealistic or excessively high. Although it is sometimes helpful to have standards that are slightly higher than your current level of performance, which can give an individual a realistic target goal to reach, perfectionism is often associated with having standards that are extremely difficult, if not impossible, to attain.

Following are some examples of all-or-nothing thinking:

- Anything less than sticking to my diet perfectly is a failure. If I eat one cookie, I may as well have eaten ten cookies.

- If I don't get an A+ in this course, I don't deserve to be in this program.

- My reports are never good enough.

- I seem to be the only person in this house who knows how to clean things properly.

- There is a right way and a wrong way to do everything.

- If I lose my temper with my children, I am a bad parent.

Exercise 3.3
Examples of All-or-Nothing Thinking in Your Life

_____

_____

_____

Some examples of excessively high standards:

- Deborah feels inadequate if she is not able to manage all the demands in her life, which include working full time, taking a night course two evenings a week, being attentive with her partner, cooking for her family, spending several hours a day with her children, visiting her parents weekly, spending time with several of her close friends, and finding time to nurture herself.

- All of his life, Mark has wanted to be an attorney. In fact, there is nothing else that he can imagine doing. Unfortunately, he is a senior in college, his average grade is C, and he is very unlikely to be accepted into law school.

- Stephen is constantly correcting his seven-year-old son's use of language, to the point that his son is sometimes afraid to speak in front of Stephen. The son cannot understand why he is always being corrected by his father, since his grades are among the highest in his class and he is often told by his teachers, friends, and other family members that he speaks very well.

- Alexis weighs 130 pounds and is 5'4" in height. Although her doctor insists that she is not overweight, and her friends tell her she looks great, Alexis feels guilty because she cannot seem to reach her goal weight of 110 pounds.

Exercise 3.4
Examples of Excessively High Standards in Your Life

_____

_____

_____

Filtering

Filtering is a tendency to selectively focus on and magnify negative details at the expense of positive details. This is often associated with a tendency to dismiss positive information. Following are some examples of filtering:

- Ella receives a two-page performance evaluation at work that is very positive overall, emphasizing that she is among the most valued employees in the company. However, she feels angry and hurt over one criticism suggesting that she try to participate more in meetings.

- When people tell Rico that he looks good, he assumes that they are being insincere and that they actually feel sorry for him or are trying to manipulate him in some way. In contrast, when someone tells Rico that he looks tired, he assumes that they find him unattractive, and he feels extremely self-conscious.

- Carrie is a tenth-grade student who has gained five pounds. She is sure that everyone at school finds her unattractive now, despite the fact that she is often asked out on dates and her friends tell her that she is attractive.

- Tim's daughter has become much better at putting away her toys in recent months. However, on one occasion, when she leaves a toy on the steps, Tim becomes very angry.

Exercise 3.5
Examples of Filtering in Your Life

Mind Reading

Mind reading involves assuming that you know what others are thinking. However, mind reading usually involves the assumption that one is being judged negatively by others. This style of thinking is common in people who are perfectionistic and may contribute to depression and feelings of social anxiety and shyness. Examples of mind reading include:

- When Evelyn's supervisor does not give Evelyn feedback on her report for over a week, Evelyn assumes this is because her supervisor thought that the report was not good enough.

- After cooking dinner for several friends, Jack is convinced that his guests are not enjoying their food when one of them excuses himself from the table to visit the bathroom.

- Ricardo is hurt and angry when a woman he is attracted to fails to return his phone call. He is certain that she is either irresponsible or uninterested in him, and he wonders if he'll ever find a partner who meets his high standards.

Exercise 3.6
Examples of Mind Reading in Your Life

_____

_____

_____

Probability Overestimations

Perfectionism is often associated with a tendency to predict that negative events are more likely to occur than they really are. We call these predictions probability overestimations. Examples of this include:

- Alex is a straight-A student; yet before every exam, he believes that he is definitely not going to pass.

- Franca is sure that she is going to come across as unprepared during her presentation, even though she is well-prepared and her co-workers usually enjoy her talks.

- Mary rarely misses work and is highly regarded by her supervisors. Yet, when she must take off a few days due to illness, she believes that her boss will not believe she is sick and that she will receive a negative performance appraisal.

Exercise 3.7
Examples of Probability Overestimation in Your Life

_____

_____

_____

Tunnel Vision

Tunnel vision is a cognitive style in which people pay too much attention to detail and therefore often miss the big picture. This can also be thought of as "missing the forest for the trees." Tunnel vision can slow people down and get in the way of task completion. Following are a few examples of tunnel vision:

- Peter spent many hours reading and taking hundreds of pages of notes in preparation to complete his ten-page paper on World War II.

- Before making any new purchase, no matter how small, David spends many hours reading past issues of *Consumer's Report*, talking to sales people, and discussing his options with friends.

- When taking multiple choice exams at school, Amy obsesses about the meaning of each question and often does not finish the exam before she runs out of time.

- Susan spends so much time organizing (e.g., making lists, filing, putting things in order) that she is often not able to finish her work.

Exercise 3.8
Examples of Tunnel Vision in Your Life

_____

_____

_____

Interpersonal Sensitivity

People who are perfectionistic are often overly concerned about the opinions of others. Most people prefer to be liked by others. However, perfectionism may be associated with an excessive concern about obtaining approval from others. Examples of interpersonal sensitivity include:

- It is very important that everyone likes me.
- If others think I am incompetent then I am incompetent.
- If someone doesn't love me then I am unlovable.

- It is very important not to make mistakes so that others will approve of me.

Exercise 3.9
Examples of Interpersonal Sensitivity in Your Life

_____

_____

_____

Catastrophic Thinking

Catastrophic thinking (also known as catastrophizing) involves incorrectly assuming that one could not cope with a negative outcome if it were to occur. This style of thinking also includes predictions that particular events would be unmanageable if they were to occur. Catastrophic thinking is common in people who are prone to experiencing problems with anxiety, depression, and anger. Examples of catastrophic thinking include:

- I couldn't handle making a mistake in front of the class.

- It would be absolutely terrible if I did not make this deadline.

- If this deal doesn't go through, I don't know how I will manage.

- If I do not stay thin, nobody will ever be attracted to me.

- If I back down or change my mind, I will be perceived as weak.

- It would be unmanageable to develop an illness that caused me to miss even a day of work.

Exercise 3.10
Examples of Catastrophic Thinking in Your Life

_____

_____

Excessively Rigid Standards and Inflexibility

Everyone has standards that not only influence their own behavior, but also help them to decide whether to attempt to influence the behavior of others (e.g., providing constructive feedback to co-workers to improve their performance on a project). When people cannot achieve a particular goal or are unable to influence someone else, they may either keep trying or lower their standards or expectations. Perfectionistic people sometimes view a decision to lower their standards as "giving up" or settling for less than they should. This view may make it difficult to be flexible with respect to one's standards for oneself or for others. It may be very hard for people who have developed an inflexible style or are critical of themselves or others to know when it is okay to break rules. Following are some examples of excessively rigid standards:

- Laura always arrives home before her midnight curfew. On the weekend of her high school prom, Laura asked her parents for permission to come home at 1:00 A.M., since the prom ended at midnight. Her parents refused to allow her to come home later, explaining that her curfew was midnight and that there could be no exceptions.

- Graham was used to winning when he played squash. When he lost to a friend from work, he was quite angry and found it difficult to accept that he had lost the game.

- Jonathan had just made a very nice dinner for his girlfriend. However, she refused to eat the dinner, because she noticed that he had forgotten to wash his hands before cooking it.

- Paul is accustomed to running five miles each day to keep fit. One week, he comes down with a bad case of the flu and ends up feeling like a failure because he was unable to run for three days.

- Angela gets very upset whenever plans are changed. For example, if she and her husband decide to see a movie and the movie ends up being sold out, Angela becomes very angry and disappointed at the prospect of having to find something else to do.

Exercise 3.11 ─────────────────────
Examples of Excessively Rigid Standards
and Inflexibility in Your Life

_____

_____

_____

Over-Responsibility and an Excessive Need for Control

Often, people who are perfectionistic believe that they have more control over events in their life than they actually do. This may lead to a sense of over-responsibility and a tendency to spend unnecessarily large amounts of time on tasks, engage in excessive checking and rechecking, or go to great lengths to protect oneself from making a mistake or from being harmed. Perfectionistic individuals may also believe that it is important to control the behavior or thoughts of other people in their lives, in order to prevent them from making mistakes or encountering harm. These beliefs can lead to relationship problems if individuals are frequently critical of the behavior of their loved ones. Some examples of over-responsibility and need for control are:

- If I spend a long time double checking the content of my letter before I send it, I can make sure that there is nothing in there that might be offensive.

- If I practice this talk enough times, I will ensure that everyone in the audience will like it.

- I can prevent my daughter from getting sick if I constantly remind her to dress warmly, eat her vegetables, wash her hands, get enough sleep, etc.

- I can control whether others like me by being very careful about how I phrase things when I speak.

- It is important for me to be able to convince people to do things my way at work.

- It is important that I correct other people when they make mistakes of any size.

Exercise 3.12
Examples of Over-Responsibility and an Excessive Need for Control in Your Life

_____

_____

_____

Should Statements

"Should" statements are arbitrary rules for how things ought to be. If others break these rules, a person may feel angry or resentful. If individuals break their own rules, feelings of guilt, sadness, inadequacy, or anxiety often occur. Statements containing the words "should" or "must" are often a sign that one is engaging in this style of thinking. Follow are a few examples of "should" statements:

- My children should always do what I tell them to do.

- My co-workers should not be late for work.

- I should never make mistakes at work.

- I should never come across as nervous or anxious.

- I should be able to anticipate problems before they occur.

- I should be assertive and at the same time never upset other people.

- I must never get a grade lower than an A.

Exercise 3.13
Examples of Should Statements in Your Own Life

_____

_____

_____

Difficulty Trusting Others

Perfectionism is often associated with difficulty trusting others to complete tasks. People who are perfectionistic might have difficulty delegating tasks to others or may feel the need to watch people closely when they are completing tasks at work or in other situations. Examples of difficulty trusting others include:

- If I let my partner cook dinner for me, I will not enjoy my food.
- I have to do everything myself because other people just don't know how to get the job done properly.
- If I send my husband to pick up a new telephone, he will probably get the wrong one.
- I don't like other people to buy me gifts because they couldn't possibly know what I want.

Exercise 3.14

Examples of Difficulty Trusting Others in Your Life

_____

_____

_____

Inappropriate Social Comparisons

One method that people typically use to evaluate their performance involves comparing themselves to other people. Everyone engages in social comparisons from time to time in order to see how they measure up compared to others whom they perceive as similar to them. For example, if you receive a raise at work, you might be interested in knowing whether other individuals doing similar jobs received comparable raises. Following a test in school, students often try to find out how other people in the class performed on the exam. Usually, people compare themselves to others whom they perceive to be similar or slightly better than themselves in the dimension being compared. So, following a term test, average students are likely to compare themselves to other average students. This would tell them more about their own performance than making comparisons to the top student in the class or the weakest student in the class.

People who are particularly perfectionistic might find themselves making social comparisons more frequently than other people and may be more likely to experience negative emotions following these comparisons. Perfectionistic individuals may also compare themselves to others in a manner that serves to maintain their perfectionistic attitudes. Thus, they may compare themselves to others who are much stronger in a particular dimension, thereby strengthening their beliefs that they have to meet an almost impossibly high standard. In fact, in any particular dimension you choose to measure (e.g., intelligence, sense of humor, creativity, athletic ability, physical appearance, etc.), there will likely always be someone else whom you perceive as being "better." Comparing yourself to others whom you perceive as much better in a specific dimension may help to maintain perfectionistic beliefs and foster a negative self-image or feelings of inadequacy. Following are examples of inappropriate social comparisons:

- Neil compares his athletic ability to that of a professional athlete and feels pressure to meet that standard.

- Sheila feels inadequate after reading a new fashion magazine and thinking that she will never be as thin or attractive as the models in the magazine.

- Danielle feels like a failure after finding out that her friend received a higher exam grade than she, even though her friend usually receives the highest grades in all her classes.

Exercise 3.15
Examples of Inappropriate Social Comparisons in Your Life

_____

_____

_____

In summary, identifying your perfectionistic thoughts and understanding the relationship between thinking and perfectionism are important steps in overcoming excessively high standards. Later in the book, we will discuss strategies for changing your perfectionistic thoughts. First, however, we will provide an overview of the ways in which certain types of behaviors can help to maintain your perfectionism. As explained in the next chapter, perfectionistic thoughts and behaviors are closely related, in that perfectionistic beliefs can lead to perfectionistic behaviors and perfectionistic behaviors can help to maintain perfectionistic beliefs. It is difficult to overcome perfectionism without addressing both the thoughts and behaviors that contribute to the problem.

Chapter 4 _____

Perfectionism and Behavior

_____

The Paradox of Perfectionism

Joanne has great difficulty making choices when shopping for clothes or other items. She fears that if she only buys one item, she will get home and feel that she has purchased the wrong one. As a result, when faced with several options, she tends to buy one of each. For example, if she can't decide between six colors of a blouse, she buys one in each color. Only by purchasing one of each can she guarantee that she has the correct item.

Unfortunately, she does this with everything that she buys. Her home is cluttered with things she doesn't need or use, including several hundred pairs of shoes, closets full of clothing, shelves filled with unread books and magazines, and cupboards overstocked with food. Joanne's difficulty making decisions when shopping is one manifestation of her belief that it is important not to make mistakes and that mistakes should always be prevented. Ironically, Joanne's struggle to avoid making mistakes leads to many different problems, including considerable credit card debt, no time to do things other than shop, and very little empty space in her home. Joanne recognizes that her compulsive shopping is controlling her life.

Reid cannot resist the temptation to correct other people when he believes they have made an error. For example, whenever someone mispronounces a word, he is quick to let the person know how the word should be pronounced. If his girlfriend is telling a story to a group of friends and leaves out details that Reid believes are important, Reid feels compelled to fill in those details, so that their friends do not misinterpret any of the information they are hearing. Most of the people in Reid's life (including his girlfriend, friends, family members, and co-workers) find him difficult to be around. They interpret his behavior to mean that he always needs to show people how smart he is and he enjoys putting others down. People feel as though they need to be careful about what they say in front of Reid.

In actuality, his tendency to correct others has more to do with the intense discomfort that he feels when a mistake has been made, leading to a feeling of intense internal pressure to set things right. Reid understands that his need to correct others has caused problems in his relationships, but he has trouble stopping himself.

These case examples illustrate the paradox of perfectionism. People who are perfectionistic often believe that in order to maintain order and control in their lives, they must engage in various perfectionistic behaviors. Perfectionistic behaviors may be divided into two main types: behaviors designed to help an individual meet his or her unreasonably high standards, and behaviors that involve avoidance of situations that may require an individual to live up to his or her perfectionistic standards. Behaviors that are aimed at meeting perfectionistic standards include checking and reassurance seeking (e.g., to make sure that a goal is being met), correcting others, repeating actions, and excessive dwelling before making decisions. Both Reid and Joanne engage in these types of behaviors. Examples of avoidance behaviors include procrastination (putting off starting a task because one's desire for perfection is likely to make the task difficult and unpleasant) and giving up on tasks prematurely (because perfectionistic standards are unlikely to be met).

Unfortunately, when performed excessively, perfectionistic behaviors can have an effect that is the exact opposite of the desired effect—they actually lead to disorder and a lack of control. Perfectionistic behaviors can increase the time needed to get things done and can make others feel uncomfortable. For example, individuals who constantly correct the work of their co-workers are likely to find that others either get angry or eventually learn to stay away. People who check and recheck their reports in order to avoid making mistakes are likely to get less done than people who are able to submit a report with minimal checking.

How Behavior Maintains Perfectionistic Beliefs

The relationship between behavior and thoughts is complex. Your beliefs, expectations, and interpretations all influence your behavior. For example, if an individual believes that being late for an appointment is unforgivable and that one should be able to plan ahead for all possible delays, he or she would likely leave the house earlier than necessary in order to guarantee a prompt arrival. People who believe that there is only one way to get a particular job done may be inclined to do the work themselves rather than allow others to help with the task. Students who believe that a term paper must be perfect may be inclined to procrastinate or put off starting their papers because they know that they cannot possibly meet the impossible standards that they have set for themselves.

The relationship between thoughts and behavior can also work in the opposite direction—there are also ways in which behaviors can affect thoughts. Behaviors often have the function of maintaining beliefs. As discussed previously, people often seek out experiences that maintain their beliefs and pay extra attention to events that are consistent with these beliefs, in comparison to the amount of their attention focused on events that challenge their beliefs. This tendency can make it especially difficult to change negative patterns of thinking. For example, people who have very strict beliefs about moral issues and values (e.g., political issues) are likely to surround themselves with friends and family members who share these beliefs. As a result, they may continually have their beliefs confirmed by others and may have trouble when encountering people who don't share their perspective.

Here's another example of how perfectionistic behavior can maintain perfectionistic beliefs: Some people who go into too much unnecessary detail when giving other people instructions (e.g., about how to bake a cake, how to get to the mall, etc.) may believe that such detailed information is necessary to ensure that the task is carried out correctly. By continuing to go overboard when giving other people instructions, the perfectionist never learns that these beliefs are not true. To test out the validity of the perfectionistic beliefs, it would be necessary to leave out some of the detail and see whether the instructions are still carried out correctly.

Another way in which behaviors can maintain perfectionistic beliefs is by preventing the individual from learning that the belief is not true. People who believe that only by checking and rechecking their work can they possibly avoid making mistakes are likely to continue checking their work and may never learn that they could probably get by with being somewhat less "careful."

Appropriate Standards versus Perfectionistic Behaviors

In order to perform effectively in the world, it is important that people behave in a way that helps to maintain their standards. For example, if after hanging a picture in the living room, a person notices that it is not hanging straight, he or she probably would take the time to straighten it. Straightening the picture might make spending time in the living room more pleasant for this individual and others who are likely to see the picture. Before handing them in, most students check over their exams and proofread their papers. Checking over one's schoolwork is likely to reduce the number of errors, ultimately leading to higher grades. It is not unusual for people to ask others for feedback or reassurance when unsure about whether they have performed well during a presentation. Asking for feedback allows people to find out how they perform and provides them with suggestions for improvement.

These are examples of methods that people use to ensure that their behavior meets certain standards. If people didn't adhere to these standards, the quality of their work would decrease, their relationships would suffer, and they would likely run the risk of getting into trouble. Problems may arise, however, when individuals apply these standards in excessive or inflexible ways.

Perfectionistic behaviors are similar in content to the types of behaviors that most people engage in to maintain their standards. However, they differ in frequency and intensity. As an example, consider behavior with the aim of being organized. You may know people whom you perceive as disorganized. These people are chronically late, are always losing things, and have trouble getting things done. This lack of organization affects all aspects of their functioning. Friends may be reluctant to lend money (or other items) to people who appear to be disorganized, for fear of never seeing their money again. They may also avoid making plans with people whom they perceive as disorganized, for fear that the person will not follow through with his or her part of the plan (e.g., showing up on time for a dinner reservation).

Most people appreciate the importance of being organized. However, if a person's level of organization is perfectionistic, it no longer has a useful function because the person may be overly concerned about organization, to the point of not being able to get things done. This type of organization can be associated with procrastination or with a tendency to spend so much time organizing and generating lists of things to do that the actual work never gets done.

Consider the following examples of behaviors that might be considered either helpful or overly perfectionistic, depending on the context, frequency, and intensity of the behavior.

Potentially Helpful Behaviors	Perfectionistic Behaviors
Skimming a credit card application once before handing it in at the bank.	Reading every word on the credit card application four or five times and having a friend read it over as well, just to make sure there are no mistakes.
Correcting a co-worker when he or she mispronounces your name.	Correcting everyone (including strangers) when they mispronounce any word at all.
Straightening up the house for an hour before guests arrive for dinner.	Taking two days off work to clean the house before guests arrive for dinner.
Changing your shirt when you realize it doesn't match your pants.	Trying on five or six different outfits each morning until you find the one that is "just right."

Perfectionistic Styles of Behaving

As discussed previously, the term "perfectionism" means different things to different people. No one person is a perfectionist in every situation or engages in every perfectionistic behavior listed in this section. On the other hand, many people do behave like a perfectionist from time to time, and it can be helpful to identify the types of perfectionistic behaviors that may be a problem for you. As you read through the following pages, identify examples from your own experience of any perfectionistic behaviors that are problematic in your life. Keep in mind that these categories of behavior overlap considerably. A particular perfectionistic behavior may fit equally well in two or more of these categories.

Overcompensating

Because perfectionism is often associated with anxiety or discomfort about the possibility of not meeting a particular standard of performance, people who are perfectionistic often overcompensate in their behavior. Overcompensation involves engaging in a behavior excessively to make absolutely sure that there is no way that harm can occur or that something can go wrong. In other words, people who are perfectionistic sometimes go too far in their attempts to get things "just right." Examples of overcompensation include:

- Natasha lives about twenty minutes from work. Nevertheless, she leaves ninety minutes before having to arrive at work—just in case there are unanticipated delays.

- To ensure that his tax return was completed correctly, Danny hired the most expensive accountant in town, even though his return was fairly straightforward.

- To make sure that his client received his communication, Thomas left the message by telephone, E-mail, fax, and regular mail. He then telephoned the client a week later to make sure that the messages were received.

- Oliver tends to tell stories in excruciating detail to make sure that nothing is left out.

- Miles believes that by keeping perfectly clean, he can avoid becoming ill. He is especially concerned about avoiding possible contamination from germs and other agents that may cause him to get sick. To be sure that he stays germ-free, he washes his hands more than thirty times a day and frequently asks his family members to wash their hands.

- Barry worries excessively about losing documents on his computer. Therefore, he tends to back up each document that he writes—on five separate diskettes.

Exercise 4.1
Examples of Overcompensating in Your Life

_____

_____

_____

Excessive Checking and Reassurance Seeking

People who tend to be perfectionistic often engage in frequent or excessive checking to make sure that they have done things correctly, no one else has made a mistake, or some standard has been met by themselves or another person. A specific form of checking involves repeatedly seeking reassurance from others that a particular task was done well enough or that some other standard has been met. Examples of excessive checking and reassurance seeking include:

- Before submitting a completed form (e.g., a credit card or job application), Dana spends hours looking it over for errors. If he is unable to check the form to his satisfaction, he sometimes experiences difficulty sleeping at night.

- Patrick cannot leave the house without checking over and over again to make sure that all the appliances in his house have been turned off and unplugged. Because of his excessive checking, he tends to be late for work and sometimes is not even able to make it in to work at all.

- Although she is often told she looks attractive, Louise is convinced that her nose is too large for her face. She spends several hours each day looking in the mirror to evaluate whether her nose looks too big.

- Ken makes a point of watching his fellow co-workers each day to see who arrives on time and who is late.

- Karyn, a pharmacist, feels compelled to check the amounts and names of all medications that she dispenses ten to twelve times each before giving them to a customer.

- Although she rarely makes mistakes, Jennifer asks her supervisor and co-workers many times daily to check over her work; she does this so that she can be reassured that she has done it correctly.

- Even though Gus is an excellent cook, he constantly doubts his ability to cook well and requires excessive reassurance from everyone in his family that they enjoyed the meal.

Exercise 4.2
Examples of Excessive Checking and Reassurance Seeking in Your Life

_____

_____

_____

Repeating and Correcting

If a behavior is perceived as incorrect or a situation doesn't "feel" right, it may seem overly important to correct the behavior or situation. At times, perfectionism can be associated with a tendency to go overboard with respect to correcting one's own behavior or that of another person, even if the consequences of not correcting the behavior are in reality minimal. In fact, the consequences of repeating and correcting one's actions are often greater than the consequences of not engaging in these behaviors.

For example, an individual who constantly points out every time anyone makes a mistake—even if the "mistake" is minor (e.g., how the other person chooses to complete a task)—can lead others to become angry or hurt. Furthermore, no matter how consistently people are corrected, they are going to continue making mistakes. Examples of repeating actions and correcting situations include:

- If Candace notices that a book on her shelf has a creased cover, she feels compelled to replace the book with a new copy. She spends several hundred dollars per year replacing things because of "defects" that most people would not even notice.

- If Nathan's laundry is not folded perfectly, he tends to refold it until he is satisfied.

- When talking to people, Phyllis tends to repeat herself to make absolutely sure that she is being understood. Unfortunately, people often become bored with the conversation and listen less and less as time goes on.

Exercise 4.3
Examples of Repeating and Correcting in Your Life

_____

_____

_____

Excessive Organizing and List Making

People who are perfectionistic may spend too much time on organizational details, such as making lists of things to do, making lists of possessions, or putting belongings in a particular order. Although some level of organization is helpful (e.g., it makes it easier to find things that you're looking for), excessive organization can get in the way of completing tasks. Following are some examples of excessive organization and list making:

- Bruce spends several hours each week organizing his family's music, books, and computer software. In addition, he keeps a detailed inventory of all his music, books, and software on his computer. Each week, he checks to makes sure that all of his cassettes, CDs, books, and diskettes are all stored in alphabetical order. If items have been misplaced or filed out of order, he tends to become frustrated with his family for not being able to put things back where they belong.

- Each morning, Maya spends more than an hour making a list of all the chores and tasks that she needs to accomplish for the day. She spends additional time making sure that the items are listed in the most efficient order, so that no unnecessary time is lost between tasks. If she misses a task or has to complete the list out of order, she feels compelled to rewrite her list so that it accurately reflects what she is doing. She keeps her lists of things to do for years, just in case she needs them.

- Jeffrey cannot get any work done until his office is completely tidy and organized. As a result, he often spends more time making his office tidy and organized than he actually spends working.

- Dar is a student who spends many hours each week planning her strategy for studying (e.g., calculating exactly how much time she should spend studying for each subject). As a result, she is left with little time to actually study.

Exercise 4.4
Examples of Excessive Organizing and List Making in Your Life

_____

_____

_____

Difficulty Making Decisions

People who are perfectionistic often have a hard time making decisions. Faced with many different alternatives, perfectionistic individuals are often anxious about making a mistake that might be irreversible and potentially catastrophic. Difficulty making decisions can affect almost any area of an individual's functioning by making it hard to do one's work, complete tasks, and even respond to questions. Examples of difficulty making decisions include:

- Ray found it very difficult to make decisions about everyday activities (e.g., choosing movies at the video store, deciding what to wear in the morning) because he feared making a wrong choice. As a result, these activities tended to take him much longer to complete, compared to other people. He often noticed that his friends and family became frustrated while waiting for him to make decisions.

- Because of his difficulty making decisions, Miguel tended to change his mind frequently. For example, after ordering a meal in a restaurant, it was not unusual for him to change his order several times before actually receiving his food.

- Linda prefers to have others make decisions for her, so that she cannot be blamed for making a wrong choice.

Exercise 4.5
Examples of Difficulty Making Decisions In Your Life

_____

_____

_____

Procrastination

Because perfection can't be reached, people who are constantly aiming for perfection may put off doing things for fear that they will never meet their targets or goals. By not starting things, perfectionistic individuals do not need to confront the possibility of doing a less than perfect job. In some cases, perfectionism may lead to complete avoidance of situations in which an individual feels as though he or she may not measure up. Following are examples of procrastination:

- Because Michelle feels such intense pressure to do well in all her classes, she tends to take her schoolwork very seriously. With each paper that she hands in, it is very important to her that she impresses her professor. She tends to put off starting her work because she fears that the task of writing the perfect paper will be too overwhelming.

- In order to lose weight, Michael has come up with a very complex list of rules for what he can and cannot eat, as well as a detailed exercise plan. However, he has serious doubts about whether he is going to be able to stick to his plan. To minimize the chances of failing, he has delayed starting his new weight loss plan until the time feels "right." So far, it's been two years and time has not yet felt "right."

- Jason has been interested in getting to know a new co-worker for several weeks. However, rather than just saying "hello," he has been dwelling on trying to come up with the best way to introduce himself.

Exercise 4.6
Examples of Procrastination in Your Life

_____

_____

_____

Not Knowing When to Quit

In order to reach a particular goal or target, people who are perfectionistic will sometimes continue to engage in a task for too long a time. This can interfere with a person's ability to complete a task and can also frustrate other people. Following are examples of not know-ing when to quit:

- Despite being very bright, Anne rarely finishes her exams on time. When she encounters a question for which she doesn't know the answer, she becomes determined to get it right. As a result of her determination, she often spends too much time on these difficult items and doesn't have time to complete later questions on the test.

- Alice finds it very difficult to accept others who do not see things the way she does. When she disagrees with another person about a matter, she usually continues trying to con-vince the other person of her point of view, often to the point of getting into arguments and compromising her relation-ships with others.

- In preparation for his wedding, Rashad had a very difficult time deciding whom to invite. In preparing his list (which was to be no more than one hundred people), he began with his immediate family, close friends, and co-workers. How-ever, as he continued to add names, he had great difficulty stopping. He worried that people might be offended if they were not invited. He ended up with a list of over three hun-dred people that included distant relatives, people at work that he hardly knew, and many friends with whom he had lost touch.

Exercise 4.7
Examples of Not Knowing When to Quit in Your Life

Giving Up Too Soon

This particular behavioral style is the opposite of not knowing when to quit. People who tend to be perfectionistic sometimes give up trying because of their anxiety over not being able to reach a par-ticular goal or standard. Examples of giving up too soon include:

- Despite being told by his guitar teacher that his playing was coming along very well, Hans quit taking guitar lessons because he felt that it was taking too long to achieve the level of competence that he desired.

- Phyllis believed that she wasn't living up to her supervisor's expectations, even though her supervisor was very happy with her job performance. Phyllis decided to quit her job, rather than wait to be fired for making a mistake.

- Danny quit his job as an interior designer because he believed that he would never be among the top designers in the country.

- Because she thought that she could never find a partner that met all her needs, Keisha gave up trying and instead decided to stay single.

Exercise 4.8
Examples of Giving Up Too Soon in Your Life

_____

_____

_____

Slowness

Perfectionism can sometimes lead people to do things more slowly than they would otherwise. Slowness is often related to some of the other behaviors discussed earlier. For example, procrastination can cause people to take longer before starting a particular project or activity. Also, people who have difficulty making decisions often take a long time to choose among several options (e.g., choosing what color to paint the living room). Finally, people who check excessively sometimes take longer to complete tasks, particularly if they continually check their performance as they go along. Perfectionism can lead to slower performance, independent of these other behaviors as well. Some individuals who are perfectionistic have a slower style of getting things done. By doing things more slowly and carefully, they may feel less likely to make an error. Examples of slowness include:

- Jed tends to read very slowly so that he does not miss any important information.

- Tia speaks more slowly than other people do so that she can think very carefully about what she says and avoid saying the wrong thing.

- Danielle spends much more time than most people do when she showers, washes her hands, or brushes her teeth. While cleaning herself, she wants to be absolutely sure that she has done it properly.

- Luke is very handy with tools. He finished his basement on his own and loves building and fixing things. He would like to have his own renovation company; however, his perfectionism tends to slow him down. He does an excellent job, but he works much more slowly than other contractors and therefore would have a hard time earning enough money working as a contractor.

Exercise 4.9
Examples of Slowness in Your Life

_____

_____

_____

Failure to Delegate

Perfectionism is sometimes associated with a tendency not to trust others to get things done properly. Individuals who have trouble trusting others may avoid delegating tasks to other people unless they are sure that the other person will complete them perfectly. Follow are a few examples of the failure to delegate:

- Louis insists on doing all of the cooking and cleaning at home, despite the fact that his wife and children often offer to help. Although Louis does not enjoy these chores, he has very strict beliefs about how things should be done and is reluctant to let others help him, for fear that the tasks won't be done correctly and his standards will not be maintained.

- Phil has just been promoted to a new managerial position, which includes a new full-time secretary. Although his new secretary is very experienced and competent, Phil has trouble asking him to do any of Phil's clerical work (e.g., typing, filing, etc.), for fear that he will not do things the way Phil likes them done.

- Hilary refused to leave her children with a babysitter because she was convinced that the babysitter would not enforce the household rules (e.g., bedtime, etc.) adequately and that her children would learn bad habits.

Exercise 4.10
Examples of Failure to Delegate in Your Life

_____

_____

_____

Hoarding

For some people, perfectionism can be associated with difficulty throwing things away. For example, people may hold on to old newspapers, magazines, or pamphlets. Other people may keep empty jars, packages, letters, broken appliances, or other trivial items. In fact, people can hoard almost anything. Hoarding is not the same as having a collection of some kind, nor is it the same as keeping things for sentimental value. People who have problems with hoarding often have their homes filled with various things that they don't need or enjoy. Hoarding can lead to problems in relationships (e.g., if an individual's partner wants to throw something away) and can make it difficult to keep one's home clean. The most common reasons why people keep things they don't need include the specific belief that the item may be needed one day, as well as a more general discomfort with the thought of throwing the item away. Examples of hoarding include:

- Donald has every bill, bank statement, and receipt that he has received in the past fifteen years. All of his papers are neatly filed in filing cabinets that fill nearly an entire room. Although he has only had to refer to an old bill or receipt a few times over the years, he keeps everything, just in case he needs them.

- Karla hates the thought of running out of things she needs. Therefore, she always has extra stores of food, tissues, toothpaste, cleaning products, office supplies, and other items that she uses regularly. However, whereas most people might have an extra tube of toothpaste in the house, Karla feels very uncomfortable unless she has many extras of each item she might require. For example, at any one time, she tends to have twenty tubes of toothpaste, fifty rolls of toilet paper, fifteen bottles of dish soap, and many extras of most other household items.

Exercise 4.11
Examples of Hoarding in Your Life

Avoidance

Because perfectionistic standards are often so difficult to meet, people who strive to be perfect will sometimes avoid situations in which they might feel compelled to meet these impossible standards. Some specific examples of avoidance were described earlier. These include failing to delegate tasks to others, procrastinating, and giving up on tasks too quickly. Following are some other examples of avoidance:

- Julie avoids weighing herself because she knows that if she has gained even one pound, it will ruin her day.

- Although he is very bright and competent, Darcy decided not to attend college because he believed that he could never be satisfied with his performance.

- Pierre, a chef, is rarely able to enjoy other people's cooking. To avoid being disappointed, he tends not to have his partner or friends cook for him and he rarely eats in restaurants.

- Naomi tends to avoid spending time around other people at work or socially because she believes that others perceive her as not being particularly entertaining, interesting, witty, or bright. Even when other people invite her to a party or gathering, she assumes that they would not enjoy her company if she did show up.

Exercise 4.12
Examples of Avoidance in Your Life

_____

_____

_____

Attempts to Change the Behavior of Others

When an individual is overly concerned about how things are done, he or she may be inclined to be overly critical of the behavior of others and may frequently engage in attempts to change their behavior. Examples of attempts to change the behavior of others include:

- On a daily basis, Amelia feels compelled to correct the way her boyfriend washes dishes. Despite her frequent reminders for him to use warmer water, use more detergent, and let the dishes soak, he continues to wash the dishes the way he has always washed them.

- Gary is uncomfortable with the fact that not everyone at work shares his religious beliefs. In hopes of converting his co-workers to his way of seeing things, he frequently brings in religious literature and invites people to attend religious services with him, even after they have declined his offer several times and do not express any interest.

- Lately, Jane finds that almost every little thing her fourteen-year-old daughter does gets on her nerves. She constantly reminds her daughter to hold her fork properly, sit up straight, take off her shoes in the house, and behave more or less the way Jane does whenever possible.

Exercise 4.13
Examples of Attempts to Change the Behavior of Others in Your Life

———————————————————————

———————————————————————

———————————————————————

Now that we've gone over what perfectionism is and you've had a chance to identify your own perfectionistic qualities, we will help you take the steps necessary to overcome your perfectionism.

Part II

Overcoming Perfectionism

Chapter 5

Assessing Your Perfectionism

The Purpose of Conducting an Assessment

Before a psychologist, psychiatrist, or other professional begins to help an individual to deal with a particular problem, there is typically a period of assessment. Assessment involves collecting information to better understand the nature and extent of a problem and, eventually, to help develop the best possible treatment plan.

The assessment phase may involve asking questions during an interview, having the individual complete various questionnaires and standardized tests, or having the person monitor specific thoughts or behaviors using diaries. For example, if a client visits a mental health professional seeking help for problems with anxiety, the clinician is likely to begin the first session (or even the first few sessions) by simply asking questions about the main problem, other difficulties the client may be experiencing, and the client's background. The client may be asked to complete a series of questionnaires that measure anxiety and related problems. In addition, diaries may be completed to measure anxiety and other reactions throughout the week, when the person actually encounters particular anxiety-provoking situations.

The assessment process helps the clinician to get to know the client and is essential for identifying and understanding the problem. In addition, the findings from the assessment are often important for choosing and recommending a course of treatment. In the same way, a detailed self-assessment will help you to understand and change your difficulties with perfectionism. Before you begin to work on changing your own perfectionism, we are going to help you do a careful self-assessment. This assessment process will have three main components: identification of key problem areas, measurement of the severity of the problem, and measurement of changes that may result from using the strategies described in this book.

Identifying Problem Areas

An important function of the initial assessment phase is to describe the features of your perfectionism and to identify the main problem areas. These include identification of perfectionistic thoughts and behaviors as well as situations that trigger perfectionistic responses.

Isolating Your Perfectionistic Thoughts and Behaviors

In chapters 3 and 4, you identified your perfectionistic thoughts and behaviors. Because perfectionistic beliefs and behaviors vary across people, it is important to identify the unique ways in which your perfectionism is manifested. Reviewing the beliefs and behaviors that you identified in chapters 3 and 4 will be helpful.

Exercise 5.1
Perfectionism Diary

Below is a diary to record episodes during which your perfectionism comes up in your everyday life. Each time you find yourself having a perfectionistic thought (see chapter 3 for your personal examples) or engaging in a perfectionistic behavior (see chapter 4 for your personal examples), complete this form. The first step to changing perfectionistic thinking is to catch yourself in the act. Completing the perfectionism diary will help you to identify times when you are thinking or behaving in a perfectionistic manner. You may want to photocopy this page so you can use the diary for every perfectionist thought or behavior during the next two weeks.

Perfectionism Diary

Date _____   Time _____

Situation

_____

_____

Perfectionistic Thoughts

_____

_____

Perfectionistic Behaviors

_____

_____

Mood (e.g., anxiety, depression, anger, etc.)

_____

_____

Isolating Situations and Triggers for Your Perfectionism

For many perfectionists, their overly high standards are more problematic in some situations than in others. For example, they may be very perfectionistic in their work, but fairly laid back at home. Therefore, as part of your self-assessment, it is important to identify the specific situations that trigger your perfectionism. For example, do your perfectionistic thoughts and behaviors occur more often with certain people, during particular activities, or in certain places?

Exercise 5.2

Identifying Your Perfectionism Triggers

Below is a list of people (part 1) and activities (part 2) that sometimes trigger perfectionistic beliefs and behaviors. For each item that reflects an area in which you tend to be perfectionistic, list some examples of the ways in which your perfectionism is manifested. Next, for each item in the list, estimate the degree to which perfectionism is a problem for you. Use a scale ranging from 0 (perfectionism is not at all a problem) to 100 (perfectionism is very much a problem). For example, a score of 50 would reflect a moderate level of perfectionism. Later, these numbers will help you to choose specific areas to work on. Areas in which perfectionism is more of a problem may be those that you will choose to focus on first.

Part 1: People with Whom You Tend to Be Overly Perfectionistic

Person	Examples	Intensity (0–100)
Partner	I tend to be overly concerned about what clothes my boyfriend wears when we go out.	65
	I get very angry if my wife arrives home even five minutes later than she said she would arrive.	70

Person	Examples	Intensity (0–100)
Spouse or partner	_____	_____
	_____	
Children	_____	_____
	_____	
Parents	_____	_____
	_____	
Siblings	_____	_____
	_____	
Friends	_____	_____
	_____	
Co-workers	_____	_____
	_____	

Strangers	_____	_____
	_____	
Other	_____	_____
	_____	
Other	_____	_____
	_____	
Other	_____	_____
	_____	

Part 2: Activities in Which You Tend to Be Overly Perfectionistic

Activity	Examples	Intensity (0–100)
Cleaning	I spend many more hours cleaning than most people in an effort to makes sure that everything is perfectly clean.	80
	I get overly angry with my children when they leave toys lying around.	80
	I get irritated when my employees are even ten minutes late to work.	45

Activity	Examples	Intensity (0–100)
Work/School	_____	_____
	_____	
Art or Music	_____	_____
	_____	
Housework	_____	_____
	_____	
Organizing things	_____	_____
	_____	

Relationships _____ _____

Small
decisions   _____ _____

Eating   _____ _____

Sports/
Fitness   _____ _____

Grooming/
Washing   _____ _____

Driving   _____ _____

Other   _____ _____

Other   _____ _____

Other   _____ _____

Measuring the Severity of the Problem

Your self-assessment should include an analysis of how severe or impairing the perfectionism is. In examining the severity of the problem, several different steps should be taken, including: distinguishing whether your high standards are helpful or unhelpful, identifying the areas of functioning (e.g., work, relationships, emotional well-being, etc.) that are impaired as a result of the perfectionism, estimating the impact of your perfectionism on others, identifying the effects of perfectionism on your emotional functioning, and identifying the extent to which your perfectionistic beliefs are flexible versus rigid.

Helpful versus Unhelpful Standards

Perfectionistic standards, as opposed to beneficial high standards, are so high that they either can't be met or they can only be met at an enormous cost to yourself or others. Making the distinction between helpful and unhelpful standards can often be difficult for people who are perfectionists. One reason for this is that a standard that is helpful for one person may be overly perfectionistic for another person. For example, a professional squash player must meet very high standards in order to make a living at the game, while an individual who plays squash in their leisure time can afford to have lower standards. In fact, having overly high standards can lead to unnecessary anger and disappointment when a mistake is made or a game is lost. For such an individual, overly high standards might be considered perfectionistic and, therefore, not especially helpful.

Exercise 5.3
Reevaluating Your Standards

The best way to identify whether your own standards are overly perfectionistic is to look at the impact of having these standards. Several questions should be asked:

Are your standards higher than those of other people?

_____

Are you able to meet your standards?

_____

Are other people able to meet your standards?

_____

Do your standards help you to achieve your goals or do they get in the way (e.g., by making you overly disappointed or angry when your standards are not met or causing you to get less work done, etc.)?

_____

What would be the costs of relaxing a particular standard or ignoring a rule that you have?

_____

What would be the benefits of relaxing a particular standard or ignoring a rule that you have?

_____

Sometimes, when you are too close to an issue, it is hard to have a realistic perspective. For example, if you have been behaving in a perfectionistic way for a long time, it might be hard to imagine thinking differently about a certain issue. If you're unsure about how to answer any or all of the above questions, try to distance yourself from the issue by imagining how someone else might look at the particular problem. You may even want to consider asking people whom you trust about their beliefs about the standard or rule in question. For example, if you are overly concerned about making a mistake when giving a presentation, you could try to imagine how another person might feel about the consequences of making mistakes during presentations. You might even ask a co-worker what he or she thinks when a presenter makes a mistake while talking. This will help you to determine whether your concern about doing a perfect presentation is exaggerated.

If you determine that a particular standard cannot be met or that the costs of having a particular standard or rule outweigh the benefits, you may want to consider loosening your standards for that particular issue. For example, some people believe that it is extremely important that their possessions remain in excellent condition—as if they are new. While most people like to keep their possessions in good working order, when standards become too strict, they begin to border on perfectionistic.

If you still feel unsure about whether your maintaining high standards or being perfectionistic, or if others continue to complain about behaviors that you feel are simply high standards and your relationships are suffering as a result, it may be helpful to visit a therapist and get a professional, third-party opinion.

Exercise 5.4
Evaluating the Helpfulness of Your Standards

Use the form below to identify standards or rules that you think are helpful and worth holding on to, as well as standards that it may be best to relax (i.e., those for which there may be some situations or times that the standard is getting in the way, slowing you down, or disturbing people who are close to you).

Standards That Are Helpful:

_____

_____

_____

_____

_____

_____

_____

_____

Standards That Are Not Helpful:

_____

_____

_____

_____

_____

_____

_____

Perfectionism and Areas of Functioning

One measure of the severity of a problem is the extent to which it interferes with a person's functioning. In chapter 2, you identified ways in which particular areas of your life are affected by perfectionistic beliefs and behaviors. Below is a list of areas that are often affected by perfectionism. For each relevant area, list some examples of ways in which your perfectionism interferes. Next, for each item in the list, estimate the degree to which perfectionism interferes with that specific area. Use a scale ranging from 0 (perfectionism causes no interference) to 100 (perfectionism is completely impairing). For example, a score of 50 would reflect a moderate level of interference in that domain. You may wish to refer back to chapter 2 for examples of how perfectionism affects these areas of your life.

Exercise 5.5
Assessing the Degree of Impairment Caused by Perfectionism in Your Life

Domain	Examples	Impairment (0–100)
Work	I am unable to get all my work done because I tend to check my work excessively.	70
	My co-workers tend to avoid me because I often correct everything they do—even when the issue doesn't affect me directly.	55

Domain	Example	Impairment (0–100)
Work/School	_____	_____
	_____	
Housework	_____	_____
	_____	
Recreation/ Hobbies	_____	_____
	_____	
Close Relationships	_____	_____
	_____	

Other
Relationships _____   _____

Diet _____   _____

Self-care _____   _____

Other _____   _____

Other _____   _____

Other _____   _____

The Effect of Perfectionism on Others

It is important to assess the impact of your perfectionism on those around you. By doing this, you can improve your interpersonal relationships by reducing the strain that can be caused by perfectionistic criticizing and directing, as well as reducing your own irritation and anger about the actions of others that you would perform differently.

Exercise 5.6
How Your Perfectionism Affects Those Around You

Try to answer the following questions to the best of your ability.

How do people react to you when you impose your standards on them?

_____

How do others respond when they observe you imposing inappropriately high standards on yourself?

Are there times when others become frustrated with your perfectionistic behaviors?

Are some people anxious around you for fear of making a mistake in your presence?

How do *you* respond to other people who tend to be perfectionistic with themselves or with other people?

If you are not sure how your perfectionism affects other people, it might be worth asking one or two people how they are affected by your perfectionistic behaviors. Choose people who are close to you and whom you can trust. Here are some questions that you might ask the other individual:

* Have you noticed ways (e.g., situations, behaviors, etc.) in which I am overly perfectionistic?

* How are you affected when I do _____ ?

* In what areas would you like to see me become less perfectionistic?

* What impact would it have on our relationship if I were to become less perfectionistic?

After you have obtained more information about the effect of your perfectionism on other people, try to process the information in a way that is helpful. Here are some questions to ask yourself:

* How do you feel after hearing about the effects of your perfectionism on others?

* Does your perfectionism affect your relationships?

* Do you want to become less perfectionistic in your relationships?

_____

_____

* Which specific behaviors or standards do you want to decrease or end completely?

_____

_____

* Which specific behaviors or standards do you want to keep the same?

_____

_____

Perfectionism and Emotional Functioning

Your self-assessment should include an examination of the ways in which perfectionism affects you *emotionally*. Sometimes perfectionism can lead to feelings of depression if the individual consistently finds that his or her high standards are never met (e.g., a person who feels depressed because his or her grades are not high enough to be accepted into graduate school).

For other individuals, perfectionism can be associated with intense anxiety, nervousness, or fear. For example, some people with unreasonably high standards for themselves report intense anxiety about being judged negatively by others if they make a mistake or do not meet their own unrealistically high standards. Finally, for some people perfectionism is associated with feelings of intense anger. This is often the case for individuals who hold unreasonably high standards for those around them.

Exercise 5.7
How Your Perfectionism Affects Your Emotional Functioning

Take a few moments to consider the ways in which perfectionism contributes to your emotional states. Can you think of times when your perfectionistic beliefs or standards led to feelings of depression, anxiety, or anger? Use the form below to record past situations in which your perfectionism led you to feel depressed, anxious, or angry. For each example, describe the situation or trigger, your reaction in the situation (e.g., your perfectionistic thoughts and behaviors), and the intensity of the emotion (using a scale from 0–100).

Times When Perfectionism Has Caused You to Feel Sad or Depressed:

Situation

_____

_____

Reactions (e.g., thoughts, behaviors)

_____

_____

Intensity of Depressed Mood (0–100) _____

Times When Perfectionism Has Caused You to Feel Anxious:

Situation

_____

_____

Reactions (e.g., thoughts, behaviors)

_____

_____

Intensity of Anxiety (0–100) _____

Times When Perfectionism Has Caused You to Feel Angry:

Situation

_____

_____

Reactions (e.g., thoughts, behaviors)

_____

_____

Intensity of Anger (0–100) _____

Flexible versus Rigid Perfectionistic Beliefs

Another important aspect of your perfectionism to consider is the extent to which your perfectionistic attitudes are flexible and therefore easily changed. Your self-assessment should include an evaluation of how rigid your perfectionistic beliefs are. The less rigid you are with yourself and your beliefs, the easier it will be to change. Just recognizing your rigidity in particular areas may motivate you to become more flexible.

Exercise 5.8
Assessing the Flexibility of Your Perfectionistic Beliefs

The extent to which you answer "yes" to the following questions may be an indication that your perfectionistic beliefs are relatively inflexible. If this is the case, you will need to work especially hard at changing perfectionistic beliefs and behaviors. You may also need to remind yourself from time to time about the costs and benefits of changing your standards (chapter 6 discusses this issue in more detail). You should also be aware if your natural tendency is to avoid alternative (i.e., less perfectionistic) ways of thinking and behaving when it comes to your standards or rules. Keeping this tendency in mind will make it easier to get some distance from the standards, which in turn will make it easier to change them. If you answer "no" to most of these questions, you will likely find it easier to change your beliefs and behaviors using the exercises described in upcoming chapters.

_____ Is it difficult for you to recognize when you are being overly perfectionistic? If so, list examples:

_____

_____

_____ Do you find it difficult to relax your standards? If so, list examples:

_____

_____

_____ Typically, are you unwilling to consider the possibility that you are being overly perfectionistic (even when your relationships are suffering and others blame your perfectionism)? If so, list examples:

_____

_____

_____ Do you often find yourself disagreeing with other people when they tell you that your standards are too high or too rigid? If so, list examples:

_____

_____

_____ Do you become very upset when you are unable to meet your own standards? If so, list examples:

_____

_____

_____ Do you become very upset when others are unable to meet your standards? If so, list examples:

_____

_____

Exercise 5.9
Putting It All Together

Throughout this chapter (as well as chapters 3 and 4), you have recorded a large amount of information about your perfectionism. The form below provides an opportunity to compile the information into one handy summary. You may wish to refer to your responses throughout chapters 3, 4, and 5 when completing this summary form.

Styles of Perfectionistic Thinking

List (from chapter 3) the styles of perfectionistic thinking (e.g., all-or-nothing thinking, filtering, etc.) that are most problematic for you. Give an example of each from your own life.

_____

_____

_____

_____

_____

_____

_____

_____

Styles of Perfectionistic Behavior
List (from chapter 4) the styles of perfectionistic behavior (e.g., overcompensating, excessive checking, etc.) that are most problematic for you. Give an example of each from your own life.

_____

_____

_____

_____

_____

_____

_____

People with Whom You Tend to Be Overly Perfectionistic
List (from this chapter) the people with whom you tend to be overly perfectionistic (e.g., partner, co-workers, etc.).

_____

_____

_____

Activities That Tend to Trigger Your Perfectionism
List (from this chapter) the activities that are most likely to trigger your perfectionistic thoughts and behaviors (e.g., work, relationships, etc.) and are the most problematic for you.

_____

_____

_____

_____

_____

Helpful and Unhelpful Standards

List the most important helpful standards, rules, or preferences that you recorded earlier in this chapter, which you may wish to maintain. Then list the most unhelpful (i.e., perfectionistic) standards that are the most problematic for you and that you may wish to change.

Helpful Standards

_____

_____

_____

_____

Unhelpful (Perfectionistic) Standards

_____

_____

_____

_____

Areas of Functioning That Are Most Impaired Because of Your Perfectionism

List (from this chapter) the areas of functioning that are most impaired because of your perfectionism (e.g., relationships, hobbies, etc.). Note that these areas are likely to overlap somewhat with the activities that trigger your perfectionism.

_____

_____

_____

_____

The Effect of Your Perfectionism on Others
List examples of how your perfectionism affects other people.

_____

_____

_____

_____

_____

Perfectionism and Emotional Functioning
List examples (see earlier section in this chapter) of how your perfectionism causes you to feel depressed, anxious, or angry from time to time.

Depressed _____

_____

Anxious _____

_____

Angry _____

_____

Measuring Improvement and Change

In addition to helping you understand the origins and nature of your perfectionistic beliefs and behaviors, another function of assessment is to measure changes in perfectionism over time. Therapists sometimes ask their clients to repeat the initial measures (e.g., questionnaires, diaries, etc.) periodically during their treatment. This is a helpful way to assess whether a person's problem is improving.

By continuing to use the assessment strategies discussed in this chapter throughout the process of changing your thoughts and behaviors, you will be able to determine whether you are in fact making progress. Here are some specific recommendations regarding how to continue to assess your perfectionism throughout the process of becoming less perfectionistic. Note that these are only suggestions. You can make changes to these recommendations based on your own needs.

- Examine your responses on the summary form (exercise 5.9) from time to time in order to assess whether there have been changes in the types of perfectionistic thoughts and behaviors you experience, as well as the intensity of your perfectionism and the ways it impacts your day-to-day functioning. When you examine the form, you may add items if you notice new triggers for your perfectionism, or perfectionistic thoughts or behaviors, that were not recorded initially.

- Note any items on the summary form that no longer belong on the list (in fact, you can complete a new, blank copy of the form periodically, in order to assess how things have changed).

- Initially, you should reexamine the summary form weekly. After six to eight weeks, when things have begun to improve, you may decrease the frequency of looking at the form to biweekly. When your perfectionism has decreased even further, you may decrease the frequency further (e.g., monthly). When you are no longer working on your perfectionism, you may stop any formal assessments. You may still want to conduct an informal assessment from time to time, by just asking yourself how things are going with respect to your perfectionistic thoughts and behaviors.

- Continue using the perfectionism diary, described in this chapter, as long as you are working on changing your perfectionistic beliefs and behaviors.

Chapter 6 _____

Developing a Plan for Change

Before beginning to use the strategies for overcoming perfectionism, there are several steps that should be taken to prepare for change. In this chapter, we will help you examine the costs and benefits of becoming less perfect so you can assess whether you really are motivated to work on your perfectionism at this time. We will also help you identify specific goals for change, so that you can choose exercises that will help you to reach those goals, and so that you can judge whether you are making the improvements that you had hoped to make.

In preparation for the process of making changes, we also discuss ways of choosing among the various treatment strategies in this book, as well as strategies for finding additional help if the techniques described in this book are difficult to implement on your own. This chapter concludes with a discussion of some possible obstacles to overcoming perfectionism and how to deal with them.

Costs and Benefits of Loosening Perfectionist Standards

If perfectionism is a problem for you, chances are that the high standards you hold for yourself or others are long-standing and ingrained. The thought of giving up these standards may be very frightening for a number of reasons. First, although you may be aware of your tendency to be perfectionistic, it may be difficult for you to determine which beliefs are overly perfectionistic and which standards are appropriate. If overcoming perfectionism involves lowering certain standards, you may be fearful of lowering the "wrong" standards.

Second, you may be reluctant to relax your standards if you believe that your performance will suffer. For example, if you believe that it is very important to be on time for appointments and therefore you always allow an extra hour to get anywhere you are going, you may be fearful of giving up this practice in case you end up being late for appointments in the future. If you tend to be very detailed in everything you do (e.g., when giving people directions, writing memos, cleaning), you may be fearful that performing tasks in a less detailed way will lead to problems. People often believe that their perfectionistic standards keep everything in their life from falling apart. They fear that giving up perfectionistic standards will lead to chaos.

A third reason why people are reluctant to become less perfectionistic is because they don't want to seem inconsistent or "wishy-washy" to others. If you have spent a lot of time and energy trying to have others do things your way or trying to create a certain image of yourself, the thought of changing your expectations or image may feel threatening to you. It may be very difficult to admit that you may have been too strict, or even worse, that you may have been wrong. It's ironic that most people admire others who can admit when they have made a mistake, yet it is often very difficult for people to admit their own mistakes.

Before making the decision to become less perfectionistic, you should consider the possible costs and benefits of changing. For some standards and rules that you hold, the costs of changing may outweigh the benefits. For other standards, the benefits will outweigh the costs. Examining the costs and benefits of becoming less perfectionistic can help you to decide which standards to relax.

Exercise 6.1
Determining Benefits and Negative Consequences of Loosening Perfectionistic Standards

List all the possible costs of becoming less perfectionistic. Examples may include: I will make more mistakes at work; I will go through a period of increased anxiety while I get used to the idea of being less rigid and perfectionistic; my level of performance at school may decrease; the level of performance of others around me may decrease;

others may think I am incompetent; my home won't be as clean and organized; I won't be able to find anything; I will gain weight; etc.

Many of the possible costs that you list will be fairly unlikely to occur. So, in addition to listing these costs, you should estimate just how likely that outcome is. To estimate the likelihood of a particular negative consequence happening, use a scale ranging from 0 (definitely will not occur) to 100 (definitely will occur). An estimate of 50 means that a consequence is equally likely to occur as it is to not occur.

Consequence/Negative Outcome	Likelihood of Occurring (0–100)
1. _____	_____
2. _____	_____
3. _____	_____
4. _____	_____
5. _____	_____
6. _____	_____
7. _____	_____
8. _____	_____
9. _____	_____
10. _____	_____

Now, list all the possible benefits of becoming less perfectionistic. Examples may include: I will be less hurtful and critical of the people in my family; people will enjoy spending time with me; I will have time to do more things; I will be less anxious about making mistakes; work will be more enjoyable; I will be less concerned about what other people think of me; my depression will decrease; etc. As in the above section on costs of becoming less perfectionistic, you should also estimate the likelihood that each positive outcome or benefit will occur if you are able to decrease your perfectionistic thinking and behavior. Use a scale ranging from 0 (definitely will not occur) to 100 (definitely will occur). An estimate of 50 means that a benefit is equally likely to occur as it is to not occur.

	Benefit/Positive Outcome	Likelihood of Occurring (0–100)
1.	_____	_____
2.	_____	_____
3.	_____	_____
4.	_____	_____
5.	_____	_____
6.	_____	_____
7.	_____	_____
8.	_____	_____
9.	_____	_____
10.	_____	_____

Identifying Goals

Before starting to overcome any problem, it is important to define the problem and to identify goals. It is not enough to say that you want to "become less perfectionistic." The only way to evaluate whether your perfectionism has improved is to set *specific* goals. Remember—your goals should not be too perfectionistic! They should be realistic and achievable. Also, you should think about both long-term and short-term goals. Long-term goals may include changes that you want to make over the next year or even longer. Short-term goals may involve changes that you want to make over the next few days, weeks, or months.

Although it is helpful to think of a few general goals, you should also try to come up with goals that are as specific as possible. For example, the goal "I will be less critical of my children" is not as specific as the goal "I will not criticize the clothes that my children wear to school." The more specific the goal, the easier it will be to come up with strategies for reaching the goal. Below are some examples of general and specific goals.

General Goals	Specific Goals
Become less perfectionistic regarding physical appearance	Be willing to gain five pounds without getting upset. Be able to tolerate missing a workout at the gym. Take no more than thirty minutes to get ready in the morning.
Become less detail oriented	Tell stories to other people without having to include every detail. Hand in papers that are no longer than they are supposed to be. Submit monthly reports without checking them over more than once.
Be less concerned about being judged by others	Mispronounce words when talking to people without becoming anxious. Be more comfortable when telling other people about what I do for a living. Be comfortable around people I perceive as smarter or more attractive than I. Be less concerned about showing signs of anxiety, such as shaking and blushing.
Become more tolerant of others	Stop caring how my housemate washes the dishes. Learn to tolerate my spouse arriving home thirty minutes late without phoning. Allow my children to make a mess when playing, as long as they clean it up by the end of each day.
Be less concerned about being clean	Wash my hands no more than five times per day. Spend no more than one hour per day cleaning. Shake hands with others comfortably. Be willing to use public rest rooms.

Exercise 6.2 ———————————————
Making Your Own General and
Specific Goals

Now, think about what types of changes *you* would like to make. Specifically, think about perfectionistic ways of thinking or behaving that you would like to decrease or stop all together. We have included forms for you to record goals for the next month as well as goals for one year from now. Of course, you may choose other time periods if you prefer. The main point to remember is that you may have different goals for the short term and the long term. Although some goals may be realistic targets for a year or two from now, they may not be realistic goals for one week or one month from now. We have also included space for you to record your general goals, as well as specific targets that may be included within each general goal.

One-Month Goals

General Goal 1: _____

Specific Goals

_____

_____

_____

_____

General Goal 2: _____

Specific Goals

_____

_____

_____

General Goal 3: _____

Specific Goals

_____

_____

_____

General Goal 4: _____

Specific Goals

_____

_____

_____

One-Year Goals

General Goal 1: _____

Specific Goals

_____

_____

_____

General Goal 2: _____

Specific Goals

_____

_____

_____

General Goal 3: _____

Specific Goals

_____

_____

_____

General Goal 4: _____

Specific Goals

_____

_____

_____

_____

What to Change First: Setting Priorities

Now that you have identified thoughts and behaviors that you would like to change, the next step is figuring out where to start. There are two general principles to keep in mind when deciding which aspects of your perfectionism to work on first: which thoughts and behaviors cause the most interference in your life, and which thoughts and behaviors are likely to be the easiest to change.

In most cases, it is best to start with the problem that interferes the most in your life or causes the most problems with other people. By choosing to work on the most important goals first, your efforts will have the largest possible impact on your life in the shortest amount of time. This will likely have the effect of motivating you to continue to work on other aspects of your perfectionism. In addition, you should also consider which goals are easiest to meet. By choosing to work on goals that are very difficult to meet, you may end up becoming discouraged and give up before making any significant changes.

Review the short-term and long-term goals that you listed earlier. Rank order them with respect to how important each goal is, as well as how attainable each goal is. We recommend beginning with the most impairing problem, but choosing goals related to that problem that are manageable and realistic. If a problem seems too big and overwhelming, it will be necessary to break it up into smaller steps.

Exercise 6.3
Choosing Your Priorities for Change

In the spaces below, list the goals on which you plan to work. List the goals in the order that you want to work on them. Note that the list may change as you begin working on these issues. You may decide that a particular goal is too difficult to work on right away. Or, a goal from the bottom of your list may become more important, depending on what else is happening in your life.

Goal 1 _____

_____

Goal 2 _____

_____

Goal 3 _____

_____

Goal 4 _____

_____

Goal 5 _____

_____

Goal 6 _____

_____

Goal 7 _____

_____

Goal 8 _____

_____

Goal 9 _____

_____

Goal 10 _____

_____

How to Choose Among Specific Strategies

Chapters 7 and 8 describe many different techniques and exercises for overcoming perfectionistic styles of thinking and behaving. It is unlikely that you will want to use each of the methods listed. Because perfectionism affects different people in different ways, this book includes a broad range of strategies that are designed to be helpful for different people. When reading the next two chapters, it is better to choose a relatively small number of techniques and to practice them frequently. Overcoming perfectionism requires learning new skills. If you attempt to use all of the techniques described in this book, you will probably not learn any of them well enough to use them effectively. On the other hand, if you choose a small number of strategies and practice them regularly, you are more likely to notice change.

We recommend that you read through chapters 7 and 8 once, marking the passages that include techniques that seem most relevant to you and then reread those sections. Also, you should choose strategies that are practical, given your lifestyle and the resources that you have available. After trying several of the strategies described in these chapters, you will quickly discover which ones are likely to help you overcome your perfectionistic thoughts and behaviors. The main point to keep in mind as you begin to implement the strategies is that it is better to do a few things thoroughly than to attempt to do everything suggested in this book.

The Importance of Regular Practice

The strategies and exercises described in the remainder of this book will require regular practice. Ideally, you should expect to conduct some sort of practice almost every day. Although some of these practices may be quite brief, others may last up to several hours. Exercises will include such activities as completing diaries each time that you experience perfectionistic thoughts, purposely making small mistakes until the thought of doing things imperfectly is less anxiety provoking, and eliminating perfectionistic behaviors such as excessive checking.

In many cases, these practices will be exercises that you can integrate into your normal activities (e.g., when talking to people, working, etc.), so they need not take up much time. For other exercises, you will need to set aside blocks of time to practice. To be most effective, practices should be regular, structured, and planned in advance. You should plan to practice regardless of whether you are in the mood to practice when the scheduled time actually comes. Also, you should have backup plans, in case a particular practice falls through.

Involving Others in Your Practices

Because perfectionism involves other people, it may be important to include other people in your efforts to overcome perfectionistic thoughts and behaviors. There are several ways in which involving others can be helpful. First, by reading relevant sections of this book, people who are close to you will develop a better understanding of the causes of perfectionism and the methods for changing perfectionistic habits. This should help the people in your life to be more patient and understanding with you while you work on becoming less perfectionistic.

Second, some of the exercises described in the remaining chapters of the book may be difficult to do alone and may depend on the cooperation of those around you. For example, if you want to become more comfortable with people in your family doing things differently than you do, you may want to make sure that your family members understand the purpose of the exercises and ask them if they are willing to assist the process by purposely doing things that you view as imperfect.

Finally, it is likely that family, friends, and co-workers have found ways of working around your perfectionism or compensating for difficulties that you may have. For example, people who fear that you will be overly critical may avoid telling you about things that they have done. If you tend to be overly critical of your own behavior, people may avoid giving you feedback for fear of offending you. If you tend to avoid certain activities (e.g., cooking, paying bills, certain projects at work, etc.), for fear of making mistakes, other people in your life may be doing more than their share of these activities. If the people around you have changed their behavior because of your perfectionism, you may want to have them try to stop behaviors that make it easy for you to continue your perfectionistic habits, such as doing things for you or purposely trying to avoid saying anything that might trigger a perfectionistic response from you.

When and How to Seek Professional Help

You may find that it is too difficult to overcome your perfectionism alone or with the help of your family or friends. It may be that the perfectionistic beliefs are too rigid and difficult to change on your own, or it may be that your anxiety is too intense to conduct the practices described in this book by yourself. Perhaps you have other difficulties such as depression or significant anxiety that interfere with your ability or motivation to work on your perfectionism. Or, perhaps you would benefit from working with another person, such as a therapist, to discuss problems that arise during treatment or to check on your progress. For many people, a trained professional can help in ways that go beyond what a book such as this can offer.

There are several advantages of seeking help from a psychologist, psychiatrist, social worker, or other mental health professional. A trained professional can help to explain various concepts, explore the causes of a problem, be involved in practices, generate appropriate exercises and practices, help solve problems that arise, and help to improve motivation. In addition, a therapist may be qualified to treat the problems that often go together with perfectionism, including anxiety disorders, eating disorders, anger, and depression. A psychiatrist, family doctor, and some psychologists can also prescribe medications that may be helpful for problems with anxiety and depression, as well as the perfectionism that can accompany these problems.

If you are interested in seeking professional help, there are several places to look for a therapist or doctor. A good place to start is with your family physician. He or she may know of other professionals who can help. Most therapists who are experienced with problems such as anxiety and depression are likely to be able to help with your perfectionism. If you suffer from a particular anxiety disorder, depression, or another specific problem, there may also be clinics in your area that specialize in your problem. Some specialty clinics (particularly research and training clinics associated with universities) offer services at reduced costs. In the third section of this book, the chapters describe the types of treatments that have been shown to be effective for particular problems. Because there are so many different types of therapies available, it will be helpful for you to have an idea of the type of treatment that you are seeking.

Another place to get information on treatment options is through national organizations that offer referrals to consumers. An example is the Anxiety Disorders Association of America in Rockville, Maryland, which offers a newsletter and referral service for members. Additional information on where to obtain treatment is available on the web site for the National Institute of Mental Health (www.nimh.nih.gov).

Obstacles to Becoming Less Perfectionistic

In order to maximize your chances of making positive changes as you start the process of overcoming your perfectionism, it will be helpful to anticipate any obstacles that might get in the way of your success.

By preparing for possible road blocks in advance, you will be less likely to be affected by these potential difficulties.

If You're Unable or Unwilling to Consider Alternative Ways of Thinking

As discussed previously, there are three reasons why it is often difficult to change ways of thinking even when your beliefs get in the way of life. First, the natural tendency is to assume that your thoughts are true. In other words, if you are like most people, your beliefs may be ingrained and difficult to challenge. Second, if you come across information that disproves your beliefs, you probably tend to view it as an exception, or even worse, you ignore the information. Instead, people tend to pay more attention to information that confirms their beliefs. Finally, even when you do begin to doubt whether a belief is true, you may still do everything you can to avoid admitting that you have made a mistake. Perfectionistic thinking is especially prone to being rigid and difficult to change. In order to become less perfectionistic, you will need to be able to make a commitment to consider the possibility that particular beliefs are not true and that particular standards are not helpful. The fact that you are reading this book suggests that you are aware that perfectionism is a problem for you, and this awareness is the first step toward being willing to consider the possibility of changing your perfectionistic thoughts.

If You Feel That Perfectionism Isn't Causing Significant Problems for You

You may feel that perfectionism is not a big enough problem to warrant spending all the time and energy needed to change your perfectionistic thoughts and behaviors. In fact, the benefits of having high standards may outweigh the costs. If this is the case, you may not want to invest too much in the strategies described in this book. Even if you feel this way, it is also possible that your high standards do cause problems of which you are unaware. For example, perhaps your perfectionism has negative effects on those who are close to you. Before assuming that your perfectionism is not a problem, you may want to check with those around you and get a second opinion.

Even if perfectionism is currently a problem, you may find that as you practice the exercises in this book, your perfectionism gradually interferes less and less. As the problem starts to be less impairing, your motivation to work on it may decrease. You may start to think, "Why bother spending all that time and effort on the problem if it isn't bothering me anymore?" It is important to continue to work on your perfectionism even when it starts to improve. This perseverance will help to consolidate the gains that you have made. Also, continuing to use the strategies in this book will help to prevent the problem from getting worse again in the future (e.g., during a stressful time in your life).

If You Don't Believe That You Can Change

Because perfectionism is part of your personality, you may feel as though becoming less perfectionistic is beyond the realm of possibilities. You may believe that it is impossible to change a person's personality. If you hold this belief, it may be helpful to remember that your personality is really just the sum of your beliefs, attitudes, and behaviors. Breaking perfectionism down into its parts will make it easier to make changes. On a cautionary note, remember that just having the belief that you cannot change may have a negative impact on your likelihood of making changes. Researchers have shown consistently that people's expectations have an effect on whether they respond positively to therapy, medication, and other medical interventions. Therefore, it will be helpful if you can try to be open-minded and optimistic until you have had a chance to see whether the strategies described in this book are likely to be effective for you.

If You Feel There Are Too Many Other Things Going On in Your Life to Focus on Your Perfectionism

You may find that there are other stresses or demands on your time that interfere with your ability to put forth the necessary effort for overcoming your perfectionism. Perhaps you are dealing with extreme stress at work or a serious problem in your relationship. Or perhaps you are suffering from another difficulty (e.g., excessive alcohol use, severe depression, a serious medical problem). Or maybe you are just too busy with work, school, or taking care of your family. If this is the case, now may not be the best time to begin working on your perfectionism. If your effort is only half-hearted, you may only see a modest improvement. You may need to decide whether it is worth beginning to overcome your perfectionism now or if it would be best to wait until you can devote more time and energy to the problem. On the other hand, if your life is always stressful and busy, now may be as good a time as any.

If You Are Too Anxious to Practice

Many of the exercises described in this book are anxiety provoking. They involve purposely relaxing rules and standards for how things "should be." For example, if an individual is overly concerned with being neat and clean, he or she may need to purposely leave things messy and purposely come into contact with things that are "dirty." The thought of allowing your standards to be lowered may be terrifying. You may fear making mistakes or having things fall apart. This fear is common among people who are using cognitive and behavioral strategies to overcome a problem. To deal with the anxiety, you need to remember that the anxiety will pass. With repeated practices, the strategies described in this book will be less scary. In fact, you will become more and more comfortable letting go of your perfectionistic thoughts and behaviors.

Chapter 7 _____

Changing Perfectionistic Thoughts

In chapter 3, we discussed the ways in which beliefs, interpretations, and predictions contribute to negative emotions such as anxiety, depression, and anger. We also discussed the ways in which negative thoughts contribute to perfectionism. You may recall from earlier chapters that people do not respond to what is actually occurring around them. Rather, they respond to their interpretations of what is happening around them. For example, if you fear making mistakes at work, it is not the possibility of making mistakes that makes you anxious. Instead, it is your beliefs regarding the *meaning* of the mistakes that causes you to feel upset or nervous. Perhaps you assume that making mistakes will lead to some terrible consequence that cannot be corrected or undone (such as being fired or ridiculed by others). Or you may believe that making mistakes is a sign of weakness or incompetence.

Sometimes your thoughts are correct, and at other times they are incorrect. Sometimes standards are appropriate, and sometimes they are too strict. Most people's standards are not universal, and therefore, other people may not share them. In other words, everyone creates their own standards for performance based on their learning and their beliefs about what level of behavior is appropriate. Beliefs and standards vary among individuals and across groups, including people from different cultures, ages, sexes, occupations, education levels, geographical locations, etc.

Although standards and beliefs are subjective, people tend to assume that their interpretations, beliefs, predictions, and standards are true. In other words, people assume that their beliefs are facts. They may believe that other people share their beliefs and high standards as well, or they may believe that although other people may have lower standards, they cannot afford to let their standards slip. Becoming less perfectionistic will involve relaxing your standards and changing perfectionistic beliefs. It will involve treating your standards and beliefs as *possibilities* or *guesses* about the way the world should be—rather than as hard facts.

Of course, you don't need to change all beliefs and standards. Some expectations are appropriately high, and there can be costs to letting go of all standards that you have for yourself or others. The trick will be trying to identify which beliefs are unrealistic or excessive and to work on changing those beliefs.

Using Thought Records and Diaries to Change Perfectionistic Thinking

Throughout this chapter, we will include examples of thought records and diaries that may be used to help you identify and change your perfectionistic thoughts and standards. You may use one or more of these, or you may prefer to develop your own diaries. Regardless of which diaries you choose to use, working through your perfectionistic thinking on paper should make it easier to become less perfectionistic. With practice, the process of changing your thoughts will become more automatic and you will no longer need to use the diaries.

Steps for Changing Perfectionistic Thoughts

Changing thoughts involves four basic steps: identifying perfectionistic thoughts, listing possible alternative thoughts, considering the advantages and disadvantages of the original perfectionistic thoughts and the alternative thoughts, and choosing a more realistic or helpful way to view the situation. Although the process may seem easy on paper, it is often more difficult in practice. Mastering these strategies will require perseverance and repetition.

Identifying the Perfectionistic Thoughts

Before your perfectionistic thoughts can be changed, you must first identify these thoughts. This can be difficult for two reasons. First, you may incorrectly view your perfectionistic thoughts as appropriate and accurate. Second, your perfectionistic thoughts may be unconscious and completely outside of your awareness.

It may be easier to identify times when you are engaging in perfectionistic thinking if you pay attention to three particular situations. First, notice when you feel that you are not living up to your own expectations (e.g., you're not performing well at work or school; other people are judging you to be unattractive, incompetent, or overly anxious; you are unhappy about some aspect of your body, such as your weight; you are anxious about saying the wrong thing, etc.). Second, notice when you feel that other people are not living up to your expectations (e.g., people at work make too many careless mistakes, your children's grades never seem to live up to your expectations, people don't know how to drive properly, etc.).

Finally, take note when you find yourself engaging in perfectionistic behaviors (e.g., checking and rechecking your work, apologizing too much for minor mistakes, exercising excessively to stay thin, spending too much time cleaning, etc.). If you find yourself engaging in perfectionistic behaviors or holding on to standards that are not being met, you may need to ask yourself, "Am I thinking like a perfectionist?" If you are not sure, ask someone you trust for another opinion.

If you have difficulty identifying your perfectionistic thoughts, we recommend that you read chapter 3 again. This chapter lists types of perfectionistic thinking styles and provides several examples of each.

Listing Possible Alternative Thoughts

Once you have identified a particular perfectionistic belief, the next step is to consider possible alternative beliefs or thoughts. This can be difficult because perfectionistic thoughts and standards are often ingrained and automatic, and it can feel almost impossible to even consider other ways of viewing a situation. One way of helping with this process is to ask yourself the question, "How might someone else view this situation?" You can even think about particular people in your life (e.g., your spouse, best friend, boss, daughter, father, etc.) and ask yourself how they might view the situation. This strategy, which we call "perspective taking," is discussed in more detail later in this chapter.

Considering the Advantages and Disadvantages of the Original and Alternative Thoughts

The next step involves identifying the advantages and disadvantages of holding on to your original perfectionistic thoughts and standards versus adopting the alternative thoughts and standards. Strategies to use here include evaluating the evidence for and against particular beliefs/standards and testing out the accuracy of your beliefs using mini-experiments (also known as hypothesis testing). These and other techniques are described later in this chapter.

Choosing More Realistic or Helpful Ways to View the Situation

After you have evaluated the advantages and disadvantages of changing your beliefs and standards, you will be in a position to choose a more realistic and helpful way of thinking about the situation. Changing your thoughts will lead to a reduction in anxiety, depression, anger, or other negative feelings associated with perfectionism.

Exercise 7.1
A Diary for Changing Your Perfectionistic Thoughts

Here is a diary that you can use to help you work through the four steps for changing perfectionistic thoughts. We include two examples of completed diaries as well as a blank diary that you can complete whenever you find yourself thinking or behaving in a perfectionistic way. If you are unable to complete the diary at the time that you notice your perfectionism getting the best of you, you may complete it later.

Perfectionism Diary (Example 1)

Date: July 17   *Time*:   2:00 P.M.

Situation: My husband is fifteen minutes late picking me up from work.

Emotions: anger, impatience, frustration

Perfectionistic Thoughts:

> * My husband should never be late to pick me up.
>
> * I should not be kept waiting, even for a few minutes.
>
> * My husband cannot be counted on for anything.

Alternative Thoughts:

> * It is okay for my husband to be late sometimes.
>
> * It is okay to be kept waiting sometimes.
>
> * My husband can be counted on most of the time.

Evaluating Perfectionistic Thoughts and Alternative Thoughts

> * My expectation that my husband *always* pick me up on time only causes me to get angry and frustrated. It doesn't seem to change the situation at all.
>
> * If I were more willing to be picked up a bit late from time to time, I would probably be less upset when it happens. The time I waste arguing and being angry is much more than the time I spend waiting for my husband when he is late.
>
> * If I plan ahead, I can deal with his being late by using the time to relax, read a book, or make a telephone call.
>
> * Even though my husband is sometimes ten or fifteen minutes late when he picks me up from work, he tends to be very responsible and considerate in most areas of our relationship.
>
> * Just because I am early for everything I do, that doesn't mean that everyone else should always be early.
>
> * The worst thing that will happen if I am kept waiting is that I will arrive home a few minutes later.

Choosing a More Realistic and Helpful Perspective

Perhaps being picked up late from work is more manageable than I originally thought.

Perfectionism Diary (Example 2)

Date: December 29   *Time:*   8:00 P.M.

Situation: I told a joke at a party and nobody found it funny. In fact, my friends seemed to ignore me and they changed the focus of the conversation to a different topic.

Emotions: embarrassment, sadness, anxiety

Perfectionistic Thoughts:

* I should always be entertaining and funny.

* If I am not entertaining, people will not like me.

* People find me to be awkward, anxious, and boring.

Alternative Thoughts:

* It is okay not to be entertaining all the time.

* People won't judge me on the basis of one uncomfortable interaction.

* People find me interesting to be with.

Evaluating Perfectionistic Thoughts and Alternative Thoughts

* Nobody is entertaining all the time. Everyone has awkward moments from time to time.

* My friends know me well and are unlikely to judge me based on one conversation. In fact, some of my friends are not terribly good at telling jokes and I still enjoy being with them.

* For the rest of the evening, people seemed to talk to me normally, suggesting that they found me interesting and enjoyed my company.

* People probably find me interesting because they continue to invite me to spend time with them.

Choosing a More Realistic and Helpful Perspective

Perhaps I need to give myself permission to make mistakes when I am talking to other people. I do not judge other people when they say something unusual or awkward. Perhaps they are not judging me when I make mistakes.

Your Perfectionism Diary

Date: _____   *Time:* _____

Situation: _____

_____

Emotions: _____

_____

Perfectionistic Thoughts:

1. _____

2. _____

3. _____

Alternative Thoughts:

1. _____

2. _____

3. _____

Evaluating Perfectionistic Thoughts and Alternative Thoughts

1. _____

_____

2. _____

_____

3. _____

_____

Choosing a More Realistic and Helpful Perspective

_____

_____

Strategies for Changing Thoughts

There are many different ways to change thoughts. In this section, we describe methods that may be helpful. As you will see, these methods overlap with one another to some extent and aren't completely separate or distinct. Ideally, you should practice using strategies such as these each time your find yourself engaging in perfectionistic thinking. You may even use these strategies before the thought occurs. For example, if you are about to enter a situation or engage in some activity that usually leads to perfectionistic thinking (i.e., a hobby, sport, or task at work), you can anticipate the thoughts and challenge them before they even occur. If you forget to use these strategies, or if it is not practical to use these techniques before or during the episode of perfectionistic thinking, they may be used later.

Examining the Evidence

One of the most useful methods of challenging perfectionistic beliefs is to examine the evidence that confirms and contradicts your beliefs. This process may involve examining your previous experiences in a given situation. For example, if you believe that it would be terrible to receive less than an A on a paper, you could try to recall what happened in the past when you received a lower grade on a paper or exam. Did you survive the experience? What happens when other people receive grades that are lower than an A? Do terrible things necessarily occur as a result? The following conversation between a therapist and client illustrates how examining evidence for and against perfectionistic beliefs can be a helpful way of changing them:

Client	It really bothers me when my children lie. Yesterday at dinner, my four-year-old son fed his broccoli to the dog. When I asked him what happened to his broccoli, he said that *he* ate it. I was up all night worrying that my son was going to grow up to be a pathological liar.
Therapist	Rather than automatically assuming that your prediction is true, let's look at the evidence. Can you think of any evidence to support your prediction that your son is going to become a pathological liar?
Client	Well, I imagine that most people who lie a lot begin their lying in childhood.
Therapist	Are there reasons to think that your prediction may not come true?
Client	I guess my son doesn't lie that often. In fact, sometimes when he does lie, he feels so guilty that he admits his lie a day or two later.
Therapist	Can you think of times when you lied to your parents?
Client	I remember when I got into a minor accident in my father's car. I told him that the car was hit in a shopping mall parking lot, while I was shopping.
Therapist	Did you grow up to become a pathological liar?
Client	No, I guess I didn't.

Therapist	No one likes to be lied to. Nevertheless, most people do hide the truth from time to time. Perhaps we can find ways of helping you to be more accepting of others when they tell small lies.
Client	But isn't it wrong to lie?
Therapist	Being lied to can lead others to feel hurt and lose trust in the person who lies. Nevertheless, the severity of the lying can be looked at on a continuum. For example, there is a big difference between telling a small lie to avoid hurting a person's feelings, like when you tell someone you like their new haircut even when you don't, and cheating on your partner and then lying about the affair.
Client	I guess I have been treating all lying as the same. I was thinking that if someone told a small lie, they were likely to lie about anything and everything. I can see how that isn't really realistic.

Examining the evidence for your beliefs can combat many of the perfectionistic thinking styles that are described in chapter 3. For example, examining the evidence for and against a particular thought can be used to combat filtering (paying attention only to information that confirms or supports a perfectionistic thought). Similarly, catastrophic thinking (the tendency to assume that things would be terrible if a particular event were to occur) can be combated by asking questions such as, "What if that event did occur?" and "How could I cope with that if it were to happen?"

Education

One reason why people sometimes maintain perfectionistic beliefs is a lack of accurate information. Seeking accurate information on a given topic can help change perfectionistic or rigid beliefs. Becoming educated is one way of examining the evidence that supports and refutes perfectionistic beliefs.

For example, education can be a helpful method of changing unrealistic standards regarding weight and physical appearance. A significant proportion of the population (particularly among women in many Western cultures) is overly concerned about maintaining a weight that is actually below what is normally considered to be healthy. These unrealistic standards are probably related in part to constant exposure to models and celebrities who themselves are underweight. To help people change their overly stringent beliefs about how much body fat is acceptable, health professionals often educate their patients and clients about their ideal weight range—that is, the weight range that has been shown to be predictive of living longer and having fewer health problems.

Perspective Taking

Taking the perspective of another individual is a powerful way of changing perfectionistic beliefs. By perspective taking, we are referring to the process of asking the question, "How do other people view this situation?" Allowing yourself to view the situation as other people might can help to change unrealistic beliefs. Consider the following conversation between a therapist and client.

Client	If people notice how anxious I am during my presentation, they will surely think I'm a complete idiot.
Therapist	How would they know you are anxious?
Client	I tend to blush when I am nervous. Also, they would likely notice me losing my train of thought and forgetting certain words.
Therapist	Put yourself in the shoes of the audience members for a moment. Can you think of a time when you have seen another person blush or lose their train of thought?
Client	I have a good friend who often blushes.
Therapist	What do you think of this person when you notice them blushing?
Client	Actually, I rarely notice. If I do notice, I don't really give it much thought. I suppose that I might think he is embarrassed.
Therapist	Do you think he is an idiot?
Client	No, but that may be because I know him.
Therapist	When you see another presenter blushing, forgetting words, or looking anxious, do you think he or she is an idiot?
Client	No.
Therapist	Do you think others would view the presenter as an idiot?
Client	I suppose it is possible, but probably not.

Therapist	Then how likely is it that you will be viewed as an idiot if you blush or forget a few words during your presentation?
Client	I guess it's pretty unlikely. But, it's still a possibility. That's what bothers me.
Therapist	What if one or more people in the audience actually did you think you were an idiot? Would there be any real consequences?
Client	I always assumed that it would be terrible, but as I think about it now, I can't think of any real consequences. I guess nothing would happen.
Therapist	Is it okay for some people not to like you?
Client	I would prefer to always make a good impression, but I imagine that it wouldn't be the end of the world if I made a less than perfect impression sometimes.

One way of making it easier to take the perspective of other people is to actually ask other people how they think about a particular situation. A client in our clinic believed that it was essential that her house be completely dusted, cleaned, and vacuumed daily. Her parents kept a very clean home and she intended to do the same. This belief led her to spend several hours a day cleaning, at the expense of being able to look for work or enjoy other hobbies or activities. It also led to frequent arguments with her family because they refused to help. From their perspective, it was enough to vacuum and dust once a week. As a homework assignment, the woman was instructed to ask several friends and neighbors how often they dusted and vacuumed. She was surprised to discover that nobody—not even people whose homes she considered to be spotless—cleaned as often as she did. After surveying her friends' cleaning habits, she was willing to try cleaning less often and her family began to help more frequently.

Compromising with Yourself and Others

Rather than being unwilling to accept anything less than perfection, try asking the question, "What level of imperfection is acceptable?" You may believe that if you lower your standards regarding a particular dimension or issue, chaos will ensue. If the thought of lowering your standards *too much* is frightening, perhaps you can consider lowering them *somewhat*. This is a good technique for dealing with all-or-nothing thinking. If you tend to view situations in terms of black and white or right and wrong, it can be helpful to compromise by viewing things in shades of gray and realize that there are different ways of doing things. Viewing things as either right or wrong can lead a person to miss out on important complexities that are inherent in most situations.

You can also compromise with others when your standards are different than those around you. For example, if you have difficulty discarding or giving away old objects (e.g., clothing, magazines, household items, etc.), and your family asks you to reduce the clutter, perhaps you could agree to throw out items that you haven't looked at or used for a certain length of time (e.g., one year, five years, etc.). This might be a good compromise between keeping everything (which is what your perfectionism may be telling you to do) and throwing out everything (which is what your family may be telling you to do).

Hypothesis Testing

An excellent way to test the accuracy of your perfectionistic thoughts and predictions is to carry out small experiments, a process also known as hypothesis testing. By choosing these experiments carefully, you can disprove your perfectionistic beliefs. For example, if you tend to write papers that are too detailed, try leaving out some of the detail and seeing what happens. Either way, you will obtain valuable information. If there is no consequence, you will learn that your beliefs regarding the importance of including all of the details are not true. On the other hand, if your boss tells you that your most recent report was not detailed enough, you will learn that the amount of detail you had in your earlier reports was appropriate and you can readjust.

Hypothesis testing can be used to test the validity of most perfectionistic predictions. By behaving in ways that do not meet your own high standards (e.g., purposely making small mistakes in your work, saying things incorrectly, leaving the house dirty, etc.), you will learn whether the standards are in fact necessary. Of course, you want to choose exercises that are relevant to your perfectionistic thoughts. If you are not overly concerned about the cleanliness of your house, there is no reason for you to purposely leave the house messy. Also, you should use good judgment when designing hypothesis-testing experiments. Do not select experiments that have a very good chance of backfiring and leading to serious negative consequences. For example, if you are a nurse who worries about giving a patient an incorrect medication unless you check it fifteen times, a good exercise might be to check it only once or twice. On the other hand, a bad use of hypothesis testing would be to purposely give a patient the wrong medication to see if anything bad happens.

Exercise 7.2
Hypothesis Testing for Your Perfectionistic Beliefs

Below is an example of a form that can be used to help in the process of hypothesis testing. Before conducting the experiment, make particular predictions regarding what is likely to happen. Then, conduct the experiment and record what actually occurs. You may be surprised at how often your predictions don't come true.

Hypothesis Testing Form

Date: May 3   *Time:*   4:00 P.M.

Experiment: Arrive five minutes late for a doctor's appointment instead of thirty minutes early.

Predicted Outcome: The receptionist and doctor will be angry with me.

Actual Outcome: Neither the receptionist nor the doctor seemed angry at all. In fact, the doctor talked to me for quite a while about her new house and ended up being ten minutes late for her next appointment.

Hypothesis Testing Form

Date: _____   *Time:* _____

Experiment: _____

_____

Predicted Outcome: _____

_____

Actual Outcome: _____

_____

Changing Your Social Comparison Habits

As mentioned in chapter 3, everyone compares themselves to other people as a way of evaluating their standing or performance in a particular area. Most people compare themselves to their peers. For example, if they want to evaluate whether they are doing a good job at work, they might compare themselves to their co-workers.

People who are perfectionists may be more likely to compare themselves to people who are much more experienced and skilled in that particular area. For example, perfectionistic beginning or amateur musicians might compare themselves to musicians who have already achieved great success (as measured by their ability to play music, their income, or their popularity). The tendency to compare oneself to people who are perceived as significantly more skilled, attractive, intelligent, physically fit, or "better" in some other way can make an individual feel more depressed or anxious about not meeting his or her own high standards. Therefore, it may be helpful to try to limit your social comparisons to people who are more similar to you in a particular dimension.

Looking at the Big Picture

Perfectionism is sometimes associated with a tendency to focus on unimportant details rather than looking at the big picture. Looking at the big picture involves assessing the overall impact of a particular event, situation, or outcome on your life. Situations that seem so important in the moment rarely end up being particularly important even a short time later. Below are some examples of perfectionistic statements followed by alternative statements that illustrate how to look at the big picture:

Perfectionistic Statement	What am I going to do? I didn't do well on my English exam.
Alternative Statement	It is unlikely that my grade on this exam will have any impact on what I am doing a year from now (e.g., my career, income, relationships, etc.).
Perfectionistic Statement	I feel terrible that the cake that I made for my daughter's birthday party did not turn out the way I hoped it would.
Alternative Statement	The children will probably still enjoy the cake, and even if they don't, it won't matter a week from now.

Perfectionistic Statement	My haircut looks terrible and I am terrified of being seen in public.
Alternative Statement	People on the street are much less interested in my hair than I am and they probably won't even notice. Besides, my hair will grow back eventually.
Perfectionistic Statement	It drives me crazy when my partner leaves her jacket lying on the floor.
Alternative Statement	I guess she only leaves her jacket lying around once a week or so. It's a small price to pay for an otherwise wonderful relationship.
Perfectionistic Statement	I'm so upset that my new car has a small scratch on the fender.
Alternative Statement	It is normal for cars to have small scratches. If it didn't happen today, it would have happened sooner or later.

Coping Statements

The process of changing perfectionistic thoughts and beliefs is complex. It involves using any of a number of techniques to identify the negative thoughts and replace them with more realistic alternative thoughts. Sometimes, you may not have the time to challenge your perfectionistic thoughts using some of the other strategies described in this chapter. Other times, you may feel so anxious, depressed, or angry that it is difficult to think clearly about the situation. Coping statements may be helpful in cases where it is difficult to use some of the other strategies discussed in this chapter. Coping statements are simple phrases that you can memorize and say to yourself when you find yourself thinking like a perfectionist. For example, saying to yourself, "It's okay to make mistakes," can make it easier to get through a stressful or difficult task. Similarly, the phrase, "It's okay if some people don't like me," can make it easier to deal with social situations that are anxiety provoking. Reminding yourself that there are many different "right" ways to fold laundry can help decrease the frustration that occurs when your family members fold the laundry differently than you like it.

Coping statements involve more than just "positive thinking." In fact, coping statements should reflect thoughts that you actually can believe, and they should be realistic—not just positive. For example, if you typically find yourself becoming anxious when giving a presentation, it wouldn't be helpful to prepare for a talk by saying to yourself, "I will not be anxious during this presentation." On the other hand, it might help to remind yourself that even if you do become anxious, there will be no real consequences, other than the temporary discomfort that you feel. If you decide to use coping statements, we recommend that you record them on an index card and carry them with you. This will help prompt your memory until these statements become second nature.

Tolerating Uncertainty and Ambiguity

Perfectionists go to great pains to control many different aspects of their lives, including their own behavior, the behavior of other people, and the environment in which they live. Although most people feel more comfortable when they can predict and control events that occur (particularly negative events), the need to know and control are often much stronger for people who have rigid, perfectionistic beliefs. For example, a person who is applying for a job may find it very difficult to wait until she finds out whether the job materializes. Similarly, arriving home to find a note from your partner saying that he or she will be home "later" may be frustrating, as it may make you uncomfortable that there is no time specified in the note. Because you often cannot control or predict things that occur, it can be helpful to find ways to tolerate some degree of uncertainty and ambiguity in your life.

One way of dealing with uncertainty involves mentally preparing for several possible outcomes. To return to the examples described above, the people who are waiting to find out about the job can make some decisions about what they might do if they get the job and what they might do if they don't get the job. Similarly, if you are impatiently waiting for your partner to come home, but have no idea when to expect him or her, you can prepare for the possibility that he or she will return in the next few minutes, in an hour, or in several hours. By preparing for different possible outcomes, the uncertainty is likely to be less frustrating or anxiety provoking.

Another way of combating the need for certainty and control is to ask yourself questions such as, "Why do I need to know what will happen?" "Can I cope with not knowing?" "Is it really as important as it feels for me to control this situation or be able to predict exactly how it will turn out?"

Difficulty Believing Your Alternative Thoughts

One of the most common complaints of individuals who try to use the strategies described in this chapter is what is sometimes called the "head/heart problem." The head/heart problem occurs when an individual knows rationally that a particular style of thinking is incorrect or inappropriate, but nevertheless *feels* that the negative way of thinking is correct. In other words, the head is able to think about the situation in a realistic way, but the heart continues to think about the situation in a perfectionistic way. For example, you may realize rationally that there is generally very little to lose by making small mistakes. Nevertheless, you may continue to feel awful every time you do certain things incorrectly.

Try thinking about the head/heart problem with two things in mind. First, you need to realize that your perfectionistic beliefs have probably been around for a long time. The techniques described in this chapter are skills that need to be built through practice. It will take a while for the perfectionistic beliefs to change. With practice, it should become easier to believe the new, more flexible ways of thinking.

Second, it is possible that trying to think rationally about situations that trigger your perfectionism may not be enough. You may actually need to do something differently rather than just try to think differently. The techniques described in the next chapter involve changing perfectionistic behaviors. Behavioral strategies are among the most powerful ways to change thoughts, because they create new learning experiences that directly disprove your perfectionistic thoughts.

Chapter 8 _____

Changing Perfectionistic Behaviors

Why Change Perfectionistic Behaviors?

Perhaps the most effective method of overcoming perfectionism is to change the behaviors that help to maintain your perfectionistic beliefs, attitudes, and predictions. If you have a tendency to set very high standards for yourself or others, you probably use some of the behaviors discussed in chapter 4, either to ensure that your standards are met or to avoid the situations that force you to confront your high standards. Examples of perfectionistic behaviors include overcompensating by doing much more than is necessary to deal with a situation, excessive checking and reassurance seeking, repeating behaviors, excessive organizing and list making, procrastination, failure to delegate tasks to others, and avoidance of anxiety-provoking situations.

Behaviors that are associated with perfectionism actually help to maintain the problem. By engaging in these behaviors, you prevent yourself from actually testing out and disproving your perfectionistic thoughts. In other words, continuing to behave like a perfectionist makes it difficult to stop thinking like a perfectionist. For example, if you believe that only by checking and rechecking your work can you maintain your high standards, the act of repeatedly checking your work will prevent you from ever finding out whether that belief is true.

Similarly, procrastinating on a project because you are worried about not being able to do an adequate job prevents you from ever ing out whether that prediction is true. In fact, procrastination ten makes it more difficult to perform well because, in the end, you have less time and are under more pressure. Therefore, procrastination can end up confirming your anxious beliefs about not being able to do a job well.

In small amounts, the behaviors we are describing as perfectionistic can be helpful. For example, proofreading an important report *once* is likely to improve the quality of your work. Putting off an unpleasant task *for a short time* may give you the necessary break that you need to later tackle the job. On the other hand, overdoing these behaviors is likely to cause problems. For example, excessive checking gives you less time to do other things and may even increase your anxiety. Correcting other people too often may lead them to feel inadequate or angry with you for not trusting them. Including too much detail in your conversations with other people can lead the other person to become bored and to start daydreaming—therefore missing most of what you are trying to say.

In this way, changing the behavior patterns that are associated with your perfectionism is an important step toward overcoming the problem. The strategies described in this chapter are especially important for people who have difficulty identifying or changing specific thoughts using the cognitive strategies discussed in chapter 7. These techniques involve trying to change thoughts by examining the evidence for and against them and by trying to replace negative thinking patterns with more realistic beliefs. In contrast, the behavioral strategies discussed in this chapter change beliefs directly by providing new learning experiences that disprove the thoughts. Therefore, changing perfectionistic behaviors leads to automatic changes in perfectionistic thoughts.

Strategies for Changing Perfectionistic Behaviors

Exposure-Based Strategies

For the past few decades, therapies based on *exposure* have been used to treat anxiety disorders such as social phobia and obsessive-compulsive disorder, and to a lesser extent, other problems such as depression and eating disorders. Basically, exposure involves confronting a feared object or situation over and over again until the fear has decreased. For people who are fearful of driving, we encourage them to practice driving until the discomfort subsides. For people who fear heights, we have them encounter high places until they no longer experience significant fear. Exposure is the best strategy to use for dealing with situations that trigger intense negative reactions, such as fear or anger. Similarly, exposure can be especially helpful for people who tend to avoid situations because of their perfectionism.

Exposure is a very effective strategy for dealing with unrealistic fears. In the case of certain phobias, such as animal phobias, up to 90 percent of individuals are able to overcome their fear in a matter of hours (Öst 1989). For other fears, changes may take longer, but still a considerable percentage of people benefit from exposure-based treatments. In our experience, exposure is also very useful for dealing with perfectionism, which is often associated with a fear of being imperfect or failing to meet some goal or standard. In dealing with perfectionism, exposure involves purposely allowing oneself to repeatedly encounter "imperfect" situations that cause anxiety, frustration, or discomfort, until they are no longer a problem.

The effects of exposure on fear and anxiety are universal. Even animals seem to become less anxious after repeated exposure to a frightening situation. For example, a new puppy may be fearful of strangers or of walking near busy streets. With repeated exposure, however, these situations become easier. In our experience, even spiders respond to exposure. When we work with people who are phobic of spiders, we encourage them to confront spiders by being near them and eventually touching them. Not only do our clients become less fearful of the spiders, but the spiders seem to become less fearful of humans. By the end of the treatment session, the spider is much less likely to run away from humans, compared to their behavior at the beginning of the session.

In order to use exposure as a treatment for perfectionism, you must first identify situations that make you uncomfortable and then create exposure practices to target those particular situations. Later in this chapter, we describe exactly how to conduct exposure practices for particular situations that may occur.

Why Exposure Works

Exposure is based on the premise that people can get used to almost anything if they are given enough time. For example, people who go camping in the wilderness get used to being dirty if they do not have access to running water for a shower or bath. During war, people may even get used to the sound of bombs going off in nearby neighborhoods. If you watched the news coverage at the start of the Gulf War in 1991, you may recall the voices of CNN reporters Peter

Arnett, John Holliman, and Bernard Shaw, reporting from Baghdad when the allied forces first attacked Iraq. When the war first began, the cameras showed the bombing outside the building, and the reporters were understandably very frightened—the fear could be heard in their voices. However, after a few days of bombing, the reporters sounded much calmer, even though the situation was more or less the same.

There are several different theories regarding why exposure works. One of the most compelling explanations is based on a cognitive model. From a cognitive view, exposure works by changing a person's beliefs about the feared situation. In other words, after repeated experiences in the feared situation, the person gradually learns that nothing bad is going to happen and eventually learns to see the situation as nonthreatening and safe. In the case of perfectionism, exposure works in part by teaching a person that even if mistakes are made, the consequences are usually not terrible. Even if your performance is not to someone else's liking, the situation is likely to be manageable. The same rule applies when someone else's behavior doesn't meet your high standards. It's bound to happen, and when it does, it's unlikely to be the end of the world. Exposure to situations where your standards are unlikely to be met is an excellent way to learn that these situations need not be threatening or that you may benefit from adjusting your standards.

Types of Exposure

Exposure-based strategies were first developed in the 1950s by a psychiatrist named Joseph Wolpe. In order to help people overcome their phobias, Wolpe (1958) used a method that he called *systematic desensitization*. This procedure began with teaching the patient exercises designed to relax the muscles of the body. After the person was proficient at conducting the relaxation exercises, he or she was instructed to imagine the feared situation while maintaining a state of relaxation. The sessions would begin with imagining situations that were mildly anxiety provoking and would gradually increase the intensity until the person was able to imagine situations that were more frightening. For example, a person who feared snakes might have been instructed to start by imagining looking at a tiny snake at a distance in a sealed aquarium and eventually work up to imagining holding a large snake.

Although systematic desensitization was a breakthrough in the treatment of phobias, exposure-based treatments have come a long way since systematic desensitization was first introduced. We now know that exposure works even better if it is done live instead of in imagination. We also know that exposure works just as well if it is not paired with relaxation exercises. Now the treatment of choice for many phobias is actual live exposure to feared situations, without any relaxation component. Exposure is also used for a broader range of problems. For example, a woman with an eating disorder who is fearful of eating certain foods may find that her fear decreases if she allows herself to eat her "forbidden" foods and finds that the consequences are not catastrophic.

There are different ways in which exposure can be conducted. As already mentioned, exposure can be conducted live (also called *in vivo exposure*) or in the imagination. Although we recommend live exposure whenever possible, exposure in imagination may be appropriate in cases where live exposure is impractical, impossible, or too frightening. For example, if you tend to be very frightened of making mistakes during presentations, we recommend first that you try live exposure by practicing making presentations and even making minor mistakes that are unlikely to cause any real harm (e.g., purposely pausing for a few moments, as if you've lost your train of thought). However, if the thought of giving a real presentation is too overwhelming, you could start by imagining that you are giving a presentation and work up to the real thing.

A second way in which exposure practices can vary is in terms of how gradually steps are taken. We don't recommend that you start by practicing in the most upsetting situation that you can imagine. Rather, we recommend that you start with easier situations and gradually work up to more difficult situations. The rate at which you take steps toward more and more difficult situations is up to you. The faster you take steps, the quicker you will learn to tolerate more difficult situations. However, taking steps more quickly may also lead to more intense discomfort during the practices.

How to Conduct Exposure

When we present the rationale for exposure to our patients, they often point out, "I'm already exposed to the situation that I fear from time to time, but it doesn't seem to help." In fact, some people report that their fear and anxiety actually becomes worse after exposure to the feared situation. For exposure to be effective, it has to be done in a particular way. For example, if you were afraid of snakes and someone threw a snake at you, that experience would not lead to a decrease in fear. In everyday life, exposure to feared situations tends to be unpredictable, brief, and infrequent. For example, when arachnophobic individuals encounter a spider, it is usually a surprise (unpredictable exposure). In addition, they usually leave the situation quickly (brief exposure) and go through a lot of trouble to make sure it doesn't happen again (infrequent exposure). Also, people who are anxious or uncomfortable in a particular situation tend to use subtle ways of avoiding the full impact of the situation (e.g., distraction, excessive checking, or other overprotective behaviors), so they don't really benefit from the exposure.

To maximize the benefits of exposure practices, there are several steps you can take. First, in preparing to conduct exposure practices, develop an exposure hierarchy. An exposure hierarchy is a list of anxiety-provoking situations that are ranked in terms of difficulty. This list can be used to help guide your practices. The items in the hierarchy should be as specific as possible and should be items that are practical and that can actually be practiced if you decide to do so. In other words, you should not choose items that would be impossible to try if you chose to do so. Following are some examples of exposure practices that can be conducted to change particular types of perfectionistic concerns:

Perfectionistic Thought	Sample Exposure Practice
I cannot handle my house being a mess.	Leave particular areas in the house messy.
I spend hours trying to get my hair perfect.	Spend no more than five minutes on my hair.
I feel compelled to correct my wife when she mispronounces words.	Ask wife to purposely mispronounce words in a way that happens to bother me.
It would be terrible to have someone else notice my hands shaking.	Carry a glass of water and let my hand shake.
There is only one right way to fold socks.	Fold socks in various "wrong" ways.
I avoid asking my secretary to do my typing because I am very particular about the way I like it done.	Ask my secretary to type my letters.

Once you have identified specific exercises that may help to challenge your high standards, the next step is to develop your exposure hierarchy. First, generate a list of ten to twenty exposure exercises. These should be practices that are of varying degrees of difficulty. They should include items that range in difficulty from mildly difficult to extremely difficult. Next, estimate (using a scale from 0–100) how uncomfortable you will be conducting the practice. The final step is to rank order the items in the hierarchy from hardest to easiest.

After developing your exposure hierarchy, you will be ready to start your exposure practices. Start with easier items and work your way up to more difficult items. As you go along, you will find that some items become too easy and you may want to delete those from the hierarchy. Some steps may be too difficult, in which case you can add some in-between steps to make the process more gradual. It is okay to skip steps as you go along. The quicker you take steps, the quicker the situations will become easier. On the other hand, quicker steps will likely lead to more discomfort during your practices. Choose a pace that provides a balance between exercises that are manageable but also challenging.

If you have several different areas of perfectionism, you can develop separate exposure hierarchies for each area. For example, if you have very high standards with respect to cleanliness and school work, you can develop a hierarchy of situations for each of these areas. Or, if you prefer, you may combine them into one hierarchy and work on them together. Deciding between these two approaches is a matter of preference. However, you should keep in mind that trying to do too many things at once may compromise your success.

Sample Exposure Hierarchy: Fear of Making Mistakes in Front of Others (Social Anxiety)

Item	Fear (0–100)
Give a formal presentation about unfamiliar material in front of people whom I don't know well (e.g., at work).	99
Throw a party for people from work and prepare a difficult dish that I have never made before.	85
Purposely forget my wallet when in line at the supermarket.	85
Ask someone to repeat themselves at my weekly staff meeting.	75

Show up for an appointment (e.g., a haircut) on the wrong day.	60
Have lunch with a co-worker and allow uncomfortable silences.	50
Answer a question in my night school class.	45
Forget my ticket when I pick up my dry cleaning.	40

Exercise 8.1
Completing Your Own Exposure Hierarchy Form

Item	Fear (0–100)

Design Practices That Are Predictable, Structured, and Planned in Advance.

Exposure works best when it is predictable and under your control as much as possible. Try to choose practices that you have structured carefully and that have predictable outcomes. This is especially important in the beginning. For example, if you are working on becoming less perfectionistic about your physical appearance, decide in advance the ways that you will practice breaking standards that you have for your appearance (e.g., spending less time on your hair, wearing clothes that don't match, etc.). Later, you can purposely build more unpredictable practices into your program.

For many practices, you can't always know the outcome. For example, if you decide to practice arriving a few minutes late for appointments (to compensate for your belief that you always need to be early for everything), you cannot always predict what will happen. Some people may not care, whereas others may be annoyed at having to wait for you. To deal with this situation, you can imagine several possible outcomes and think about how you can deal with them if they occur. Of course, you don't want to choose practices that are likely to get you into big trouble, like not showing up for work at all or completely missing a final exam. If you are not sure whether a practice is appropriate and safe, ask a few people whom you trust for their opinion.

Continue the Practice Until Your Anxiety Has Decreased

The goal of exposure is to learn that you can be in a situation and eventually feel comfortable. Exposure works best when the practice is prolonged. So, if you are nervous about being around people you don't know because you may say something "stupid," try spending an extended period with someone who makes you anxious (e.g., have a long lunch) until the anxiety decreases. If you are uncomfortable leaving a mess in your house, try leaving things messy until you get used to it. Although prolonged exposure works best, some exposures are necessarily brief (e.g., asking a question in a meeting). In other situations, you may feel too overwhelmed to stay in the situation until the fear decreases. That's okay. However, the best way to compensate for brief exposures is to repeat them often. If you absolutely must stop an exposure practice, the best thing you can do is to repeat the practice as soon as possible.

Practice Frequently and Schedule Your Practices Close Together

Exposure works best if the practices are spaced close together. For example, if you are afraid of speaking in front of groups because you may make a mistake, giving presentations once a year may never lead to a reduction in your fear. On the other hand, if you practiced giving presentations for five or ten days in a row, you would notice a substantial reduction in fear over the course of the practices. Weekly practice works better than practicing once a month. Daily practice works better than once a week. We recommend that you try to practice at least four or five days a week for an extended period each time. Or, if the situation is one that comes up even more frequently, try to practice whenever you have the opportunity.

Expect to Feel Uncomfortable

Often, when we ask people to practice exposure, they return the next week and tell us that it didn't go well because they were anxious during the exposure practice. Remember, if you have chosen an appropriately difficult situation, you *should* feel anxious. That's why you are doing the exposure practices in the first place. If you feel anxious during an exposure practice, it's a sign that you need to continue practicing, rather than a sign that things are not going well. If you are not anxious during a practice, we recommend that you choose a more difficult situation the next time.

With repeated practices, your anxiety will decrease. However, that doesn't mean that there will be a decrease in anxiety each time you practice. Occasionally, some practices will be more difficult than previous ones. This may be because it is a more difficult situation or because you are feeling less prepared (e.g., more tired, less confident, etc.). For every few steps forward, there may be a step back. It's part of getting over any fear. Also, it is possible that on days when you confront situations that make you anxious, your overall level of stress will be higher. You may even be more irritable with people who are close to you. As your anxiety decreases, other stress-related feelings such as irritability will decrease as well.

Don't Use Subtle Avoidance Strategies

Subtle avoidance strategies are techniques that you may use to make encountering an anxiety-provoking situation more bearable. These may include distraction, reassurance seeking, checking, and other "tricks" for managing the discomfort. These techniques may help to manage your discomfort in the short term. However, like more overt forms of avoidance, they prevent you from learning that your perfectionistic thoughts are exaggerated or untrue. In addition, subtle avoidance techniques can undo the effects of your exposure practices. Therefore, try not to use these techniques if at all possible.

Use Cognitive Strategies to Cope with Discomfort During Practices

What you tell yourself, or how you interpret the situation, can have an enormous impact on your experience during an exposure practice. Therefore, it will be helpful to use some of the cognitive strategies discussed in chapter 7 to deal with negative thoughts that may occur during exposure practices. For example, you may decide to use the process of hypothesis testing as a way of dealing with negative predictions. Using this method, you can treat your exposure practices like small experiments, designed to test the validity of your perfectionistic thoughts. There are a few other specific strategies that can be helpful for dealing with anxiety or discomfort experienced during your exposure practices. If you are purposely entering situations where you fear that you may behave imperfectly or incorrectly, make a decision to allow yourself to be imperfect. Ask yourself the question, "Can I handle imperfection in this situation?" Also, you can remind yourself that the anxiety is temporary and will gradually decrease. In most cases, the worst thing that will happen during an exposure practice is that you will feel uncomfortable.

Exercise 8.2
Your Exposure Diary

Use the form below to record the outcome of your exposure practices. In the first column, record the date and time of the practice. In the second column, record the nature of your practice, including the specific exercise, the duration of the exercise, and other relevant details. In the third column, record your average discomfort level during the practice (using a scale from 0–100). You should notice a decrease in your anxiety as you continue to practice exposure.

Date/Time	Situation	Anxiety (0–100)

		Anxiety
Date/Time	**Situation**	**(0–100)**
_____	_____	_____
_____	_____	_____
_____	_____	_____
_____	_____	_____
_____	_____	_____
_____	_____	_____
_____	_____	_____

Response Prevention

A second strategy for changing perfectionistic behaviors is response prevention. Response prevention involves taking steps to stop yourself from engaging in problematic perfectionistic behaviors. By preventing these behaviors, you will learn that many of these actions serve no real function, other than to decrease your anxiety or discomfort for a short time. For example, if you tend to check your work over and over, preventing the rechecking will teach you that if you stop checking excessively, the quality of your work will not suffer. Other perfectionistic behaviors for which response prevention can be helpful include correcting or checking the behavior of other people, looking at your watch or clock often (to make sure that you are on time), checking your weight or physical appearance, arguing with teachers or professors to have a point or two added to your course grade, excessively washing or cleaning, or participating any other repetitive behavior that you use to make sure that your standards are met or to reduce your anxiety about not meeting your standards.

It is important to do what you can to prevent these behaviors. At first, you may find that your anxiety or discomfort increases significantly when you prevent the behaviors. You may worry about the consequences of not checking, cleaning, or correcting. However, after a while, the discomfort should decrease as you learn that nothing terrible happens when you start to eliminate these behaviors.

The behaviors associated with your perfectionism may be so ingrained and habitual that you are not even aware of when you are doing them. There are a number of ways that you can make yourself more aware. First, you can use a diary to record times when you engage in behaviors such as checking, repeating, correcting, cleaning, counting, or asking for reassurance. Pay special attention to the specific situations, moods, and places that trigger these behaviors, as well as the way you feel after you engage in these behaviors. This exercise should make you more aware of the perfectionistic behaviors that need to be stopped. If you still have trouble identifying these behaviors, ask someone who is close to you to help point them out. With practice, you should eventually become more aware of your perfectionistic rituals.

Communication Training

A third strategy for changing perfectionistic behaviors is communication training. Communication training is useful when perfectionism affects the way you communicate with other people. For example, perfectionism causes some people to communicate in a disapproving or judgmental way with others who do not meet certain perfectionistic standards. If this is a problem for you, it may be important to examine how you communicate your high expectations to other people in your life. Often, perfectionism is associated with an intense drive to change the behavior of other people so that they conform to your high standards. This drive may cause you to constantly nag, correct, or even offend other people with the message that their behavior is not good enough. This message can cause them to feel angry or hurt.

For individuals who are more self-focused in their perfectionism, communication may be affected by a tendency to communicate passively and have difficulty listening to what other people are saying. A full discussion of how to change communication patterns is beyond the scope of this book; for a more detailed discussion of this topic, we recommend the book *Messages* (McKay, Davis, and Fanning 1995), listed in Further Readings at the end of this book. There are, however, a few general guidelines that we can provide for you.

Be Assertive

Everyone encounters situations in which the behavior of other people is inconsistent with their own expectations. However, perfectionism can lead people to communicate their disapproval in a way that is not terribly helpful. By understanding how you communicate and by working on your communication skills, you can lessen the risk of alienating others.

There are three general styles of communication. The first style, known as *passive communication*, involves communicating indirectly and putting the needs and rights of others ahead of your own needs.

For example, rather than expressing disagreement about a particular topic, a person who communicates passively may be more likely than others to pretend to agree, in order to avoid being criticized. Similarly, a passive communicator may find indirect ways to express his or her needs and desires. Some perfectionists (particularly people who tend to feel depressed or socially anxious) may constantly feel that they are not living up to their own standards. They may be at risk for using passive communication if they believe that other people will find what they have to say to be uninteresting or unimportant. Passive communication is not terribly effective. Other people are unlikely to hear your message if it is communicated passively.

A second style of communication is known as *aggressive communication*. Aggressive communication involves putting your own needs ahead of the needs of other people. Aggressive communication often involves putting too much pressure on other people to do things your way. It may be associated with being hurtful or insulting to those around you and usually leads to the other person shutting down and not listening to you or becoming very angry with you. People who have perfectionistic beliefs regarding how other people should behave may become quite pushy and aggressive in their attempts to have other people conform to their high expectations.

The third and most effective style of communication is called *assertive communication*. Being assertive involves taking into account both your own rights and needs as well as the rights and needs of the other individual. Assertive communication involves three main components: describing the situation in the most objective, nonbiased, and nonjudgmental way possible; describing how the situation affects the way you feel (e.g., the emotion that you are experiencing); and describing how you would like the situation to change. Although assertive communication is not guaranteed to work, it tends to be more effective than passive and aggressive communication styles. Following are illustrations of how each of the three communication styles might be used to tell a child that his or her bedroom needs to be cleaned:

> *Passive*: Look into the room, let out a sigh and role your eyes.
>
> *Aggressive*: Say to the child, "You are a complete slob. You are never going to amount to anything unless you can learn to be more organized."
>
> *Assertive*: Say to the child, "Your toys are all over your floor. I feel frustrated when I have to clean your room. I

would like you to clean your room before you go out today, please."

Unlike passive communication, assertive communication is likely to be heard and understood by the other individual. Unlike aggressive communication, assertive communication is less likely to lead the other person to automatically disagree or feel hurt.

Listen

An important part of any communication is listening to the other person. Listening involves hearing what the other person has to say and making a genuine attempt to understand his or her point of view. Perfectionism can get in the way of listening. If you are overly critical of the other person, you may tend to focus your attention on mistakes that the other person makes rather than on the entire communication. If you are overly critical of yourself, you may miss important aspects of the other person's communication if you are paying too much attention to how you are coming across or are thinking about what you are going to say next while the other person is talking.

A helpful way of making sure that you have heard and understood what the other person has said is to repeat back to the person what you have heard and to ask for clarification if there is a misunderstanding. However, moderation is the key. If you happen to be a person who compulsively asks for reassurance and checks excessively to make sure you are understanding other people, we recommend that you cut back rather than increase this behavior.

Pay Attention to Nonverbal Communication

The words people say are only a small part of their communication. Nonverbal communication plays an enormous role in how others interpret what you say. Nonverbal communication includes such things as voice quality (e.g., tone, volume, inflection, rate of speech), facial expressions, and body posture. Even if your words are not critical of the people around you, your perfectionism may lead you to communicate your disapproval in nonverbal ways (e.g., frowning, crossing your arms, leaning back). If you can be aware of your nonverbal communication patterns, you can also take steps to ensure that you are not inflicting your perfectionistic standards on others in nonverbal ways.

Prioritizing

Do you have difficulty getting things done on time? Or, do you spend so much time trying to get everything done that you sacrifice other important areas in your life? A fourth strategy for changing perfectionistic behaviors involves prioritizing. Prioritizing is important for individuals who always feel like they have to get everything done right away. It may also be helpful for people who have problems deciding what to do first (in case they make a "wrong" decision). The process of prioritizing involves three steps.

The first step involves generating lists of tasks that need to be completed. Ideally, this should be done on paper. You may include separate lists for things that need to be done today (e.g., take out garbage, finish report, get haircut, etc.) and things that need to be done some time, but not right away (e.g., invite neighbors over for dinner, buy new lamp, get new passport, take up tennis, etc.).

The second step involves examining the list (or lists) and ranking the items in terms of importance. Just because it feels important that you finish a task doesn't mean that it is important. To assess the importance of the tasks, you need to assess the possible consequences of not completing an item. When you ask the question, "What will happen if I don't finish the task?" you will come to realize that many of the items are not as important as they seemed.

The third step is to begin completing the tasks in order of importance. You should try to be realistic about what can be done and about the possible consequences of not completing certain tasks. If you have problems deciding which task to do first, it may be because it doesn't matter which one you do first. If that is the case, pick one task (flip a coin) and start with it.

Overcoming Procrastination

The final strategy for changing perfectionistic behaviors is geared toward overcoming procrastination. People procrastinate for a variety of reasons including not enjoying the particular task or job, not having time to work on the task, being fearful of not being able to complete the task well, and not knowing where to start. In the case of perfectionism, the last two reasons are particularly relevant. If you tend to procrastinate, some of the strategies that we have discussed already (e.g., prioritizing, exposure) may be helpful. We recommend that you break up the task into smaller, more manageable tasks. Rather than thinking about how overwhelming the entire job is, try dividing the job into smaller jobs that are easily completed. This strategy has been essential in helping us write this book. Below is a description of how we managed to divide the task of writing a book on perfectionism into smaller, manageable tasks.

Steps for Writing this Book

1. Develop a table of contents

2. Develop a list of main headings for chapter 1

3. For each main heading, generate a list of subheadings for each topic

4. Write a first draft of the information that belongs under the first subheading

5. Repeat step 4 for each subheading in chapter 1

6. Proofread and make revisions to chapter 1

7. Repeat steps 2 through 6 for each of the other chapters

You can use this same strategy for any task. For example, if you are procrastinating about writing a letter, you can break the task into small jobs, such as getting out the paper, addressing the envelope, developing a brief outline, writing the first paragraph, and so on. Each step in isolation is unlikely to be overwhelming. If you come across a particular step that is overwhelming, break it down into even smaller steps.

Part III

Working with Specific Problems and Perfectionism

Chapter 9 _____

Perfectionism and Depression

_____

The Nature of Depression

You have probably experienced a period of sadness or depression following a significant loss in your life. Perhaps it was following the breakup of a relationship, death of someone close to you, loss of a job, or inability to achieve some goal. For most people, losses such as these tend to trigger periods of sadness, depression, or grieving. Most people also experience sadness from time to time, even in the absence of a significant loss. They may feel overwhelmed with work, hurt by the behavior of a significant person in their lives, or lonely for no particular reason. Sadness and depression are universal emotions.

Although sadness is a normal experience for all people, sometimes feelings of depression can be so intense or chronic that they begin to interfere with a person's ability to enjoy life or function in his or her environment. The severity of depression (e.g., the intensity, frequency, and impact of feeling sad) is on a continuum from very mild to very severe. Although this chapter is written for people who experience a level of depression that interferes with their lives, people who experience depression at mild levels may still find the information helpful, particularly if their depressed feelings are related in part to not meeting their own expectations for themselves or for other people.

Normal Feelings of Sadness

Psychologist Sidney Blatt and his colleagues (1976) have identi-fied three components of normal depressed mood: dependency, self-criticism, and inefficacy. Although these components are present in normal depressed mood, they also tend to be present in clinical depression, often at a much greater intensity.

Dependency

Dependency is the perception of needing help and support from other people. When people are feeling sad, they tend to want to affili-ate with other people. So, after doing poorly on an exam or receiving a poor evaluation at work, you may feel inclined to go out with friends or to spend a quiet evening at home with your family or your partner. Or, when feeling sad, you may be inclined to phone a close friend just to talk. Of course, not everyone responds this way when feeling down. Some people may isolate themselves when feeling sad, particularly if the depression is more severe. Even so, there still may be a perception of helplessness and a desire for support from other people.

Self-Criticism

Self-criticism is a tendency to exaggerate one's faults. A number of researchers have demonstrated a phenomenon known as *state-dependent memory*. In general, when people are in a particular emo-tional state (e.g., feeling sad), they are more likely to recall previous periods when they felt the same way, as well as past events that are consistent with their low mood. For example, if you are feeling sad following the breakup of a relationship, you may tend to remember all of the problems with your previous relationships. You may also exaggerate all of your own shortcomings that are perceived as having contributed to the breakup. Similarly, if you are feeling sad about doing poorly on a job at work, you may dwell on all the ways that you don't measure up to your co-workers' performances or to your own standards.

Inefficacy

Inefficacy is a sense that important events are independent of your actions. In other words, you may feel at times that no matter what you do, you cannot influence the outcome of events (i.e., being rejected by other people, losing close people in your life, doing poorly in school, having financial problems, or experiencing other significant life stresses). This feeling of helplessness or a lack of control often goes along with feeling sad or depressed.

Although sadness is a normal part of life for everyone, some people experience levels of depression that may interfere with their ability to function properly at work, at home, or in their relationships. When depression is severe enough to cause significant impairment, it is often referred to as *clinical depression*.

Clinical Depression

Researchers and clinicians in the mental health field have identified a number of specific problems, collectively known as *mood disorders*, that are defined in part by the presence of depression. In this chapter, we limit our discussion to two of these disorders that are most often associated with perfectionism. These are *major depressive disorder* and *dysthymic disorder*.

Major Depressive Disorder

Major depressive disorder is a mood disorder in which an individual has experienced one or more major depressive episodes. A major depressive episode is a period lasting at least two weeks, in which a person consistently experiences depressed mood or a loss of interest in almost all of his or her normal activities. In addition, the person must experience several additional symptoms, which may include such things as changes in weight or appetite, changes in sleep, feeling very restless or very slowed down, loss of energy, feelings of worthlessness or excessive guilt, poor concentration or difficulty making decisions, and thoughts about death or suicide (American Psychiatric Association 1994).

Although major depressive episodes must last at least two weeks by definition, they more typically last up to several months. The average age at which major depressive disorder begins is in the mid-twenties, although the problem can begin at any age, including during childhood. Some people experience only a single episode of major depression, perhaps triggered by a stressful life event. For other people, depression may be long lasting or may be associated with a series of briefer episodes. For people who experience more than one major depressive episode, mood may return back to normal between episodes, or there may still be some minor symptoms of depression left over after the full episode has improved.

Dysthymic Disorder

People with dysthymic disorder experience sadness and depression over a longer period, and usually at a milder level, relative to people with major depressive disorder. Technically, to meet criteria for dysthymic disorder, a person must experience a period of two years or longer in which he or she feels sad or depressed most of the day, on most days. Although the minimum duration is two years, people with dysthymic disorder often report having felt down and blue for many years. In addition to the low mood, people with dysthymic disorder must experience at least two additional symptoms, which may include changes in appetite, changes in sleep, low energy, poor self-esteem, poor concentration or difficulty making decisions, and feelings of hopelessness.

As you can see, major depressive disorder and dysthymic disorder share many features. Nevertheless, there are important differences. Major depressive disorder is typically associated with discrete episodes, whereas dysthymic disorder is generally more long lasting. Second, a major depressive episode must be associated with depressed mood (in addition to the other associated symptoms) day after day for the required period of two weeks or longer. In contrast, people with dysthymic disorder do not necessarily feel down every day—just most days. Finally, the intensity of the depression tends to be much worse in major depressive disorder than in dysthymic disorder.

Causes of Depression

If you have had significant problems with depression, you may have had one professional or another tell you that your depression is caused by a chemical imbalance in your brain, problems in the way your parents brought you up, genetics, or any number of other factors. Despite the many different theories that have been proposed to explain depression, we do not know *the* cause of depression. In fact, it now seems that depression is caused by many different factors and that different people may experience depression for different reasons. Although researchers are beginning to get a clearer understanding about the variables that contribute to depression, they still cannot determine the cause of depression for any one person. However, the problem does seem to be due to a complex interaction of both biological and psychological processes.

Biological Factors

Genetics

A number of studies have demonstrated that depression runs in families. For example, averaging across studies, a person is up to three times more likely to suffer from major depressive disorder if he or she has a parent who suffers from the problem than if there is no depression in the immediate family. Of course, the fact that depression runs in families does not, in and of itself, mean that depression is inherited genetically. It could be that depression is learned from growing up in a home with other people who are depressed. To demonstrate a genetic basis for a problem such as depression, psychologists must turn to twin studies, adoption studies, and studies that directly measure the presence and absence of genes that are believed to be related to depression (i.e., genetic linkage studies). In general, there is some evidence, particularly from twin studies, that depression is in part genetically based. However, the evidence from other genetic research methods has been mixed. Although genetics may be important in the development of depression for some individuals, it should be pointed out that depression is not inherited in the same way as traits (i.e., eye color). Genetics may predispose people to develop depression, but it is no guarantee. Even in pairs of identical twins (who are genetically identical), it is not unusual for one twin to experience depression and the other one to be free of depression.

Neurotransmitters

Many studies have examined the relationship between neurotransmitter levels and depression. Neurotransmitters are chemicals in the brain that are responsible for sending messages from one nerve cell to another. In general, the neurotransmitter model of depression that has obtained the most support suggests that depression is associated with low levels of serotonin and/or norepinephrine. Neurotransmitter models of depression are based in part on the fact that medications that raise levels of these substances seem to improve depression. In addition, there is other evidence supporting a role for these transmitters in depression. However, the relationship between neurotransmitters and depression is complex, and doctors cannot simply measure how much serotonin or norepinephrine there is in the brain to see if there is an imbalance.

Other Biological Factors

Numerous other biological processes are thought to be involved with depression in some people. Hormonal levels probably play a role in some types of depression. In addition, abuse of alcohol and other drugs can increase a person's likelihood of developing depression. Finally, factors such as the amount of exposure to sunlight and even sleep patterns may have an effect on depressed mood.

Psychological Factors

Many studies have shown that psychological factors are important in the development and maintenance of depression. For example, various life stresses (e.g., physical or sexual abuse, divorce, unemployment) may put certain people at risk for depression. Also, a person's style of thinking can increase his or her chances of feeling depressed. One of the most influential psychological theories of depression describes how thinking contributes to feeling depressed. This model, proposed by Dr. Aaron Beck and colleagues (1979), is known as the *cognitive theory of depression*. In short, Beck proposes that depression is associated with a tendency to think negatively about the self (e.g., "I never seem to achieve anything I set out to do"), the world (e.g., "Nobody cares about me"), and the future (e.g., "Things will never improve"). In addition to these three types of thoughts, Beck also emphasized the role of other negative beliefs (e.g., "I have to be perfect") and tendencies to interpret situations in a negatively biased way.

There are other psychological theories of depression as well, several of which overlap considerably with Beck's approach, in that they propose that thoughts and interpretations play an important role in maintaining depression. You may wish to review chapter 3 regarding the role of thoughts in perfectionism. Many of the thoughts and beliefs that contribute to perfectionism are relevant to depression as well.

Perfectionism and Depression

Recall from chapter 1 the three types of perfectionism: self-oriented perfectionism (a tendency to set unreasonably high standards for one's own behavior), other-oriented perfectionism (a tendency to demand that others meet your unrealistically high standards), and socially prescribed perfectionism (the belief that others have impossible standards and that you must meet these standards in order to win their approval) (Hewitt and Flett 1990, 1991a, 1991b).

Hewitt, Flett, and their colleagues have examined the relationship between these types of perfectionism and the symptoms of depression, and they have reported four interesting findings. First, they found that people who score high on a measure of self-oriented perfectionism (compared to those that score low on the measure) may be more susceptible to problems with depression, particularly if they experience achievement-related stresses (e.g., stresses related to work, school, or other related areas), as well as experiences related to failure (Hewitt and Flett 1990). For example, people who are high on self-oriented perfectionism may be susceptible to problems with depression at a time when they have a lot of tests at school, especially if they don't do as well on some of these tests as they would have liked.

Second, these investigators have shown that people who score high on a measure of socially prescribed perfectionism (compared to those who score low on the measure) may be susceptible to depression if they experience achievement-related stresses and/or interpersonal stresses (e.g., stresses involving relationships, intimacy, etc.) (Hewitt and Flett 1993). In other words, people who are high in socially-prescribed perfectionism may be at risk for developing problems with depression if they have significant stress at work or difficulties with their relationships at home.

Third, socially prescribed perfectionism is also associated with feelings of helplessness and hopelessness, both of which have been shown to be components of depression. Finally, perfectionism appears to be related to other specific aspects of depression, such as a tendency to exaggerate one's own faults and a tendency to believe that important events are independent of one's actions (Hewitt and Flett 1993).

In these ways, perfectionism can put people at risk for developing depression, particularly if the person has experienced certain life stresses or failures. The relationship between perfectionism and depression is not surprising. Perfectionism is the tendency to set unrealistically high standards. Because these standards are unlikely to be met, a person who holds such high standards is bound to fall short of meeting them. Frequent experiences of failure can make a person feel helpless and inadequate, and may eventually make a person feel hopeless about things ever improving. Therefore, if perfectionism and depression are both problems for you, you may find that learning to accept lower standards helps you to feel less depressed.

Treatments for Depression That Are Supported by Research

Cognitive Behavioral Therapy

Chapters 7 and 8 discuss many of the components of cognitive behavioral therapy (CBT) in detail, so we will only provide a brief recap here. Basically, the "cognitive" part of CBT refers to techniques used to help people change their negative and unrealistic beliefs, attitudes, and expectations. These techniques include teaching people to identify their negative beliefs, examine the evidence supporting and refuting their beliefs, and engage in small experiments to test out the validity of their beliefs. Behavioral strategies are designed to change behaviors that maintain negative feelings and thoughts. These may include exposure to situations that are anxiety provoking, role playing or practicing difficult interactions that are likely to come up in the future, and learning to communicate more effectively.

Interpersonal Psychotherapy for Depression (IPT)

Interpersonal psychotherapy for depression (IPT) (Klerman et al. 1984) is one of the only psychological treatments other than CBT that has consistently been shown to be effective for depression. This approach to treatment is based on the premise that depression stems from problems in interpersonal relationships. Treatment usually lasts fifteen to twenty sessions and tends to be focused on one or more of the following areas of interpersonal functioning: interpersonal role disputes (e.g., problems adjusting to the demands of a particular social role, such as being a father, employee, daughter, etc.), interpersonal losses (e.g., the loss of a close friend or relative), interpersonal deficits (e.g., difficulty communicating effectively with your spouse), and interpersonal role transitions (e.g., difficulty coping with life changes such as graduation, divorce, retirement, etc.). In studies comparing IPT to medication and CBT, IPT appears to be at least as effective as these other approaches.

Antidepressant Medications

Below is a partial list of medications that have been shown to be useful for treating clinical depression. As you can see, the list is quite long. These drugs are organized with respect to their effects on particular neurotransmitter (i.e., brain chemical) systems that are believed to be involved in depression, such as the ones that involve serotonin, norepinephrine, and dopamine. We have included both the generic name as well as the brand name (in parentheses) for each medication.

Selective Serotonin Reuptake Inhibitors (SSRI) Fluoxetine (Prozac) Fluvoxamine (Luvox) Paroxetine (Paxil) Sertraline (Zoloft)
Selective Dopamime Reuptake Inhibitors (SDRI) Buproprion (Wellbutrin)
Selective Serotonin Norepinephrine Reuptake Inhibitors (SNRI) Venlafaxine (Effexor)
Nonselective Cyclic Antidepressants **(Sometimes called tricyclic and heterocyclic antidepressants)** Imipramine (Tofranil) Clomipramine (Anafranil) Amitriptyline (Elavil) Desipramine (Norpramin) Nortriptyline (Aventyl or Pamelor) Trazodone (Desyrel) Nefazodone (Serzone)
Monoamine Oxidase Inhibitors (MAOI) Phenelzine (Nardil) Tranylcypromine (Parnate)
Reversable Inhibitors of Monoamine Oxidase-A (RIMA) Moclobemide (Manerix)

All of the medications listed in the table are associated with side effects, which may include such symptoms as dry mouth, headache, dizziness, upset stomach, sexual difficulties, insomnia, or other symptoms, depending on the medication. Some antidepressant medications may interact with other medications, drugs, alcohol, or even certain foods (in the case of MAOI antidepressants). We recommend that you discuss possible side effects and drug interactions with your doctor if you are interested in trying an antidepressant (or any medication, for that matter). Although side effects are relatively common, many people are able to tolerate antidepressant treatment with no side effects. Furthermore, when side effects do occur, they are often mild and tend to improve with time or adjustment of the dosage. Nevertheless, in rare cases, some medications may be associated with more severe side effects. Ask your doctor about the side effects of any specific medication that he or she recommends.

With such a long list of available antidepressants, how does one choose one antidepressant over another? There are several factors that come into play. The first is effectiveness. Your doctor should choose a medication that has been shown to be effective for your pattern of symptoms. Second, your doctor should take into account the side effect profile of the medication. If you are already feeling fatigued and experiencing some sexual difficulties, it might be important to select medications for which these are not common side effects. Third, your doctor should consider possible interactions with other medications that you may be taking, as well as interactions with alcohol and other drugs that you may use occasionally. Fourth, the cost of the pills varies from medication to medication. If cost is an issue (e.g., if you don't have a drug plan), you should mention it to your doctor. Finally, the decision of which medication to use should be influenced by your past responses to particular medications. If one medication was effective and well-tolerated in the past, it might make sense to try it again. If you have a history of not responding to an adequate dosage of a medication in the past, perhaps this time you should try a different medication.

If a particular medication does not work for you, don't give up. First, you should make sure you are on an adequate dosage. It is not unusual for doctors to be cautious and recommend dosages that are too low to be effective. If you are not sure whether you are on an adequate dosage, obtain a second opinion from another general practitioner (family doctor) or specialist (psychiatrist). Second, antidepressants take a few weeks to work. It is not uncommon for people to be taking these medications for up to six or even eight weeks before noticing any benefit. Third, if a particular medication does not work for you, there are still other options. There may be another medication that is effective for you. Or, you may benefit from a psychological treatment such as CBT or IPT. Finally, it is possible to boost the effects of some antidepressants using other medications such as lithium carbonate. Lithium is normally used to treat bipolar disorder (a problem in which people experience both manic and depressive episodes). However, when used in conjunction with an antidepressant, lithium has been shown for some people to augment or improve upon the benefits achieved by an antidepressant alone.

Electroconvulsive Therapy

Electroconvulsive therapy (ECT) is typically administered after all other treatments for depression have been attempted and failed. This treatment is still very controversial and is often discussed in a negative light by the media. Today, ECT is very different than the way it has been portrayed in movies such as *One Flew Over the Cuckoo's Nest.* It is done under anesthetic and involves inducing brief convulsions by delivering a shock to the brain lasting less than a second. The main side effect of ECT is confusion and loss of short-term memory that lasts for about a week or two. Despite these side effects, many individuals who do not respond to medications may find ECT to be effective for depression.

How to Change Perfectionistic Thinking and Behavior in Depression

For a detailed review of all the strategies for overcoming perfectionism, see chapters 7 and 8. In this section, we will highlight some of the techniques that may be helpful for you if you suffer from depressed mood or if you tend to feel down when your expectations are not met.

Changing Perfectionistic Thoughts That Contribute to Depression

You may recall from chapter 7 that we recommend following five steps for changing perfectionistic thoughts: identifying perfectionistic thoughts, listing more reasonable alternative thoughts, reassessing the advantages and disadvantages of the original thoughts and the alternative thoughts, and choosing a more realistic or helpful way of viewing situations. In addition, we suggest a variety of specific techniques that can be helpful for changing perfectionistic thoughts. Several of these will be particularly helpful for individuals who tend to feel sad or depressed. These include: examining the evidence, perspective taking, compromising with yourself, hypothesis testing, changing patterns of social comparison, and looking at the big picture. Others may be helpful as well, so it is worth looking over the material in chapter 7 for further possibilities.

In the case of depression, you should pay particular attention to depressive beliefs about yourself, such as beliefs that you are worthless, incompetent, or generally deficient in some way. If you hold these beliefs, you may find it helpful to think carefully about what these labels mean. Sometimes, attempting to define labels such as worthless and incompetent will lead you to realize that these words do not really capture who you are (or who anyone is, for that matter). Consider the following therapy vignette. In this vignette, the therapist uses the strategy of perspective taking to help the patient to evaluate his own worth using the same criteria that he uses to judge other people.

Client	Most days, I feel completely worthless. I just sit around the house and nothing seems to get done.
Therapist	Let's look at the word "worthless." Exactly what does that word mean to you?
Client	Well, I suppose that a worthless person is someone who doesn't contribute to society and doesn't do anything—someone like me.
Therapist	Can you think of anyone else who you would describe as worthless?
Client	Actually, no. I can't.
Therapist	If you were to meet someone else who is worthless, how would you know it?
Client	I don't really think of other people as being worthless.
Therapist	What if you met a person who, like yourself, was unemployed and not spending time with friends? Would you consider that person to be worthless?
Client	Not at all. If anything, I would feel empathy for that person.
Therapist	It seems that you have different standards for yourself than you do for other people. Is it possible to change your view of yourself to match the view that you might have of another person who is similar to you?
Client	I guess it's possible that I am not worthless, although I still believe that there are lots of things in my life that need to change.

Following is another therapy vignette that illustrates how to change social comparison strategies that may contribute to depressed feelings:

Client	My daughter's report card just arrived and it was just average. To make things worse, my nephew is doing very well in school. I know my brother is going to tell me about my nephew's report card and I am going to feel terrible.
Therapist	Why will you feel terrible?
Client	My daughter should be doing at least as well as my nephew. I feel that her report card reflects badly on me.
Therapist	How do your nephew's grades compare to everyone else's in the class?
Client	He is always at the top of the class. That just makes it worse.
Therapist	What effect does it have to compare your daughter's report card to that of the top student in the class?
Client	It makes me feel miserable.
Therapist	People can be measured in many different dimensions, including physical appearance, intelligence, artistic talent, physical fitness, aptitude for sports, knowledge of particular topics, physical health, income, school performance—and the list goes on and on. In fact, each of these dimensions can be subdivided into other dimensions. For example, physical appearance includes such things as height, weight, hair color, complexion, and so on. Each of us performs well in some of these dimensions. In other dimensions, we may perform poorly, compared to most people. However, in most dimensions, we tend to be somewhere in between—in other words, *average*.
Client	Now that you mention it, there are lots of ways in which my daughter really outshines my nephew. He just studies all the time, but my daughter has lots of outside interests and is quite good at sports.

In addition to changing negative thoughts about yourself, you should also examine your negative thoughts and absolutes about the world (e.g., "People should always be interested in what I have to say") and about the future (e.g., "I will never find a relationship that makes me happy"). Not only are thoughts such as these usually untrue, but they also contribute to feelings of depression.

Changing Perfectionistic Behaviors That Contribute to Depression

A number of strategies may be helpful for dealing with perfectionistic behaviors that are associated with depression. Exposure exercises designed to disprove perfectionistic beliefs can reduce the intensity of these beliefs. Exposure can help reduce depression in other ways as well. Often when people are feeling depressed, they tend to become socially withdrawn and uninterested in their usual hobbies and activities. Therefore, they begin to avoid doing things because they believe that they are unlikely to enjoy themselves. The net result of the avoidance, however, is to decrease the person's enjoyment of life, thereby contributing to the depression and the lack of motivation to do things. Exposure can have the effect of breaking the cycle. By forcing yourself to do things that normally are interesting to you, chances are that you may enjoy them more than you might expect. Going places and doing things, despite not having the energy or interest in being active, may help to increase your interest in doing things over time. For more details on how to conduct exposure practices, see chapter 8.

In addition to exposure, several of the other behavioral strategies discussed in chapter 8 may be helpful. For example, if you tend to have difficulty communicating directly and assertively when you are feeling down, you may find some of the suggestions regarding assertive communication helpful. In addition, procrastination can often be a problem for people who are feeling depressed. Check out chapter 8 for methods of overcoming procrastination.

Chapter 10

Perfectionism and Anger

Like sadness and fear, anger is a universal emotion that is experienced by everyone. Despite the fact that people all feel anger from time to time, most people don't enjoy feeling angry and they may even feel embarrassed about expressing anger in front of other people. The experience of anger is often associated with other feelings, such as irritation, disappointment, rage, or a feeling of hatred and dislike toward another person, a situation, or even yourself.

When angry, you may also experience a desire to be aggressive or destructive, or you may feel the urge to seek revenge toward another person who has let you down. Almost always, anger is associated with a sense of blame. That is, when you feel angry, you are probably assigning blame to another individual or yourself for behaving in an unacceptable way. Also, anger is typically associated with strong beliefs about the way a situation *should* be.

Although anger can increase the likelihood of aggression, there is little evidence to support a strong relationship between anger and aggression. Anger prepares you to be aggressive if the need arises, but it does not cause aggression directly. Most people, across situations, are able to control their anger and prevent it from leading to verbal or physical attacks on others. Furthermore, even when a person is aggressive, it is often not related to anger, bur rather to a need for dominance or control. For example, people who injure their victims during a robbery have probably not been provoked in any way and probably aren't angry at the victim. Similarly, when children tease or hurt other children in the school yard, it probably has little to do with anger and more to do with a desire to dominate the other person or look strong in front of peers.

People differ with respect to their threshold for feeling anger. An experience that might cause anger for one person may not have the same effect on another individual. Although some drivers become very angry when other drivers make mistakes—such as cutting off another car, tailgating, driving too slowly, or going through a red light (this anger toward other drivers is often referred to as "road rage" in the media)—other drivers tolerate these situations without much reaction.

As discussed in previous chapters, perfectionism puts people at risk for becoming angry more easily. If you tend to have high standards that are rigid and inflexible, you are at risk for not having your standards and expectations met. Not being able to achieve a goal is one of several common triggers for anger.

Common Triggers for Anger

Psychologist Carroll Izard (1991) identified three common triggers for anger: restraint, interruption of goal-oriented behavior, and aversive stimulation. We will consider each of these in turn.

Restraint

Restraint involves some force blocking your desired actions in a particular situation. Restraint can be physical or psychological in nature. Physical restraint involves actually holding a person down in order to prevent him or her from doing something or going somewhere. Studies show that even infants as young as four months old respond with anger when their arms are restrained. Psychological restraint involves being prevented from doing something by some social or psychological force (for example, having to follow particular rules or regulations to avoid getting in trouble). You probably recognize the experience of becoming angry when you are restrained or prevented from doing something that you want to do. As a teenager, you may have become angry when your parents prevented you from going out with friends. As an adult, you may become angry when you get into your car, only to realize that the tire is flat and you are going to be late for an appointment.

Interruption of Goal-Oriented Behavior

Interruption of goal-oriented behavior is very similar to restraint, in that a person is prevented from reaching a particular goal. An example is feeling angry when you are interrupted while concentrating on a task, such as reading a book, watching a good movie, or filling out your income tax forms. Although most people enjoy breaks from time to time, uninvited interruptions may be less welcome for some people, especially when there is a perceived pressure to finish a task by a certain time. Because perfectionism can often be associated with high standards for performance or a drive to finish jobs quickly, being interrupted is more likely to be a trigger for anger among perfectionistic people.

Aversive Stimulation

Aversive stimulation involves being exposed to an unpleasant stimulus, such as extreme cold or heat, intense pain, a loud noise, a nasty odor, or a morally offensive comment. For example, if you are shopping in a crowded shopping mall, you may become irritable following several hours of exposure to noise, crowds, and uncomfortable stuffiness (especially if you're wearing warm clothing).

Other Triggers for Anger

There are many other possible triggers for anger. For example, most people feel angry when they have been deceived, treated poorly, or hurt by another person. In addition, you probably have had times when disapproval from others has led you to feel angry. You may also feel anger toward others even when their behavior is not directed at you (e.g., feeling angry at your best friend's boss when you find out that you best friend was unjustly fired; feeling angry at a politician for making a decision that you don't agree with).

Anger can be directed at yourself as well. If you make a mistake on an important job at work, you may feel angry for not doing the "perfect" job that you had anticipated. You may even feel angry about feeling angry. It is not unusual for people to experience anger toward themselves if they lose control when feeling angry toward another person.

When Is Anger a Problem?

Chronic problems with anger can contribute to high blood pressure, heart disease, excess stomach acid, and other physical problems. Interpersonally, anger can lead to less intimate relationships, as friends, co-workers, and family members learn to avoid talking about certain issues in order to prevent themselves from being the victims of your anger. In extreme cases, people may avoid you completely, leading to complete social isolation. Finally, continual displays of anger can affect your self-esteem by making you feel guilty, embarrassed, out of control, or inadequate.

Although anger is a normal emotion that everyone experiences, it can be problematic under the following circumstances: when it happens too frequently, when it happens too intensely, when it leads to physical or psychological aggression, when it leads to relationship difficulties, and when it leads to any other types of significant impairment in a person's life (e.g., individuals who are so angry that they cannot work on their term paper that is due the next day; people who get fired for telling their boss what they really think of him or her).

The Development of Anger

The experience and expression of anger is mediated by a complex interaction among various biological and psychological factors. As mentioned earlier, there is evidence that the capacity to express anger is present from infancy. In addition, many animals are capable of expressing anger, often in ways that are very similar to the expression of anger in humans. From a biological perspective, the limbic system (including the hypothalamus and amygdala) have been implicated in the expression of anger.

In addition, your learning experiences during childhood probably have a large impact on how you express anger. There is evidence that parents are more tolerant of anger in boys than in girls. Researchers have found that parents of boys tend to respond to anger with attention, which may reinforce the angry behavior. In contrast, parents are more likely to tell their daughters that their anger is inappropriate and instruct them to stop being angry. The extent to which this is true may help to explain stereotypes regarding differences in the ways men and women express anger as adults (e.g., that men express anger more readily than women—even men who have difficulty expressing other emotions, such as fear and sadness) (Radke-Yarrow and Kochanska 1990).

Other research has lent further support to the view that parental behavior contributes to the expression of anger in children. For example, one study found that toddlers are more likely to express anger frequently if their parents respond to their problem behaviors with anger (Crockenberg 1985). In contrast, parents who respond to toddlers with other emotions, such as fear or sadness, are more likely to have children with fewer behavioral problems and a well-developed capacity to empathize with other people. It should be noted that parental behavior is not the only social influence on the way a person expresses anger. There is also evidence that a child's peer group has a large impact on the development and maintenance of anger and anger-related behavior (Lemerise and Dodge 1993).

Because anger is a universal emotion influenced by such factors as brain functioning and childhood learning experiences, you may be tempted to assume that there is nothing you can do to change your angry behavior. Nothing could be further from the truth. More than fifty studies have investigated the effectiveness of cognitive and behavioral treatments for anger, and overall this approach to treating anger has been shown to be quite effective. Learning to change the thoughts and behaviors that help to maintain your difficulties with anger is the best way to overcome the problem.

The Role of Thoughts in Anger

When you respond with anger, it is not the situation or event that leads you to react, but rather, your interpretation of the situation or event. For example, imagine that your child arrives home from school and hands you a midterm report card. Upon examining the report card, you notice failing grades in math and science. How would you respond to this situation? What emotions would you be feeling? What thoughts might you be having? Now, imagine how other people you know might respond to this situation. Think about specific people, such as your partner, family members, co-workers, etc. Would any of them respond differently to this situation than you? Can you imagine another parent feeling differently when confronted with this situation? There are many different ways that a parent might respond. Furthermore, the specific reaction is likely to be influenced by the person's beliefs about the situation, as indicated in the table below.

Emotion	Thoughts
Angry	My child did not study hard enough.
	My child should have performed better.
	My child is making me look bad by not doing well in school.
Sad	If I were a better parent, my child would be doing better in school.
	My child will never amount to anything.
Concerned	My child must be feeling terrible about this.
	What if my child cannot pull up these grades by the end of the year?
Neutral	There is still time for these grades to improve.
	Perhaps a tutor could help my child raise the math and science grades.
	I had some poor grades when I was in high school. A couple of poor grades won't matter a lot in the long run.

In this example, you can see how the specific beliefs that you hold affect your emotional response to the situation. By examining the accuracy of your angry beliefs and trying to change them to be more realistic and moderate, you will find it easier to control your anger.

Perfectionism and Anger

Perfectionism can lead to anger when you apply your unreasonably high expectations and standards to other people. You may also become angry at yourself when you do not meet your own specific goals or expectations. Any belief that you have about how you or other people *should be* puts you at risk for feeling angry if these expectations are not met. Beware of statements or thoughts that include words such as "should" and "must," especially when they are accompanied by words such as "always" and "never." Examples of perfectionistic expectations that may lead to anger when they are not met include the following:

- I should never be late for appointments.
- My doctor should be able to diagnose and treat any symptom that I have.

- My children should always dress the way I want them to.

- People should never tell white lies.

- Nice people never talk about others behind their backs.

- I should lose five pounds.

- My children must never swear.

- People should never eat with their hands.

- People should always do exactly what they say they will do.

Changing Perfectionistic Thoughts and Behaviors That Contribute to Anger

Chapters 7 and 8 contain many different strategies that are useful for combating the thoughts and behaviors that are associated with perfectionism, including those that contribute to anger. You may wish to review these chapters. The remaining sections of this chapter highlight several of the strategies that are especially helpful for dealing with anger. Also, we describe several additional techniques (to the ones discussed in earlier chapters) that you may find helpful.

Become Aware of Your Anger Before It Becomes Intense

People are often unaware of their anger, especially when it is at low levels. Therefore, the first step to reducing your anger is to increase your ability to detect anger before it gets out of hand. Be aware of subtle signs that you may be feeling angry. These may include a tendency to use sarcastic comments or put-downs, a feeling of tension in your body, being grouchy or irritable, or being overly sensitive to comments from other people. If you are in a situation where things are not going your way, be aware of whether you are becoming angry and take steps to keep the anger from getting the best of you (some possible strategies are described throughout the rest of this chapter). When anger is very intense, it may be hard to think clearly, so catching it early can be helpful.

In fact, you can even deal with the anger before it happens. If you anticipate being angry in a situation, try to challenge your angry thoughts before they occur. For example, if you are expecting a negative performance appraisal in an upcoming meeting with your boss, plan how to deal with the situation before it happens. Before the meeting, brainstorm possible ways of dealing with the situation that are unlikely to be damaging to you or your situation at work.

Challenge Your Perfectionistic Thoughts

Rather than accepting your angry thoughts as facts, test out their validity by using the strategies discussed in chapter 7. Examine the evidence supporting your angry beliefs. Search for other ways of interpreting the situation. The following therapy vignette illustrates how to make your standards more flexible in order to become more tolerant and decrease your angry feelings.

Client	My daughter just came home from college with a lip ring, and I'm absolutely furious.
Therapist	What bothers you about the piercing?
Client	It looks repulsive. Also, I'm worried that when other people see it, it will cause problems for her. Nobody will ever find her attractive with that thing.
Therapist	The thought that you just mentioned is a "worry" thought. What "anger" thoughts are you having? For example, do you believe that you've somehow been hurt by your daughter getting her lip pierced?
Client	Well, she knows that I don't approve of it, and she did it anyway. We've talked about it in the past, and I let her know how I feel. She has completely disregarded my feelings, and I believe that she has no respect for my opinions.
Therapist	So, you interpret the lip piercing as evidence that your daughter doesn't respect your opinions. Are there other possible interpretations?
Client	Not that I can think of.
Therapist	Would you say that any time a person decides to purchase a piece of clothing or adopt a new hairstyle that another person does not find attractive, it is a sign of disrespect?
Client	Of course not, but this seems different. This is such a radical change.

Therapist	Can you think of anything that you may have done in the past that your own parents thought was radical or inappropriate?
Client	Actually, when I got my ears pierced, my parents didn't talk to me for a week.
Therapist	Today, the role of body piercing is not very different from that of ear piercing thirty years ago. If you look around the city, there are many people your daughter's age who have a piercing in one place or another.
Client	What if she can't find a job after graduation because of her lip ring? It's possible that employers out there will see it the way I do!
Therapist	Let me throw the question back at you. What if she can't get a job because of the lip ring?
Client	I guess she will take out the lip ring or find a place to work where it doesn't matter. I can see what you're getting at. Even though I don't like it, it's not as bad as I thought at first.

In general, asking yourself some of the following questions may help you to challenge the perfectionistic thoughts that contribute to your anger:

- Is this situation as important as it feels?
- What if this situation doesn't go my way? Does it really matter?
- Do I need to control this situation?
- Is my way the only way to view this situation?
- Would another person necessarily see this situation the same way as I do?
- What if things don't work out the way I want them to?
- Do I know for sure that things will turn out badly if I don't get my way?
- Will getting angry result in the outcome that I want?

Allow People to Be Different Than You

People like to be around other people who share important beliefs, attitudes, and values. People who are overly perfectionistic, however, may *insist* that other people conform to their way of thinking and doing things, even for matters that aren't terribly important. To be less of a perfectionist, you will need to allow other people to be themselves, even if it means that you don't agree with their choices in clothing, hairstyle, career, relationships, etc.

This doesn't mean that anything goes. In all relationships, there are limitations to what people find acceptable. Most people do not tolerate being lied to or stolen from by friends or co-workers. Similarly, parents generally don't allow their children to do things that are very dangerous. The goal should not be to have no standards, but rather to have more flexible standards. If you can distinguish between standards that are appropriate and others that are unrealistic or excessively high, you will run less of a risk of experiencing unwarranted anger toward other people.

Avoid Using Angry Language

Angry language can help fuel angry feelings. For example, labeling other people as jerks, idiots, incompetent, irresponsible, etc., can make it difficult to change the way you think about them. If you are tempted to label another person, try labeling his or her behavior instead. For example, if your housemate has not taken out the garbage in weeks, rather than saying, "My housemate is lazy and inconsiderate," try saying "My housemate has not taken out the garbage recently."

In addition to avoiding labeling, it can be helpful to make it a habit to think before you speak, particularly when you are angry. Before saying what is on your mind, imagine hearing the words that you are about to say. Would you find the words helpful if someone said them to you? If not, keep your thoughts to yourself. You don't have to say everything that you are thinking.

Assume Responsibility for Your Actions

As discussed earlier, anger is often caused by blaming another person for a problem or holding on to rigid beliefs regarding how something *should* be. To overcome a problem with excessive anger, it is important to understand all of the different factors that contribute to a situation, including your own role. Situations are often complex, and rarely is a particular person entirely responsible for a problem or situation.

Imagine that you confided in your friend Tom that you didn't like his friend Alison. If Tom told Alison how you felt about her, you might feel angry and betrayed because Tom has talked about you behind your back. Although it is true that Tom may have made a mistake in this situation, it would be important for you to assume some responsibility for what happened as well. By telling Tom about your feelings toward Alison, you would also be guilty of gossiping. Also, you would be in part responsible for the information getting back to Alison.

Similarly, arguments and disagreements are rarely the fault of any one person. Rather, they are usually determined by a complex interaction of many different factors, including the specific situation that two people are arguing about, the manner in which each person is discussing the topic (e.g., tone and volume of voice, body language, use of sarcastic comments and insults, etc.), the personal state of each person (e.g., fatigue, hunger, anxious or depressed mood, previous stresses during the day, etc.), and possible miscommunication. During a disagreement, it is easy to notice all the ways in which the other person has contributed to the argument. It is much more difficult to take responsibility for your own behaviors that may have helped fuel the disagreement.

Admit When You Are Wrong

People often believe that it is important, above all else, to be consistent. You may fear that if you back down on a particular issue or if you change your mind, you will appear uncertain, others will not take you as seriously, and your opinion will be less respected in the future. There are situations in which this may be true. For example, a politician who makes a commitment (e.g., "no new taxes") during an election campaign and then breaks the promise after being elected may be perceived as dishonest, manipulative, or indecisive. However, in most cases, people respect other people who are able to change in the face of new information or after realizing that they have made a mistake. If you realize that your expectations have been unreasonable, people will appreciate you admitting that you were wrong. People generally appreciate an apology when it is sincere.

Exposure Exercises

If you tend to overreact to other people doing things differently than you, structured exposure to the situation may help you to be more tolerant. For example, if it upsets you to have your partner clean up after dinner (because it is never done to your high standards), arrange for your partner to clean up every day for a couple of weeks (of course, this will depend on your partner's agreeing to participate). During the practices, your job will be to refrain from making any comments or criticisms. Over the course of the practices, you will probably become more tolerant of your partner's cleaning standards.

Before beginning any exposure practices, we recommend that you review the relevant parts of chapter 8 to make sure that the exercises are structured in a way that maximizes their effectiveness.

Take Some Time Out

Time out involves physically or mentally taking a break from a situation. This may include such things as lying down, taking a walk, phoning a friend, watching TV, or any other activity that gets you out of the situation. Sometimes, you won't have the opportunity to physically get away from a situation. In these cases, just taking the time to count to ten may be enough of a break to prevent you from saying something that you might regret later. Your anger is likely to decrease if you get away from the triggers that remind you of why you are angry. After a break, you are likely to see the situation in a more realistic light. Often, by the time you return to the situation, the anger will have subsided. Time out is especially helpful when your anger is too intense to make use of some of the other anger-management strategies, such as challenging your angry thoughts.

There are helpful and unhelpful ways of taking time out. It's best to never storm out of a room or hang up the telephone on another person. Even though this may make you feel better, the other person is likely to become more angry or hurt, and the problem will escalate. If you need to take a break, explain to the other individual that you are feeling angry, and that you want some time to think about things. Be specific about how much time you need (e.g., "I'll be back in an hour," or "I'll phone you tomorrow"). If the other person wants to continue the conversation, make an appointment to talk at a later time when your anger is likely to have decreased—and make sure you keep the appointment.

Physical Exercise

Physical exercise (e.g., running, walking, cycling, swimming, aerobics, sports, etc.) is a good way to blow off steam. With regular exercise, you may also feel more energetic and healthy, which in turn will make it easier for you to tolerate situations that otherwise might be annoying or frustrating.

Relaxation

Research has shown that relaxation training can be an effective way to manage anger. There are many different methods that can be used to induce a state of relaxation. Progressive muscle relaxation involves learning to relax the muscles of the body to decrease feelings of tension, stress, and anxiety. Imagery, another method that is sometimes helpful, involves learning to imagine particular scenes that are relaxing. Meditation and mindfulness training can also help a person deal with anger and other negative emotions. Finally, learning to breathe slowly and smoothly can help a person relax. A full description of each of these relaxation methods is beyond the scope of this book. However, there are a number of places where you can learn more about relaxation if you are interested. Check out the Further Readings at the end of this book. Also, you may have access near your home to classes for relaxation training, yoga, or some other activity that includes a relaxation component.

Use Problem-Solving Strategies

When you are faced with a conflict or problem, try taking the following steps to solve the problem, rather than losing your temper or stewing in anger:

1. Define the problem. Until you understand exactly what the problem is, you will not be able to solve it.

2. If the problem is complex, break it down into smaller problems. Then, choose one problem to work on at a time.

3. Brainstorm all possible solutions to the problem—even solutions that aren't likely to work.

4. Evaluate each solution by listing the potential costs and benefits.

5. Choose the best solution(s) to the problem.

6. Develop a plan for implementing the solutions (e.g., decide what steps need to be taken to make the plan work).

7. Solve the problem by implementing the solution you have chosen.

8. Evaluate the effectiveness of the solution. If the solution was not effective, repeat the problem-solving steps until you find a solution that works.

Consider the following example. Imagine that you are a manager in an office where you supervise several clerical staff. One of your staff members has a tendency to arrive ten or fifteen minutes late for work almost every day. As the supervisor, you believe that lateness is unacceptable and are determined to address this problem. Start by defining the problem. In this case, the problem is that one of your staff is late every day and that lateness makes you angry. Note that the problem has two parts to it—the fact that the employee is late (and the effects of the lateness on his or her work), and your reaction to the person being late. In this example, the lateness is only a problem because it bothers you.

Step 2 involves breaking down the problem into smaller problems if necessary. However, in this case, the problem is relatively simple and doesn't need to be broken down any further. Step 3 involves brainstorming possible solutions. For example, possible solutions include: fire the employee, only pay the employee for the time spent at work, ask the employee to make up the time later, completely relax your rules regarding lateness (i.e., decide that all lateness is okay), relax your rules somewhat regarding lateness (e.g., decide that being up to ten minutes late for work is acceptable), or simply ignore the problem.

Next, evaluate the costs and benefits of each solution. For example, one benefit of firing the employee is that you would no longer have to be angered by the situation. On the other hand, firing the employee might lead to a wrongful dismissal lawsuit, as well as making you feel very guilty and making your other staff unhappy. Conversely, choosing the solution of somewhat relaxing the rules may work well. This solution will accommodate the employee's morning schedule without really affecting productivity in any way. If the employee believes that you are flexible, he or she may be more inclined to work harder. A potential cost of this solution is that other staff may start to arrive late as well. Or perhaps if you give staff permission to arrive ten minutes late, they will start arriving thirty minutes late.

Once you evaluate the costs and benefits of each solution, you may find that none of the solutions are perfect. In the end, however, you will need to choose the best solution. If no solution seems potentially useful, take a break from the problem and come back to it later. Perhaps involving another individual in the problem-solving process will help. Another person may be able to generate solutions that were not obvious to you.

Once you are able to choose one or more solutions that are likely to be effective, begin to develop a plan for implementing them. For example, if you decide to relax the rules regarding lateness, so that being ten minutes late is acceptable, how will you implement the rule? Will you make an announcement to all staff about the new rule? Or will you wait until someone is more than ten minutes late to tell them about the new rule for acceptable and unacceptable lateness? When you have chosen a plan for action, carry it out as soon as possible. The longer you wait to solve the problem, the harder it may be to make the changes.

Chapter 11

Perfectionism and Social Anxiety

The Nature of Social Anxiety

If you've ever felt uncomfortable in the presence of another person or nervous about making a negative impression on other people, you've experienced social anxiety. Most people experience anxiety or fear in certain social situations. Perhaps you have felt uneasy in a situation where you were the center of attention (i.e., getting married, acting in a play, or giving a formal presentation at work). Or perhaps you have felt uneasy at a big job interview or meeting your partner's parents for the first time. Like any situation that triggers anxiety and fear, social situations can be uncomfortable when they are perceived as dangerous in some way. In other words, you are more likely to be anxious when you believe that you have something to lose if you say the wrong thing, behave inappropriately, or seem uncomfortable.

Social anxiety is on a continuum. Some people may appear to never experience anxiety in any social situations, whereas other people avoid all social contact, including going to work and spending time with their family. Most people are in between these two extremes. You may be tempted to avoid social situations that make you uncomfortable. If you don't avoid these situations, you may rely on certain coping strategies to help get you through the situation. For example, a client seen in our clinic was a university professor who had an extreme fear of public speaking—including teaching her classes. Although she was unable to avoid teaching, she found subtle ways to get through her classes. For example, she always taught her students in the dark, using overhead transparencies, so they would not notice her anxiety symptoms. Also, she always wore turtleneck sweaters so that the blushing on her neck wouldn't be visible.

Most social situations that trigger anxiety can be categorized into two main types: performance situations and social interaction situations. Performance situations are situations in which you are likely to be observed while performing some task. Social interaction situations involve speaking or interacting with another person. Below are some examples of each:

Performance Situations That Sometimes Trigger Anxiety

- Public speaking (e.g., formal presentations)
- Participating in meetings at work, answering questions in class, etc.
- Singing, acting, dancing, or reading aloud
- Using a public rest room with someone else in the room
- Doing aerobics or playing sports
- Writing with other people watching
- Eating or drinking with other people watching
- Going out in public without dressing "nicely"
- Sexual situations

Social Interaction Situations That Sometimes Trigger Anxiety

- Going to parties (especially when the other guests are strangers)
- Being introduced to new people
- Talking with people in authority (e.g., a boss or teacher)
- Being assertive
- Initiating casual conversations
- Maintaining casual conversations
- Going out on a date
- Going to job interviews
- Sharing private details about your life with another person
- Talking on the telephone

- Confronting another person about a problem

In anxiety-provoking social situations, people are typically apprehensive about two different aspects of the situation. First, they have anxious thoughts about the situation itself. For example, they may worry that others will find them to be incompetent, unattractive, unintelligent, or boring, despite the fact that they are actually unlikely to be judged negatively in the situation. Second, they have anxious thoughts about looking nervous in front of other people. For example, they may worry that other people will notice specific anxiety symptoms (i.e., shaky hands or sweaty palms). People who are socially anxious often see their anxiety as a sign of weakness and take great pains to make sure that other people don't notice the symptoms.

Because people who are socially anxious often avoid social situations, they may lack certain skills that are needed to perform well in these situations. For example, a person who is uncomfortable talking to other people may lack certain conversational skills that others take for granted (e.g., how to make appropriate eye contact, how to ask questions of the other person, etc.). Similarly, people who completely avoid sports or dancing are unlikely to be extremely talented at either of these activities until they have opportunities to practice and develop their skills.

Like other emotional states, social anxiety may be thought of as having three main components: the physical, the cognitive, and the behavioral. The physical component includes all the physical symptoms that people experience when anxious, including racing heart, irregular breathing, dizziness, shaking, sweating, blushing, or an unsteady voice.

The cognitive component includes the beliefs, interpretations, and predictions that contribute to the anxiety (e.g., "This person will think I'm an idiot"). This component also includes a tendency to pay too much attention to information that confirms the anxious beliefs. For example, if you are nervous while giving a presentation, you are more likely to notice the people in the audience who seem bored or unhappy than the people who seem interested in your talk. Also, when confronted with an ambiguous situation (e.g., a person who seems uninterested in what you are saying), you are more likely to interpret the situation in a way that is consistent with your anxiety (e.g., "This person finds me boring") than with a more neutral interpretation (e.g., "This person must be very distracted").

The behavioral component of social anxiety usually involves avoidance of the feared situation. This may include complete avoidance (e.g., not going to a party), or more subtle forms of avoidance (e.g., going to a party, but only talking to certain "safe" people). In addition, social anxiety may be associated with other behaviors, such as checking your appearance in the mirror and constantly trying to figure out whether people are reacting negatively in response to your behavior.

Social Phobia

Social phobia is a term used to describe social anxiety that is extreme enough that it bothers a person or causes significant interference in the person's life. The criteria that professionals use to define social phobia include the following:

- The person experiences an intense fear of one or more social or performance situations, in which the person fears that he or she will do something embarrassing or show signs of anxiety.

- The person becomes very anxious or panicky when exposed to a feared social situation.

- The person recognizes that the fear is out of proportion to the real danger.

- The person avoids the situation or endures it with intense discomfort.

- The social anxiety bothers the person or leads to significant interference in functioning.

- If the person is under eighteen years old, the problem has lasted at least six months.

- The social anxiety is not due to another problem (for example, the person is not avoiding social situations simply because he or she is feeling depressed and is uninterested in socializing).

Note that social phobia may involve many different situations or as few as one situation (e.g., public speaking) in some cases. The features of social phobia are very similar to those described earlier for more general social anxiety. The main difference between social phobia and normal levels of social anxiety and shyness are that in social phobia, the anxiety usually occurs more frequently and more intensely, and the anxiety causes problems for the person, by interfering with work, relationships, or other activities. Most people who are fearful of public speaking would not meet criteria for social phobia because the fear does not impact their life in any meaningful way. On the other hand, if a person has to make frequent presentations for work, a fear of public speaking might very well meet criteria for social phobia.

Recent epidemiological studies have estimated that up to 13 percent of the general population meet the clinical criteria for social phobia at some time in their life (Kessler et al. 1994). In addition, social phobia is often associated with other problems, including depression, eating disorders, and substance abuse. Fortunately, social phobia often responds quite well to treatment. We will review the treatment options for this problem later in this chapter.

Causes of Social Anxiety and Social Phobia

Social phobia seems to run in families. People who have an immediate family member with social phobia are two to three times more likely to develop social phobia compared to people without social phobia in the family. The fact that social phobia runs in families is probably related to both the genetic heritability of social anxiety, as well as the process of learning anxious behaviors from parents or other family members. In fact, evidence is now pointing to the fact that social phobia probably stems from an interaction of both biological and psychological processes.

Biological Factors

Twin studies that have attempted to separate out the effects of learning and genetics have yielded inconsistent results, with some studies showing that genetics plays a moderate role in the development of social phobia and other studies finding a relatively small genetic contribution (Antony and Barlow 1997). Nevertheless, two personality traits that are associated with social anxiety have been shown to be highly heritable. These include neuroticism—a tendency to feel anxious, tense, and worried, as well as to react emotionally to a variety of stresses—and introversion—a tendency to be relatively quiet and socially withdrawn compared to other people.

Although research on the biological basis of social anxiety is still in its infancy, there is indirect evidence that brain chemistry may play a role. For example, metabolite levels of a neurotransmitter called dopamine have been shown to correlate with introversion. In addition, mice that have been bred to be timid appear to have lower levels of brain dopamine than mice who are not timid. Finally, certain antidepressant medications that influence dopamine levels appear to reduce anxiety in people with social phobia. However, medications that affect neurotransmitter systems other than dopamine can also influence social anxiety, suggesting that other neurotransmitters play a role as well.

Psychological Factors

Although a person's biology plays a role in the development and maintenance of social anxiety, psychological factors are also very important. A psychologist by the name of S. Rachman (1976, 1977) identified three different pathways to developing fear: traumatic conditioning, which involves experiencing some negative event that triggers the fear (e.g., being teased after a class presentation may induce a fear of public speaking); observational learning, which involves developing a fear by watching someone else behave fearfully in the situation (e.g., developing social anxiety by growing up in a family of shy parents and siblings); and informational learning, which involves developing a fear by being told that a particular situation is dangerous (e.g., being told to "watch your back" when around other people).

A number of research studies support the view that these methods of learning can influence the development of social anxiety. Compared to people who are comfortable in social situations, people with social phobia are more likely to grow up in homes where other family members are socially anxious (an example of observational learning), parents use shame as a means of discipline (traumatic conditioning), family members place great importance on the opinions of other people (informational learning), and children are discouraged from socializing (informational learning).

In addition, many researchers believe that people's beliefs play an enormous role in whether they feel anxious in social situations. Common beliefs held by people who are socially anxious are listed as follows (notice that many of these beliefs reflect perfectionistic standards and beliefs):

- I should not appear anxious in front of other people.
- I should always appear to be brilliant.
- I should always be entertaining when I am talking to other people.
- It is awful to blush, shake, or sweat in front of others.
- People can tell when I am anxious.
- I will not be able to speak if I am too anxious.

- People find me unattractive.
- I will look incompetent if I speak to my boss.
- People will become angry with me if I make a mistake.

Perfectionism and Social Anxiety

Compared to all other types of anxiety and fear, social anxiety may be the most closely linked to perfectionism. Research from our clinic and elsewhere has found that people who are socially anxious are more likely than other people to be overly concerned about making mistakes, particularly in social situations. For example, they may hold the belief that if they make a mistake or fall short of their standards, they are complete failures. In addition, social anxiety is associated with a tendency to doubt one's abilities in social situations, including one's ability to make a good impression on other people.

If you have a tendency to set overly high standards for yourself, it is likely that you will be unable to meet your strict expectations. If you can't accept the possibility of another person finding you boring, unattractive, or incompetent, you put yourself at risk for feeling anxious when interacting with other people who you perceive as threatening. In addition, if your perfectionism causes you to avoid certain social situations, you prevent yourself from ever finding out whether your anxious predictions are correct.

Treatments for Social Phobia That Are Supported by Research

Although professionals may use many different treatments to help people overcome social anxiety, only two main types of strategies have been tested out in controlled research studies. These include medication treatments and a variety of different cognitive and behavioral techniques. In the few studies that have compared these two general approaches, both seem to work equally well in the short term (Antony 1997). However, there is evidence that cognitive and behavioral treatments have longer-lasting effects compared to medications, once treatment has ended (Heimberg et al. 1994). Currently, there are no published studies investigating the benefits of combining medications with psychological treatments for social phobia, although several studies are underway.

Cognitive Behavioral Therapy

Many studies have now established that cognitive behavioral therapy (CBT) is effective for helping people overcome social phobia. These treatments include three main approaches: using cognitive techniques to identify and change anxious thoughts and predictions regarding social situations, using behavioral techniques (e.g., exposure) to help a person confront feared situations until they are no longer frightening, and using social skills training to teach individuals the skills needed to perform effectively in social situations. Some of the skills that may be taught during social skills training include how to be more assertive, effectively using eye contact and nonverbal communication, and learning to get close to new people. Cognitive and behavioral methods for dealing with perfectionism are described in chapters 7 and 8 in detail.

Medication Treatments

Following is a list of medications that have been shown in controlled studies to be effective for treating social phobia. We have included both the generic name as well as the brand name (in parentheses) for each medication.

Medications That Have Been Shown to Be Effective for Social Phobia
Monoamine Oxidase Inhibitors (MAOI antidepressants) Phenelzine (Nardil)
Reversable Inhibitors of Monoamine Oxidase-A (RIMA antidepressants) Moclobemide (Manerix)
Selective Serotonin Reuptake Inhibitors (SSRI antidepressants) Fluvoxamine (Luvox) Sertraline (Zoloft)
Benzodiazepines (anti-anxiety medications) Clonazepam (Klonapin, Rivotril) Alprazolam (Xanax)

In addition to these medications, several additional drugs have been studied in uncontrolled trials and appear to be effective for treating social phobia. Although additional research is needed to further establish their effectiveness, some of these medications include the SSRI antidepressants paroxetine (Paxil) and fluoxetine (Prozac), as well as the antidepressants venlafaxine (Effexor) and nefazodone (Serzone).

You may notice that many of the medications that have been shown to be effective for social phobia are actually antidepressants. Antidepressant drugs appear to be helpful for most types of clinical anxiety, even in people who do not feel depressed. Chapter 9 discusses various issues related to taking antidepressant medications (e.g., how to choose from the various options, side effects, etc.).

Many of the issues discussed in chapter 9 are also relevant to the antianxiety medications (e.g., clonazepam, alprazolam), although there are a few important differences between antidepressants and antianxiety medications. First, the side effects of antianxiety medications are typically different than those for antidepressants. For antianxiety medications, the most common side effect is fatigue, which usually improves during the course of treatment. Second, compared to antidepressants, antianxiety medications are often more difficult to stop taking because they tend to be associated with withdrawal symptoms, particularly when stopped too quickly. Withdrawal symptoms typically include symptoms of increased anxiety and arousal (i.e., racing heart and dizziness). These symptoms can be minimized by decreasing the dosage gradually.

Changing Perfectionistic Thoughts and Behaviors in Social Anxiety

Challenging Perfectionistic Thoughts

Rather than assuming that your perfectionistic thoughts are true, it is important to treat your beliefs as possibilities or guesses. Unless you are able to accept the possibility that your standards for performance are too high, it will be difficult to shift your expectations to be more realistic. Chapter 7 describes methods of changing your perfectionistic thoughts. Several of these strategies are likely to be helpful for dealing with your anxiety in social situations, including examining the evidence supporting your thoughts, perspective taking, hypothesis testing, changing social comparison habits, and using coping statements. We suggest that you review the techniques described in chapter 7 to help replace your anxious thoughts with more realistic thoughts. The following examples illustrate how to replace anxious thoughts with more neutral, realistic thoughts.

Example 1: I'm nervous about going to the party.

Anxious Thought

I really don't want to go to that party tonight. I'm not going to know anyone, and the other guests will think I'm boring.

Realistic Thoughts

Because I don't know these people, I don't know how they are going to react to me. Often, I have a better time at parties than I expect to have. Maybe it will be okay. If some people find me boring to talk to, it doesn't mean that everyone will feel that way. Besides, even if people don't enjoy my company at this party, it doesn't mean I'm boring. Sometimes I'm bored when I talk to another person, but it doesn't mean that the person is boring.

Example 2: I feel intimidated and nervous while on a date.

Anxious Thought

I am not smart enough to be dating this person.

Realistic Thoughts

I have no idea whether or not I'm smarter than this person. In fact, there are so many different ways that intelligence can be measured, I'm sure there are some areas in which I'm smarter. Even if this person is smarter than me, that doesn't mean I'm not smart. I will always encounter people who are better than me at one thing or another.

Example 3: A co-worker comes by my desk to chat, but I have nothing to say.

Anxious Thought

She's going to think I'm an idiot. She'll see me blushing and think there is something wrong with me.

Realistic Thoughts

Even if she notices me blush, that doesn't mean that she'll think I'm strange. I certainly don't care when I notice someone else blushing. My sister blushes all the time, and no one seems to even notice. If I have nothing to say, she may think I'm nervous, but she may not. Instead, she may think that I'm busy or preoccupied. Even if she suspects that I'm a bit nervous, it doesn't mean that she will care a whole lot, and she probably won't think any less of me. Besides, it's not my responsibility to entertain people all the time. It's okay if someone thinks I'm strange once in a while.

Example 4: I'm having friends over for dinner.

Anxious Thought

They will hate my cooking, and the evening will be ruined.

Realistic Thoughts

I've cooked for people in the past, and usually people enjoy my cooking. Even if they don't like what I've prepared, it doesn't mean that the evening will be ruined. There are many times that I have had dinner at another person's home and not enjoyed my food. I am still able to enjoy the evening, and I certainly don't think less of my host if the meal is not to my liking.

Changing Perfectionistic Behaviors

Chapter 8 includes a number of strategies for changing perfectionistic behaviors. In the case of social anxiety, communication training may be a useful method for improving important interpersonal skills. However, the most important strategy for decreasing social anxiety is exposure to feared situations. Repeated exposure to anxiety-provoking social situations will eventually lead to a decrease in anxiety. Exposure practices should be frequent (at least several times per week) and should last long enough to experience a decrease in anxiety.

You may need to be creative to come up with appropriate situations in which you can practice. For example, if you are fearful of giving presentations, there are a number of different places where you can conduct exposure exercises. You can join an organization called Toastmasters, which gives members opportunities to improve their public speaking skills. Or you can take a public speaking course or an acting class. Another possibility is volunteering to speak about your career in front of a group of students in a high school or college. You can even ask a group of friends or family members to be your audience.

If a situation is too frightening, you can begin by conducting role-play simulations. For example, if you are frightened of going to a job interview, you can practice simulated interviews with a friend or family member. You can even ask your "interviewer" to be purposely difficult so that the real interview will seem like a piece of cake in comparison. After practicing in simulated interview situations, you can work your way up to interviewing for jobs that don't interest you especially. These practices will help you be more comfortable in interview situations, so that when the interview for the job you really want comes up, you'll be ready.

If you are afraid of drawing attention to yourself, practice doing just that during your exposure practices. For example, if you are anxious about having your hands shake while you are holding a drink or writing, let your hands shake on purpose. Let your glass shake until you spill your water. Or, when you are filling out a check at a store, let your hand shake enough that the check is unreadable and has to be rewritten. If you are afraid that other people will see you sweat when your are feeling anxious, purposely wear warm clothes so that you are more likely to perspire. The goal of exposure is to learn that the situations that you fear are not dangerous. Even if someone sees you shake or sweat, there are no long-term consequences.

Take Frequent Risks in Social Situations

People who are fearful of social situations often fear rejection from other people. If you are fearful of rejection, one of the best things you can do is take social risks more frequently. You may end up being rejected from time to time, but you will learn not to care about the rejection as much.

For example, if you tend to fear rejection when applying for a job or asking someone out on a date, you may find that it takes you months or years to get up the courage to do these things. You may fear that the person you ask out or the employer who reads your application will find you unappealing or unacceptable. When you finally do find the courage to take the risk, you may end up feeling very discouraged if you are rejected. You may take this as evidence that your anxious beliefs were true. The experience may "prove" that you are not good enough, just as you believed.

There is a problem with this logic. The truth is that most dates do not lead to long-term relationships and most job applications do not lead to jobs. Most people occasionally have the experience of being rejected in social situations such as these. To have the experience of not being rejected, a person has to take risks frequently. For example, if the probability of getting a job is one in twenty (for every twenty jobs that you apply for, you get one job offer), it will take you years to get an offer if you only apply for a job every few months. On the other hand, if you apply for several jobs per week, it probably won't be long before you have an offer.

More frequent social risks will lead to more frequent rejection. However, frequent risks will also lead to things working out from time to time. Remember, if you are looking for a job, you only need one offer. The number of rejections is not important in the long run. The same is true of dating. Therefore, we recommend that you expose yourself to anxiety-provoking social situations as often as possible. It won't always go smoothly. However, over time the situations will become easier, you will become more skilled at dealing with people in these situations, and your chances of success will increase.

Chapter 12 _____

Perfectionism and Worry

Everyone worries from time to time, particularly about events over which they have little control. They all endure daily stresses that affect their jobs, school performance, relationships, and other areas of their lives. In these circumstances, it is common to worry about possible negative outcomes. Just like sadness, anger, and other emotional states, worry is a normal part of life. However, worry can become a problem when it interferes with functioning (e.g., concentration, sleep), causes a lot of distress, or continues even in situations where there is no realistic reason to be so worried.

This chapter is written primarily for people who find that they worry often, for long periods of time, and with such an intensity that they experience physical symptoms such as appetite loss, headaches, or sleeplessness. The information here may also be of value to people who find themselves getting overly tense, irritable, and restless when they are faced with real problems to solve.

What Is Worry?

Normal worry is characterized by a state of apprehension, foreboding, and uneasiness. Typically, people worry when there is a reason to be concerned about the outcome of some situation or problem. Most people deal with this sort of worry by assessing the problem they face, getting advice if they need it, and solving the problem if they can. If the problem can't be solved right away, they can usually put the problem out of their minds, at least temporarily, while they go about their business. They may say to themselves, "I will worry about that later; there's nothing I can do about it right now." This type of self-talk can be helpful and is one strategy that many people use to deal with normal day-to-day worries

Perfectionism and Worry

Frequently, the basis for excessive worry is a need to completely predict and control negative events, combined with a belief that failing to control events will lead to some disaster that might otherwise have been avoided. Because perfectionism is associated with standards and expectations that are impossible to meet, people who are perfectionistic are at risk for having events not turn out as desired. For example, if you believe that everyone should always be fifteen minutes early for every appointment, it may be difficult for you to have to deal with a partner or child who is always running five minutes late. The more intolerant you are of lateness, the more likely you are to be disappointed by other people, and the more likely you are to have a perceived "reason" to worry.

Generalized Anxiety Disorder

Although most people are able to put their worries aside when necessary, some people have difficulty turning their worries off. In a condition called *generalized anxiety disorder* (GAD), worry is difficult to control and occurs at an intensity and frequency that leads to significant impairment. Among people with GAD, worry is excessive, unrealistic, or out of proportion to the actual threat. In addition, the worry is present most days and lasts for an extended period of time. In fact, many people with GAD report that their worry has been a problem for as long as they can remember. Along with the worry, people with GAD experience a range of other symptoms, including feeling restless, keyed up, or on edge; being easily fatigued; having difficulty concentrating or having their mind go blank; experiencing irritability; having muscle tension; and experiencing sleep problems (e.g., trouble falling asleep, staying asleep, or feeling rested in the morning). Often, it's the physical complaints, such as insomnia, muscle pain, and headaches, that bring people with GAD to seek help from their doctor or another professional.

GAD affects about 5 percent of the general population and is slightly more common among women than men. It often has a gradual onset, beginning quite early in life. However, for some people, the problem begins after some significant life stress, such as a death in the family or the loss of a job. The intensity of the worry may fluctuate over time. As you might expect, the worry is often worse during times of stress or when there is some realistic threat. Paradoxically, however, some people with GAD describe themselves as very calm and capable during actual emergencies or when there is a real threat to be confronted.

Common Worry Topics Among People with GAD

Most "worriers" tend to be anxious across different areas of their life, rather than worrying about just one or two topics. In fact, when asked what they worry about, people with GAD often report that they worry about "everything." Following are a few areas that are common sources of anxiety for people who are prone to worry:

- Work or school performance (e.g., worries about getting fired, failing exams, etc.)

- Household chores (e.g., excessive worry about not being able to get everything done)

- Money and finances (e.g., anxiety about going bankrupt or not being able to pay the bills)

- Health and safety of self (e.g., fear of contracting an illness)

- Health and safety of family and friends (e.g., worry about the children's health)

- Relationships (e.g., unnecessary anxiety about spouse being unfaithful)

- Other minor matters (e.g., worry about finding a parking spot when driving to work)

The Nature of Worry

Research has consistently shown that people who worry excessively pay more attention to threat-related information than people who are less prone to worry. In other words, if you are a worrier, chances are that you frequently look out for possible cues that something is about to go wrong. This tendency to be on guard for threat contributes to other problems that are associated with worry, including difficulty concentrating or thinking clearly and difficulty falling asleep at night. For a perfectionist, there may be the added demand of having to scan the environment well enough to catch *each and every* indicator of possible threat or danger.

Where does this tendency to always be on guard come from? There is evidence that a history of unpredictable negative events may play a role. Several studies demonstrated that the ability to predict the onset of stressful events affects whether an organism will experience chronic arousal later on (Kandel 1983). In this series of experiments, two different groups of sea slugs were exposed to mild electric shocks. In one group, the sea slugs were exposed to shock only when a light was turned on, but not when the light was off (the presence of the light made the shock predictable). In the second group of sea slugs, shocks were administered randomly, regardless of whether the light was on or off (the shock was unpredictable). The purpose of the study was to evaluate the effects of predictable versus unpredictable shock on arousal.

After experiencing the predictable shocks, the first group of sea slugs developed a pattern of arousal that was linked to whether the light was on or off. When the light was on, they showed signs of arousal; when the light was off, they were in their normal resting state. In contrast, after only a few shocks, the sea slugs that received unpredictable shocks became aroused constantly, regardless of whether the light was turned on or off. This group also showed measurable nervous system changes that were not present in the sea slugs that received predictable shocks. The chronic arousal seen in the "unpredictable shock" group is analogous to the chronic arousal reported in people suffering from GAD. Muscle tension is an indirect indicator of arousal and is perhaps the most characteristic physical symptom among chronic worriers. Instead of having peaks and valleys of muscle tension, people with GAD have heightened tension that tends to change relatively little over time.

The implication of Kandel's research for humans is that a history of predictable stressful events may make it easier to turn off worry when the danger or threat has passed. In contrast, for people who experience a series of unpredictable stressful events, there may be increased risk for developing problems with chronic anxiety and worry. Although it may seem like a bit of a leap to generalize from sea slugs to humans, there is also evidence from research on people showing that unpredictable negative events are a risk factor for developing problems with anxiety (Barlow 1988) (Barlow et al. 1996).

Procrastination and Worry

Worriers have difficulty sorting out real problems from a background of possible problems that might come along. As a consequence, they may procrastinate and avoid solving problems that arise. It is hard to settle down to sort out one difficulty if you are predicting that there will be other problems that will demand your attention. In fact, you may believe that your attempt to solve one problem will lead to several new problems that will just make things worse. For example, a perfectionistic student might be frightened to ask for help with an assignment, in case the teacher thinks he or she is lazy or incompetent. The student may therefore avoid working on the assignment completely, and in the end create even more problems as a result. In this example, perfectionistic worry is associated with the belief that "It is better to do nothing than to take a risk and fail."

Avoidance and procrastination are often reinforced or rewarded, especially in the short term. By avoiding an anxiety-provoking situation, you may temporarily feel relief from not having had to deal with the problem. You may be rewarded further if the person who had asked you to do the job forgets to check that the work was completed or changes his or her mind. Nevertheless, despite the short-term benefits, procrastination may well lead to negative consequences down the line. For example, you may be left with having to complete your work in a much shorter time than was originally available and under a lot more pressure. In these circumstances it is unlikely that you will do your best work, and you will probably feel dissatisfied in the end. The need to feel perfectly in control over the outcome and the tendency to avoid taking certain risks may actually make it harder to do a good job.

Overcompensating and Worry

Overcompensating involves taking steps above and beyond those that most people might take to prevent some dreaded event from occurring (see chapter 4 for a more detailed description). For example, parents who are constantly worried about the health of their children may insist on checking their child's temperature at the first sign of any physical symptoms and may even take the child out of school whenever another child in the class is ill. Consider the following case examples:

> Joan had two female friends who were both diagnosed with breast cancer several years ago. Although both friends were successfully treated for the illness, Joan sub-

sequently developed intense worry about the possibility of developing cancer herself or of a family member becoming seriously ill. She began to ask for reassurance constantly from her husband and children. She was married to a physician, who initially agreed to examine her and their children as often as Joan requested, in order to reassure her that she did not have cancer. Eventually, Joan's husband lost patience with her daily requests for reassurance. Her children also refused to answer her continual questions about their health. Joan began to worry that her husband's refusal to examine her was because he had found something wrong with her health and was hiding it from her. Joan avoided seeing her family physician for fear that the doctor might confirm her fear that she was seriously ill. As a result of Joan's constant requests for reassurance, there was considerable strain in the family and she worried that her husband was losing interest in their marriage.

Randall was the father of two daughters in their late teens, both of whom were very successful students. Randall had always worried about how well they did in school and kept very close tabs on their homework. He was also concerned about their safety when they were walking home after school (a total of two blocks). When they were accepted into college, they both decided to move to a city on the other side of the country. Randall tried to get a transfer in his company to be near his children, but his wife did not want to interrupt her career and also felt that their daughters should have the freedom to spend some time away. When they left home, Randall found he could not stop worrying about their safety and became very distracted at work. He tried to cope with his anxiety by calling his children as many as three times a day. This irritated his daughters, cost him a lot of money, and did not stop him from worrying for more than a few minutes at a time.

Treatments for Generalized Anxiety Disorder

Three general types of treatment have been shown to be effective for treating GAD and excessive worry: medications, relaxation training, and cognitive behavioral therapy.

Medication Treatments

The earliest medications shown to be effective for treating GAD were the benzodiazepines (also known as tranquilizers), which are also used sometimes as muscle relaxants or sleep medications. The benzodiazepines include such drugs as diazepam (Valium), lorazepam (Ativan), alprazolam (Xanax), clonazepam (Klonopin, Rivotril), and others. These drugs work very quickly and tend to be quite effective in the short term. Although some people find that these drugs are useful for long-term treatment, their effectiveness usually decreases as time goes on, unless the dosage is increased. Increasing the dosage of these medications puts people at risk for intense side effects, including drowsiness. In addition, because the withdrawal symptoms for these drugs can include intense anxiety, many people have difficulty discontinuing benzodiazepines. Today, most physicians do not use these drugs for more than a few weeks at a time.

Another type of antianxiety medication is a drug called buspirone (Buspar). This medication is derived from a completely different family than the older tranquilizers and does not produce drowsiness or dependence. It takes a few weeks to have an effect and therefore is not used for acute anxiety. It is as effective as the benzodiazepines and may work better for people who have not previously used traditional antianxiety medications (e.g., Valium, etc.).

Recently, antidepressants such as fluoxetine (Prozac) and sertraline (Zoloft) have been shown to be helpful for reducing worry. People who are anxious are often very sensitive to the side effects of antidepressants and can become very agitated from the first few doses. Therefore, they should be started at very small doses which then are slowly increased. Treatment should continue for at least several months, and there is a strong risk of relapse after stopping the medication. See chapter 9 for additional information on antidepressant medications.

Psychological Treatments

Relaxation Training

Chronic worry can be lessened by learning to relax. Several relaxation methods are available. Progressive muscle relaxation involves learning to relax the muscles of the body to decrease feelings of tension, stress, and anxiety. A second method, known as imagery, involves learning to imagine particular scenes that are soothing. Meditation, yoga, and mindfulness training may also help to decrease chronic worry. Finally, learning to breathe slowly and smoothly can help a person to relax. For more information on relaxation training, check out the Further Readings at the end of this book.

The main difficulty with relaxation training is that people often forget to practice. Scheduling regular periods to practice, at the same time each day, will increase the chances of benefiting from this approach. For example, you could try scheduling the practices just before or after other activities that come up throughout your day (e.g., having a drink of water, going to the bathroom, traveling to and from work, etc). Even taking a few minutes to breathe slowly from the abdomen, two or three times a day, is a very useful way of breaking up the seemingly never ending stream of tension and anxiety.

Cognitive Behavioral Therapy

Cognitive behavioral therapy involves teaching people first to become more aware of their anxious beliefs and then to replace their worries with more realistic thoughts and predictions. This is accomplished using the techniques described in chapters 7 and 8, including examining the evidence concerning anxious beliefs and testing the validity of anxious predictions by conducting small experiments. For example, one of the best ways to stop worrying about what might happen if you are a few minutes late for class is to try showing up five minutes late and evaluating the consequences. Another strategy that researchers have recently begun to examine involves scheduling specific times for worry. Because people with GAD often have difficulty controlling their worry, scheduling an hour each day to worry is one way of initially gaining control. If the person begins to worry at times other than the scheduled worry time, he or she is instructed to put the worry aside for the time being and return to it later at the scheduled time.

Overcoming Perfectionism Associated with Worry

Chapters 7 and 8 provide detailed descriptions of cognitive and behavioral strategies that are useful for overcoming perfectionism. In this section, we highlight some of these strategies that are particularly helpful for dealing with perfectionistic thoughts and behaviors that are often associated with worry.

Examining the Evidence

Worry is usually associated with two main types of thoughts. The first type of thought is a tendency to overestimate the probability of some unlikely event. In the case examples presented earlier in this chapter, Joan overestimated the likelihood of developing a serious illness. Randall overestimated the likelihood of something bad happening to his children.

The second common style of thinking involves overestimating just how bad it would be if a negative event were to occur. An example of such a thought is, "It would be an absolute disaster if I arrive at the movie theater and there is nowhere to park." In reality, this situation would probably be manageable if it actually occurred.

In order to combat negative thinking that contributes to worry, it can be helpful to examine the accuracy of your beliefs. This process involves asking yourself a series of questions that help you to assess the situation in a more realistic way. Following are some anxious thoughts and some questions that you might ask yourself to challenge anxious thoughts.

Anxious Thoughts:

- I am going to fail the exam.

- I have not studied enough for this exam.

- I don't know the material for this test.

- If I fail the test, I will never get into graduate school, and I will never amount to anything in life.

Questions for Examining the Evidence:

- Do I know for sure that I will fail the exam?

- Have I done well on past exams, even when I thought I would fail?

- Did I study less than I usually do for similar exams?

- What is really likely to happen if I fail the exam?

- Are the results of a single exam likely to have a huge impact on my overall average?

- Is it possible for a person to fail a single exam and still do well in life?

Attempting to answer questions such as these is a powerful method for challenging the perfectionistic beliefs that contribute to your worry. Following is an example of how to use this method for challenging anxious thoughts regarding money and finances:

Client	I am constantly worried about not having enough money to pay the bills. It drives my wife crazy, because I am always trying to control the way she spends her money.
Therapist	Specifically, what are you predicting will happen?
Client	I am afraid that I won't have enough money to pay the rent or to make my car payment. I also worry about my credit card bills getting out of hand. Sometimes I even think that I will go bankrupt. I worry that the whole family will end up living on the street.
Therapist	Do you have any evidence to support these predictions?
Client	No, not really. In fact, I pay off my credit card balance each month. I'm even two payments ahead on my car loan.
Therapist	Can you think of any evidence that contradicts your worries about money?
Client	To start, I have never been in debt before. Also, I've never missed a bill payment in the past, even though I worry about it all the time.
Therapist	What if you were short for several of your bills on a particular month?
Client	That would be terrible.
Therapist	What would actually happen?
Client	I imagine that my debts would start to double and triple. I might never get out of debt.
Therapist	Do you know anyone who once missed a bill payment?
Client	My brother misses payments from time to time.
Therapist	What happens when he misses a payment?
Client	Nothing seems to happen. He usually just makes it up the next month.
Therapist	Do you know anyone who has declared bankruptcy?

Client	Someone I work with declared bankruptcy about a year ago.
Therapist	Did this co-worker end up living on the street?
Client	No. In fact, she was under much less stress after the bankruptcy than before. *(pause)* I guess even if I had a temporary financial setback I could manage it.

Perspective Taking

It is often easier to solve another person's worries than your own. Therefore, a helpful strategy for dealing with your own worries is to imagine that you are giving suggestions to a close friend or relative who has similar worries. Consider the following case example:

Client	I am terrified to go to sleep at night. One of these days I am worried that a stranger is going to come into my home in the middle of the night. It's even worse when my partner and children are away.
Therapist	When you get into bed, how likely do you think it is that someone will break into your home?
Client	Realistically, I know that chances are low. It's never happened before. But, when I am lying there, trying to fall asleep, it feels much more likely. Maybe 50 percent likely.
Therapist	Do you worry that people might break into your friends' and neighbors' homes?
Client	No, not really. It feels like it's more likely to happen in my home, although I know that doesn't make any sense.
Therapist	What would you say to neighbors who were fearful of having someone break into their house?
Client	I would probably say that it is unlikely. I would remind them that they have lived there for several years and there has never been a break-in before.
Therapist	Can you apply that same logic for your own situation?

Tolerating Uncertainty and Ambiguity

Learning to tolerate uncertainty can combat your tendency to worry about unpredictable and uncontrollable situations. There are many situations that you can't predict or control. Fortunately, however, it is not terribly important that you be able to control most situations. A helpful way of tolerating unpredictable events is to generate a list of possible outcomes and to consider ways of dealing with each outcome. For example, if you are stuck in traffic and are late for an job interview, you have two options. You can worry about how terrible it is that you are late, or you can accept the fact that you are late, even though you don't know what the outcome will be. Perhaps the interviewer will be understanding and squeeze you in at a later time. Perhaps the interviewers will reschedule the appointment for another day. Perhaps the interviewer will confront you about being late and send you home without the opportunity to interview again. Regardless of what happens, chances are that the outcome will be manageable.

Hypothesis Testing

If you tend to make unrealistic predictions about negative things that might happen, testing the validity of your predictions using mini-experiments can be a helpful way of challenging your anxious thoughts. Before conducting the experiment, make one or more explicit predictions regarding the outcome. Then, conduct the experiment and evaluate the outcome. Did your predictions come true? If so, was it as bad as you expected? For example, if you are worried about an airline losing your luggage on your next trip, check your luggage at the gate and see what happens. If your luggage doesn't get lost, you will have gained valuable information about the likelihood of losing your luggage. If your luggage does get lost, you may learn that the situation is not as bad as you feared it would be (e.g., lost luggage is often found a few hours later).

Ritual Prevention

Try to ride out your worry without engaging in perfectionistic behaviors such as checking or seeking reassurance. As discussed in chapter 4, these behaviors block you from learning that your anxious thoughts are unrealistic. By preventing these behaviors, you will learn to tolerate uncertainty and imperfection. For more details on how to use ritual prevention, see chapters 8 and 13.

Chapter 13 _____

Perfectionism and Obsessive-Compulsive Behavior

There are two psychological problems that fall under the general heading of obsessive-compulsive behavior. The first is *obsessive-compulsive disorder* (OCD), which is an anxiety disorder associated with persistent disturbing thoughts (obsessions) and repetitive behaviors aimed at decreasing the discomfort caused by these thoughts (compulsions). Many people diagnosed with OCD have perfectionistic standards for certain activities. The second problem, called *obsessive-compulsive personality disorder* (OCPD), is characterized by a tendency to be overly perfectionistic, orderly, and inflexible. Although these are two different conditions, they overlap to some extent, and it is not unusual for a person to experience symptoms from both disorders. Even if you don't have all of the symptoms of either disorder, you may still experience some symptoms from one or both of these problems.

Obsessive-Compulsive Disorder

What Is an Obsession?

To most people, the word "obsession" refers to any persistent thought, desire, or drive that controls a person's behavior. Die-hard fans of a music group or celebrity are often said to be obsessed with their idols. A doctor who works around the clock to discover a cure for a serious disease may be considered obsessed with his or her work. Even people who love a particular food so much that they eat little else are often said to be "obsessed" with that food. In contrast to this common use of the word "obsession," mental health professionals have a very specific meaning for this term.

An obsession is defined as a recurrent and persistent thought, image, or impulse that is experienced as intrusive and inappropriate and causes significant anxiety or distress. In other words, people who have obsessions (in the psychological definition of the word) are very distressed by these thoughts and do not want to have them. In this way, obsessions are different than other types of repetitive thoughts that a person may enjoy having (e.g., fantasies). To be considered a true obsession, the thought cannot simply be an excessive worry about everyday problems such as job performance, money, or relationships. The person must also try to make the disturbing thoughts go away by ignoring them, pushing them out of consciousness, or undoing their effects by some other thought or action.

Obsessions are very common in the general population. In fact, up to 90 percent of people experience intrusive obsessive thoughts from time to time. Common themes for these thoughts include worries about becoming contaminated by some object or substance (e.g., germs, cleaning products, bodily fluids), urges to do something aggressive or hurt another person (e.g., stabbing a close relative, shouting obscenities at someone in public), thoughts about accidentally harming another person, disturbing religious thoughts, disturbing sexual ideas, and repetitive doubts about whether a task has been completed correctly (e.g., whether the stove has been turned off, whether a mistake was made in a report or term paper). Typically, people who experience obsessions usually realize that the thoughts are not realistic. Also, even though the person may fear acting on the obsession, obsessive urges are almost never actually acted upon. For example, it would be highly unusual for a person with aggressive obsessions to actually carry out the thought, unlike a person who actually has problems with aggressive behavior.

What Is a Compulsion?

Compulsions are behaviors that are repeated over and over again in response to an obsession or according to rigidly applied rules. Compulsions are aimed at preventing harm from occurring or at decreasing anxiety or distress. They may include physical behaviors (e.g., washing) or mental behaviors (e.g., silently repeating words in your head). Like obsessions, compulsions are very common in the general population. More than 50 percent of people report engaging in compulsive behaviors from time to time.

The types of compulsions that people have are often closely related to the content of their obsessive thoughts. For example, people who have obsessions about contamination or cleanliness typically engage in compulsions to prevent themselves from becoming contaminated or dirty. These may include frequent hand washing and cleaning, as well as avoiding situations where contamination may occur (e.g., public rest rooms). Other common compulsions include checking (e.g., appliances, locks, accuracy of work), counting, repeating actions, putting things in order, asking for reassurance, praying when you don't really want to, or repeating certain words, explaining or confessing, and hoarding.

What Is OCD?

For most people in the general population, intrusive thoughts and compulsive behaviors are not especially problematic. For example, you may avoid certain situations because of concerns about contamination (e.g., eating a candy that has fallen on the floor, sitting on a public toilet seat) or engage in some mild checking (e.g., checking your locks and appliances a couple of times). Or you may have distressing thoughts that come and go occasionally. Most people experience these symptoms from time to time, with little distress or interference in their life.

In contrast, people with OCD experience obsessions and compulsions more frequently and more intensely than the average person. They are also bothered more by their obsessions and take greater pains to resist or suppress their upsetting thoughts. To be diagnosed with OCD, the obsessions or compulsions must be bothersome, time consuming (e.g., more than an hour per day), or interfering in a person's life. For example, it is not unusual for a person with OCD to experience obsessions throughout the day. For some people, compulsive behaviors such as washing or checking can take up so much time that the person is unable to work, socialize, or be involved in other important activities. OCD affects between 1 and 3 percent of the general population and appears to be equally prevalent in men and women. Although the problem tends to begin in early adulthood, it is not unusual for people with OCD to have the problem begin in childhood.

OCD and Perfectionism

Perfectionism is often a feature of OCD. For example, a client who was seen in our clinic had contamination fears related to eating foods that may have gone bad. Specifically, she was afraid that if she ate something that was contaminated, she might become ill. As a result, she had strict standards regarding what she was willing to eat. There were many different foods that she avoided eating completely (including all foods containing meat, certain fruits and vegetables, and certain dairy products). In addition, if an item looked anything less than perfect (e.g., if there was a small spot on her food), she refused to eat it. Her fear was worse when eating in restaurants than at home, because she could not be sure about the quality of the food or of the chef's standards for cleanliness. She realized that her fears were excessive and unreasonable, and yet she had difficulty putting them aside. Her approach to food was perfectionistic, in that she had inflexible rules about which foods she could and could not eat, and she refused to eat anything that didn't meet her strict standards.

Another person seen in our clinic was worried that other people might misunderstand what he told them and that something terrible might happen as a result. For example, when making plans with friends, he was fearful that either he or his friends would show up at the wrong location or time. As a result of his fear, he needed to repeat things several times when he spoke to other people. Also, he tended to check that the other person understood everything properly. After speaking to someone, he often phoned them back several times to ensure that all the details from their conversations were clear. Whereas most people are able to tolerate the possibility that a mistake may have occurred during a conversation, for this person, mistakes were unacceptable. His perfectionistic beliefs were manifested in his unwillingness to risk making an error or being misunderstood.

Causes of OCD

Biological Factors

Three different lines of research support a role for biological factors in the cause and/or maintenance of OCD. First, there is indirect evidence of altered functioning in the brain neurotransmitter called serotonin. For example, medications that increase levels of serotonin in the brain appear to be effective for many people who suffer from OCD, whereas medications that affect other brain neurotransmitters do not have much of an impact on OCD symptoms. Second, there is evidence that genes inherited from parents play a role in OCD.

Finally, there appear to be differences in brain functioning in people with OCD compared to people without OCD.

Studies using *positron emission tomography* (a method of measuring brain activity) show that OCD is associated with increased blood flow in the brain areas known as the *prefrontal cortex* and *basal ganglia*. Medication that increases levels of serotonin appears to reverse this abnormality. Interestingly, psychological treatments (including cognitive behavioral therapy) also seem to cause the blood flow in brains of people with OCD to return to normal. Thus, it may be the case that the abnormal blood flow is a result of the disorder.

Psychological Factors

Several researchers have provided evidence that a person's learning experiences and beliefs influence the onset and course of OCD. The most influential psychological theories of OCD to date are those proposed by psychologists Paul Salkovskis and S. Rachman. According to these experts, OCD is not so much a problem with obsessions as it is with people's interpretation of their obsessions. Remember that most people experience thoughts that are obsessional in nature from time to time. The difference between people who experience the occasional obsessional thought without being bothered by it and those who become very distressed by their obsessional thoughts has to do with what people think the obsessional thought means. People who are bothered by obsessional thoughts often have lots of negative beliefs about what the thought means. For example, Salkovskis (1998) points out that many people with OCD believe that their obsessive thought might come true in real life unless something is done to counter it. Rachman (1997) observes that many people with obsessional problems believe that having thoughts about deeds that are morally wrong is just as bad as actually committing those acts. Other researchers such as Adrian Wells (1997) and David A. Clark and Christine Purdon (Clark and Purdon 1993) have observed that obsessions are problematic when the person believes that he or she can and should have absolute control over their thoughts.

Beliefs such as these cause people to feel that they must do something about the thought, such as washing, checking, or other such rituals. At the very least, they cause the individual to want to suppress the thought. These acts have a number of effects that serve to increase the frequency of obsessions and subsequent compulsions. First, when the thought is suppressed, exposure to the thought is terminated. This means that the person doesn't get the chance to get used to the thought, and the thought remains upsetting. Second, some research suggests that thought suppression has the ironic effect of increasing thought frequency later on (Salkovskis and Campbell 1994; Trinder and Salkovskis 1994). Third, attempts to neutralize upsetting thoughts typically reduce the anxiety associated with the obsession in the short term.

Because behaviors that reduce anxiety are more likely to be repeated, the more a person engages in the compulsion, the more he or she is likely to continue engaging in the compulsion. The sense of relief associated with anxiety reduction can lend credibility to the idea that the ritual is the only thing that keeps the thought from becoming harmful in some way. Finally, by engaging in the ritual, the individual never has the opportunity to learn that the obsessional thought is not, in fact, dangerous. Thus, the thought continues to be upsetting, and the ritual continues to be used as a means of coping with that distress.

Treatment of OCD

Two general treatment approaches have been shown in controlled studies to be effective for helping people who suffer from OCD: medications and cognitive behavioral therapy. Medications that increase serotonin levels in the brain have been shown to decrease OCD symptoms. These include the tricyclic antidepressant clomipramine (Anafranil), as well as the selective serotonin reuptake inhibitor (SSRI) antidepressants fluoxetine (Prozac), fluvoxamine (Luvox), sertraline (Zoloft), and paroxetine (Paxil).

In studies comparing these medications to one another, they appear to be equally effective for treating OCD. The decision to choose one medication over another should be based on factors such as side effects, cost, and a history of response or nonresponse to one or more of these medications in the past. Although these medications are antidepressants, they appear to be effective for people with OCD, even if depression is not a significant problem. For more information on these and other antidepressant medications, see chapter 9.

In addition to medications, cognitive behavioral strategies have been shown to be effective for helping people overcome OCD. Specifically, exposure to feared situations and prevention of compulsive rituals seems to be the treatment of choice for this problem. Some researchers have also found that teaching people to challenge their unrealistic thoughts using cognitive techniques (such as those described in chapter 7) is sometimes helpful.

Studies that have compared medicinal approaches to exposure and ritual prevention have generally found that both approaches are equally effective in the short term. However, after treatment ends, the effects of exposure and ritual prevention tend to be longer lasting than those for medication. For more details on how to conduct exposure and ritual prevention, see chapter 8. In addition, the end of this chapter includes a section on how to apply these strategies to obsessive-compulsive symptoms in particular.

Obsessive-Compulsive Personality Disorder

What is OCPD?

The hallmark of OCPD is an excessive concern with order, organization, rules, lists, and trivial details. People with OCPD are often perfectionistic to the point of not getting anything done. For example, they may spend so much time making lists of things that need to get done (and refining their lists), that the tasks on the list don't get completed. Or they may devote so much energy to including every small detail when they tell a story that the main message of the story is lost.

In addition, individuals with OCPD typically spend excessive amounts of time and energy on their work, often at the expense of other important aspects of their life, such as having fun and enjoying time with friends and family. People with OCPD tend to be overly conscientious, rigid about their views, and inflexible about issues related to ethics and morals. They have difficulty delegating jobs to other people, for fear that tasks will not be completed correctly. They may also have difficulty throwing things away, just in case they are needed in the future. In many ways, OCPD is the psychological disorder that is most closely related to perfectionism.

Research on OCPD

Compared to OCD, very little research has been conducted with people suffering from OCPD. Therefore, we know very little about the causes of this problem and almost no controlled studies have tested the effects of specific treatments for OCPD. In fact, we do not even have reliable data on the prevalence of this disorder. Despite the lack of adequate research, it is likely that both biological and psychological factors contribute to OCPD. Despite the lack of treatment research, interventions have generally focused on helping people change the perfectionistic thoughts and behaviors using the strategies described in this book (chapters 7 and 8).

Overcoming Perfectionism Associated with Obsessive-Compulsive Behavior

Ritual Prevention

As mentioned earlier, exposure to feared situations, combined with ritual prevention, is the key to overcoming obsessions and compulsions. This approach is likely to be helpful for OCPD behaviors as well, such as excessive organizing and list making. Recall that rituals have a number of negative effects that serve to maintain the fearfulness of the obsession and are self-perpetuating. Thus, the first step to decreasing your obsessive-compulsive behavior is to stop all rituals. This is because any rituals that are performed during or following an exposure practice can "undo" the benefits of the exposure. For example, if you are learning to overcome obsessive fears of contamination from germs, touching "contaminated" objects will do you no good if you wash your hands after every exposure practice. To benefit from exposure, you must first cut out all rituals.

A man in his mid-twenties who was seen in our clinic had an intense fear that he might lose something or accidentally throw something important away. Over time, his doubts broadened to include thoughts that he might purposely throw something away and then forget that he had done it. As a result of these fears, he engaged in a broad range of checking behaviors, particularly when going from one place to another. Before getting out of his car, he checked throughout the car for items that he may have left in the trunk, under the seats, between the seats, or anywhere else that he could think of. He even checked under the hood, even though he knew rationally that he had not opened the hood. Before entering his home, he checked outside his house and behind the bushes in his front yard. Before leaving his home, he checked in all drawers, cupboards, closets, and garbage cans in each room. In addition to spending many hours per day checking, he also asked people for reassurance. For example, he typically asked his partner whether she had emptied the garbage cans in the house, fearing that some important papers may have been thrown out.

As illustrated in this example, the rituals may be quite complex. Before you can begin to prevent your rituals, you will need to become aware of the specific rituals that you use and the situations and feelings that trigger your rituals. What types of repetitive behaviors do you engage in? These may include checking, cleaning, washing, counting, list making, reassurance seeking, repeating certain behaviors, purposely thinking a particular thought (e.g., a prayer, a safe word), or engaging in any other behavior that you feel compelled to do.

Are there particular situations where you are most likely to engage in these rituals? Are they more likely to happen when you are in a particular mood (e.g., anxious, sad, angry, bored)? When you are tired or hungry? When you are in a certain place (e.g., home, work, outside)? When you are with certain people (e.g., strangers, relatives, children, co-workers, alone)? If you are unsure which situations trigger your rituals, try using the monitoring form below to track your compulsive behaviors for a few days or longer.

Exercise 13.1
Using a Compulsive Ritual Record

Date/Time	Ritual	Trigger

Once you have identified the rituals that you want to stop, the next step is to find ways to prevent the rituals. At first, this task may be very difficult. The urges to do the ritual may be very intense. Over time, however, the urges will gradually decrease. Anything you can do to prevent the rituals in the beginning will pay off in the long run. Remember, the worst thing that is likely to happen if you don't complete a ritual is that you will feel uncomfortable. Below are some strategies that you can use to prevent yourself from engaging in your compulsive rituals. Remember, if you can get through the first few days, resisting the urges should become easier.

Strategies for Resisting Rituals

- You will experience anxiety when you begin resisting your rituals. Remind yourself that the anxiety is unpleasant but not dangerous.

- Do something that makes it impossible for you to perform the ritual (e.g., turn off the water from the main source in your basement so you won't be able to wash your hands; mail a letter immediately after writing it so you cannot check what you wrote).

- Remind yourself that your anxiety will decrease eventually, and that the more frequently you resist the ritual, the easier it will be to resist it.

- Remind yourself when you are doing fine and are not experiencing the obsession—or performing the rituals—that this proves that the ritual really doesn't help. By focusing on your successes when you are not performing the rituals, you will be better able to see that your desire to perform the ritual is driven by anxiety rather than by genuine necessity.

- Ask friends and family members to point out when you are performing a ritual or compulsive behavior.

- Ask friends and family members not to participate in your rituals (e.g., ask them not to give you reassurance, even when you ask for it, but rather to remind you that performing the ritual is not a good idea).

- If you "slip" and actually perform a ritual, try to undo the effects of the ritual as soon as possible. For example, if you are practicing learning to tolerate having a less organized desk, and you give in to your urges and spend four hours organizing your desk, mess it up again as soon as possible and continue your practice.

- If the urge is completely overwhelming, and you feel as though you are about to give in and perform the ritual, take yourself out of the situation. Go for a walk, watch TV, or do something else until the urge subsides.

Exposure Exercises

After you have successfully resisted performing your compulsive rituals for a few days, the next step is to begin exposure to situations that you find anxiety provoking or uncomfortable. Exposure may be conducted gradually. That is, you can begin with easier situations and work your way up to more challenging situations.

Chapter 8 is worth reviewing because it discusses in detail exactly how to conduct your exposure practices. However, the main principles to keep in mind include: continue your exposure practice until your anxiety or discomfort has decreased significantly (this can take a few minutes to several hours); if your anxiety decreases quickly, move on to a more difficult practice; repeat exposure practices frequently (conduct longer practices at least four to five days per week, as well as minipractices throughout the day); expect to feel uncomfortable—over time, your discomfort will decrease; and continue to try more and more challenging practices until you can comfortably handle the situations near the top of your hierarchy.

Following is an example of how to use exposure and ritual prevention for a perfectionistic behavior:

Problem:	You feel compelled to correct anyone who makes a mistake when speaking (e.g., mispronounces a word, presents an inaccurate statement, etc.).
Treatment Plan:	Tell people who are close to you that you have decided to stop correcting other people. If necessary, ask others to point out when you inadvertently correct them. To start, it is very important to resist all urges to correct others. If the urge is overwhelming, take a break from the situation (e.g., excuse yourself to go to the bathroom) until the urge to correct the other person passes. Pay attention to how long it takes for the urge to decrease. Over time, you will notice that it is not so important after all that you correct people about trivial mistakes or disagreements.
	After you have successfully resisted the urges to correct other people, try purposely exposing yourself to situations that trigger your urge to correct others. For example, spend time with people who make frequent errors when they are talking and people who, in the past, have tended to trigger your urges most strongly. You could even ask some people to purposely make errors on occasion, in order to provide you with opportunities to practice preventing your "correcting" rituals.

Setting Time Limits

Most people have been told at one time or another that they didn't take their time to do a job properly. In general, the more time that is spent on a project, the better the quality of the work. However, there is a point at which the benefits of spending more time on a job become fewer and fewer. For example, spending two minutes brushing your teeth will clean your teeth much more effectively than spending only ten seconds. However, for every additional minute that you spend brushing beyond the first two minutes, the benefits become smaller and smaller. In fact, if you spend too long brushing, you can destroy the enamel that protects your teeth and actually put yourself at greater risk for developing dental problems.

Another cost of spending too much time on a particular task is that it leaves you too little time to do other things. Taking the time to do very good work is not worth much if you never complete the job or if it interferes with your ability to get other important things done. On the other hand, rushing through a task so that the quality of your work is very poor can also lead to negative consequences. Ideally, you should try to balance the quality of your work with the amount of work that you get done. There may be times when it is better to do a fair job on several different tasks than an outstanding job on only one task. You will need to evaluate your priorities in order to decide whether it is worth spending less time on certain activities.

Do you tend to spend much too long completing certain tasks, such as washing, cleaning, writing a letter, filling out a form, or even telling a story? If so, setting time limits for specific activities will be very helpful. This can be done in two ways. You can gradually decrease the time that you allow for the activity. For example, if you normally spend an hour in the shower each day, you can reduce the allowed time by ten minutes per day until you reach the point of spending no more than ten minutes in the shower. Alternatively, you can make the change more abruptly by immediately reducing the allowed time to a more average level (e.g., ten minutes for a shower, fifteen minutes to write a short letter, etc.). To help you end tasks at the proper time, set a timer or have a friend let you know when the time has ended. When time is up, stop what you are doing, even if the task feels incomplete. Next time, you will have the opportunity to pace yourself differently if you need to work more quickly. If you are not sure what an appropriate time is for a particular task, ask several people how long they would take.

Using Cognitive Strategies to Change Obsessional Beliefs

In chapter 7, we described a number of techniques that are useful for changing perfectionistic thoughts. The techniques that are most likely to be effective for changing thoughts that are associated with OCD and OCPD include: evaluating the evidence for your beliefs, learning to compromise, perspective taking, hypothesis testing, looking at the big picture, using coping statements, and learning to tolerate uncertainty (see chapter 7 for detailed descriptions).

Following is an example of how learning to change thoughts can reduce obsessive-compulsive thinking:

Client   It seems like all of my spare time is spent doing housework.

Therapist   Why do you spend do much time cleaning?

Client   I grew up in a home where cleanliness was very important. I guess I worry that if the house is not clean, guests will think I'm a slob.

Therapist   How much cleaning do you actually do?

Client   On weekdays, I clean for about an hour before work and for about three hours after dinner. On weekends, I spend up to six hours a day cleaning. Each day, I try to wash the floors, vacuum my carpets, dust the entire apartment, and clean inside and under the stove and fridge. On weekends, I do bigger jobs like cleaning the windows and cleaning out the fireplace.

Therapist   Do your friends spend as much time cleaning as you do?

Client   No. In fact, when I visit friends there are often dishes in the sink and sometimes the floors are quite dirty.

Therapist   What do you think of friends who have homes that are not as clean as your apartment?

Client   It doesn't really bother me, as long as it is someone else's home.

Therapist   Do you think that other people are offended when they visit your friends and see dishes in the sink.

Client   Probably not.

Therapist	Then how likely is it that people will be offended or judge you negatively if your floors are not washed daily or if there is a dish or two in your sink.
Client	I guess it is unlikely. It just doesn't feel right to have people over without spending the day cleaning first.
Therapist	Is it possible that your tendency to be overly clean might make people uncomfortable?
Client	Actually, several people have commented on how clean my apartment is and how they were fearful of spilling a drink or making a mess. I have several friends who seem less relaxed at my apartment than when we get together at another home.
Therapist	Perhaps you could test out the accuracy of your predictions by inviting several friends over after a few days of not vacuuming, dusting, or cleaning the floors. Leave some dishes in the sink and leave the couch cushions messy. Seeing how people react to this change will help you to determine whether all your cleaning really makes a difference in what people think of you.

Chapter 14

Perfectionism, Dieting, and Body Image

Dieting and Body Image Concerns in Western Culture

Anyone influenced by Western culture is likely aware that they live in an appearance-obsessed society. Thin is in, and people go to great lengths to attain the thin beauty ideal. This culture has equated thinness with beauty and furthermore, has come to associate thinness with all sorts of positive character traits. The most common way to gain control over one's physical appearance is through dieting. Dieting is a thirty billion dollar industry in the United States. According to some estimates, the American public spends more on diet-related products (books, videos, pills, etc.) than the government spends on education, employment, and social services combined (Brownell and Rodin, 1994). Dieting can also put people at risk for developing certain problems, including eating disorders.

The drive to be thin appears to be a sociocultural phenomenon. Variables such as a person's culture and the period in which he or she grew up have an enormous impact on the way body shape and dieting are viewed. It has been estimated that 40 percent of women and 24 percent of men in the United States currently describe themselves as dieters. These numbers are considerably higher than the 7 percent of men and 14 percent of women who described themselves as dieters in the year 1950 (Brownell and Rodin 1994).

The prevalence of eating disorders has also increased dramatically over the past few decades. In addition, cultural differences appear to affect the incidence of eating disorders as well. One study (Nasser 1986) assessed the prevalence of eating disorders among Egyptian women studying in Cairo universities and Egyptian women studying in British universities. Whereas 12 percent of the women studying in England met criteria for an eating disorder, there were no instances of eating disorders among women in the Egyptian universities. Not surprisingly, there is evidence that the prevalence of eating disorders is increasing in non-Western countries, as their economies become more industrialized and their people become more influenced by Western cultures.

Perfectionism and the Drive to Be Thin

People who diet restrict their food intake not only in the hopes of losing weight, but also in order to avoid becoming fat. As much as thinness is viewed as a positive trait in our culture, fatness is viewed as negative and is associated with all sorts of negative character traits. From a young age, children tend to discriminate against overweight children, and this carries into adulthood, where overweight people suffer from prejudices in many areas of life.

These societal standards encourage perfectionism. This perfectionism is often carried out in the way that people eat. Many people engage in black-and-white thinking when they think about food. They consider some foods forbidden (e.g., cookies and ice cream) and others permissible (e.g., salads and fruits). We often hear people remark that they have "been good today" if they have adhered to their diets and are "failures" if they have eaten some of those forbidden foods. In effect, this perfectionistic style of thinking sets people up for difficulties with eating.

Psychologists Peter Herman and Janet Polivy (1984) devised a boundary model of eating that explains how dieters (people who restrict their food intake in order to prevent weight gain) and nondieters (people who do not engage in such behaviors) eat. Nondieters, on a simple level, eat when they feel hungry and stop when they are full. In other words, satiety (fullness) acts as a boundary, or a "stop-eating" mechanism. Dieters, on the other hand, have set up for themselves a diet boundary. Dieters decide in their minds that if they eat a certain amount they have maintained their diets, but if they eat more than that amount they have broken their diets. Usually, the diet boundary acts as a "stop-eating" mechanism, but if the diet is broken, dieters will eat lots of food, often until they are overly full. Herman and Polivy have called this the "what the hell" effect; once the diet is broken, dieters think that they may as well eat to abandon, usually indulging in foods that are considered forbidden.

Biological factors also play a role in causing dieters to break their diets. An important reason for which dieters fail to stay on their diets is the body's powerful drive to meet its basic energy needs. By definition, dieters chronically take in less energy (food) than the body requires to meet its energy needs—with the goal of lowering the overall body weight. The body's natural defense against starvation is to overeat, having endured severe caloric restriction.

A great deal of self-control is required to fight the body's natural drive to feed itself. There are many factors that can undermine this self-control, including experiencing social pressure not to eat fattening food, drinking alcohol, and feeling depressed. Dieters also tend to engage in overeating when they feel anxious, particularly when they are made to feel bad about themselves. Polivy, Herman, and their colleagues (Polivy and Herman 1993) have suggested that overeating serves as a way of escaping self-awareness. It is less distressing to focus on food (how it tastes, smells, etc.) than to focus on feeling bad about oneself. However, this strategy is helpful only in the short term. After overeating, dieters tend to feel guilty and even worse about themselves than before they started eating. The failure to maintain the self-control required in dieting, and the bad feelings that result from this failure, can precipitate episodes of overeating and further bad feelings. Therefore, dieters get caught in a vicious cycle.

In general, dieters are more perfectionistic than nondieters. As we already mentioned, dieters set up for themselves a beauty ideal that they would like to attain. Often, this ideal is unrealistic and based on what people see in the media. Dieters also set up unrealistic standards for eating, often restricting their intake to dangerously low levels. As mentioned earlier, the body's natural defense against starvation is to overeat. In one study conducted by Keys (Keys et al. 1950), a group of healthy men (with no previous issues around eating or body weight) were put on a severely restricted diet. Interestingly, these men ended up having episodes of overeating after having endured severe caloric restriction. In addition, the men in this study became preoccupied with food. Their conversations and daydreams often revolved around eating, food, and related topics.

Although a tendency to be overly concerned with body shape can affect anyone, woman are especially prone to have unrealistic standards regarding weight. In one study, Killen and colleagues (1986) found that one third of tenth grade girls believed they were overweight, even when they were not. In another unpublished study by Dr. Michelle Laliberté, 22 percent of normal-weight female college students believed they were overweight, and 48 percent of this sample overestimated their weights.

Stunkard and colleagues (1980) reported a study in which women and men were each asked to estimate their current body shape and their ideal body shape. In addition, study participants also rated the extent to which they found various body shapes to be attractive on other men and women. Several interesting findings emerged from the study. First, women estimated their current body shape to be significantly heavier than their ideal body shape. Second, women tended to find other women more attractive if they were thin (close to the woman's own self-rated ideal body shape). Third, men tended to rate other women as most attractive if they were slim, but not as slim as the body shape preferred by women. Fourth, there were almost no differences in men's ratings of their own current body shape, their own ideal body shape, and the shape that they find most attractive on other men. And fifth and finally, women tended to find men more attractive if they were thinner than their current body shape. To summarize, women are more likely than men to hold high standards for thinness, both for themselves and for others.

Perfectionistic Thoughts Related to Eating and Weight

Researchers have consistently shown that a person's beliefs about dieting and weight have an enormous impact on eating-related problems, including tendencies to be underweight; engage in binge eating; or engage in various purging behaviors such as self-induced vomiting, laxative abuse, and excessive exercise. Following is a list of perfectionistic thoughts that contribute to concerns about eating and weight. As you read the list, pay attention to particular beliefs that you hold:

- Some foods are forbidden, some are permissible.
- If I eat a forbidden food, I have messed up my diet.
- If I eat a bit of a forbidden food, I may as well eat tons of it, since I already broke my diet.
- If I eat a forbidden food, I'll get fat.
- If I start to eat, I'll lose control.
- I can never be too thin.
- I feel fat, therefore I am fat.

- If my clothes are too small, it is because I am fat.

- I have to exercise (purge, take laxatives, etc.) after eating, or I'll get fat.

- You can't get anywhere in this world if you're fat.

- I'll never find a boyfriend/girlfriend (or a job, friends, etc.) unless I'm thin.

- I'll only be special and unique if I'm thin.

- If I gain a few pounds, I'll keep going until I'm obese.

- I have to look like _____ (model, actress, etc.).

Perfectionism and Other Concerns About Your Physical Appearance

Although weight and body shape are among the most common sources of body dissatisfaction, people are often unhappy with other aspects of their physical appearance. You may believe that the curve of your nose is unattractive or that your balding head is a turnoff to other people. In fact, people's tendency to be displeased with the way they look helps to fund an entire industry of plastic surgeons, as well as manufacturers of cosmetics and other products designed to help people look their "best." Being unhappy with your physical appearance is often caused by setting unnecessarily high standards regarding how you *should* look, despite the fact that other people are typically much less critical of your appearance than you might think. Following are some physical features that tend to be a source of dissatisfaction for some people:

- Receding hairline or baldness

- Too much hair (on face, chest, back, arms, etc.)

- Unhappy with hair type (e.g., curly versus straight hair)

- Wrinkles, graying hair, sagging facial features, and other signs of aging

- Being too short or too tall

- Body parts that are too big or too small (e.g., nose, ears, breasts)

- Poor complexion

- Unhappy with face (e.g., double chin, small cheekbones, asymmetrical face)

- Unhappy with other body parts (e.g., feet, hands, legs)

- Unhappy with other physical features (e.g., voice, body odors, posture)

Perfectionistic Behaviors That Contribute to Body Image Problems

Almost everyone likes to look their best. Because it feels good to be complimented on your physical appearance, most people try to look good. However, people who are overly concerned about their physical appearance tend to rely too often on strategies for improving or masking perceived physical flaws. In addition, they tend to engage in behaviors that maintain their unrealistic standards by preventing them from disproving their perfectionistic beliefs. Chapter 4 describes various behaviors that contribute to perfectionism.

Following is a list of behaviors that are particularly relevant to body image problems. Most people engage in these behaviors from time to time. However, if you have particularly strong beliefs regarding the importance of your physical appearance, you may be using these behaviors excessively, to the point that they are costing you in terms of their financial impact (cosmetics, salon services, and cosmetic surgery are expensive), the time they take up (spending several hours a day trying to look perfect doesn't leave much time for other things), and their potential threat to your health (being underweight can be dangerous) or emotional well-being (withdrawing socially and so reducing the number of pleasurable activities you experience). Some examples of perfectionistic behaviors linked to body image are:

- Frequent checking and measuring (e.g., looking in the mirror, weighing self)

- Excessive grooming (constantly fixing hair, removing blemishes)

- Wearing clothes that are too small (this can maintain the belief that you are overweight, even if you are not)

- Hiding body parts that you believe are unappealing (e.g., wearing large clothes to hide your figure, long pants to hide your legs, a hat to hide a balding head, etc.)

- Avoiding contact with other people (because you fear rejection because of your appearance)

- Excessive weight-loss behaviors (e.g., dieting, exercise, purging, diet pills)

- Cosmetic surgery

- Excessive use of cosmetic products and services (e.g., makeup, hair dye, frequent expensive haircuts, electrolysis, tanning salons)

- Reading and information seeking (e.g., reading fashion and beauty magazines)

- Comparing your appearance to that of other people

Psychological Problems Associated with a Distorted Body Image

A number of psychological disorders are associated with distorted attitudes and perceptions regarding body shape and physical appearance. These include the eating disorders *anorexia nervosa* and *bulimia nervosa*, as well as *body dysmorphic disorder*, which is classified as a *somatoform disorder*.

Anorexia Nervosa

Anorexia nervosa is diagnosed when a person refuses to maintain a weight that is at least 85 percent of that expected for the individual's height and age. In addition, people with this condition have an intense fear of becoming fat, even though they are underweight. Individuals with anorexia nervosa also have distorted beliefs regarding their body shape, including denial that they are underweight or a tendency for their self-esteem to be almost entirely tied to their weight. To fully meet the criteria for this disorder, the individual must have stopped menstruating for at least three months, which is an indicator of starvation. At very low weights, the female body is unable to produce the hormones necessary for menstruation. Of course, this criterion does not apply to males, who make up about 10 percent of the people who suffer from anorexia nervosa.

The most serious problems associated with anorexia nervosa involve complications associated with being severely underweight. These include low blood pressure, lowered levels of potassium and sodium, heart problems, low iron, decreased bone mass, hormonal changes, hair loss, brittle fingernails, dry skin, and in some cases death. In fact, complications of anorexia nervosa were responsible for the deaths of musician Karen Carpenter and gymnast Christy Henrich, among others. In addition, anorexia nervosa is often associated with other psychological problems, such as depression, obsessive compulsive disorder, and substance abuse.

Treatment of Anorexia Nervosa

Although findings from treatment studies have been mixed, most experts believe that medications are relatively ineffective for treating anorexia nervosa. Instead, nonmedical treatments are typically used. The first stage of treatment involves helping the person to gain weight. If the person is severely underweight, this stage may occur on an inpatient basis so that possible medical complications can be managed.

Weight gain is achieved by structuring all food intake and ensuring that the person eats regular meals and snacks. Helping the patient gain weight is often relatively easy, especially if the person's meals are supervised. Ensuring that the person does not relapse is more difficult. Unless the individual learns to change his or her beliefs about eating and body shape, it is unlikely that the weight will be maintained. Typically, the second stage of treatment involves cognitive behavioral therapy (to change attitudes and problem behaviors) and sometimes family therapy (to improve patterns of family communication that may contribute to the problem).

Bulimia Nervosa

Bulimia nervosa is associated with frequent binge eating combined with behaviors designed to prevent weight gain (e.g., self-induced vomiting, laxative use, exercise, fasting, diet pills). Binge eating involves eating a very large amount of food in a relatively short period of time, along with a perceived lack of control over eating during the binge. In some cases, a binge can include more food than the average person eats in an entire day. In bulimia nervosa, the binge eating and associated purging behaviors must occur at least twice per week for a period of three months or more. In addition, the person's self-evaluation is tied to body shape and weight.

People with bulimia nervosa tend to be embarrassed about their episodes of bingeing and purging and go to great trouble to prevent others from finding out about their problem. In addition, bulimia is often associated with other problems including depression, anxiety disorders, substance abuse, and various medical complications (e.g., electrolyte imbalances, dental problems, gastrointestinal problems) related to binge eating and purging.

Medications for Bulimia

Treatment with selective serotonin reuptake inhibitors (SSRIs) such as fluoxetine (Prozac) appears to be helpful for decreasing binge eating, purging, and depression among people suffering from bulimia nervosa. Other types of antidepressants, including tricyclic antidepressants and monoamine oxidase inhibitors, also have been shown to be effective for treating the symptoms of bulimia.

However, there are several reasons to consider a psychological approach before trying medication for this problem. First, studies comparing treatments involving medication to psychological approaches such as cognitive behavior therapy have generally tended to favor the psychological treatments or a combination of medication and therapy. Second, patients tend to drop out of medication treatments more often than cognitive behavioral therapy. Finally, the relapse rates tend to be higher when bulimic patients stop taking their medications, compared to when they stop cognitive behavior therapy (Wilson et al 1997). For more information on antidepressant medications, see chapter 9.

Psychological Treatments for Bulimia

A number of studies have demonstrated that cognitive behavioral therapy is an effective treatment for bulimia. This approach includes educating people about the consequences of restricting their food intake, binge eating, and purging. In addition, patients are taught to set goals to gradually develop healthy eating habits and to challenge their perfectionistic and inaccurate attitudes regarding body image, weight, dieting, and eating. Finally, people are helped to recognize the situations, emotions, and thoughts that trigger their urges to restrict, binge eat, or purge, and they are encouraged to develop healthier coping skills.

Another psychological treatment that is effective for treating bulimia is called interpersonal psychotherapy (IPT). This approach (described in chapter 9) focuses on helping people find new ways to manage their relationships with other people.

Body Dysmorphic Disorder

Body dysmorphic disorder is a preoccupation with a perceived defect in one's appearance. Sometimes the defect is completely imagined, and other times the perception may be based on a small anomaly (e.g., a larger than average nose, a barely noticeable scar, etc.), but the person's preoccupation is very much out of proportion to the nature of the actual defect or body feature. The concern about the perceived defect is bothersome or interferes significantly with the person's ability to function at work, in social situations, or in other important life domains.

The areas that are most commonly a focus of concern among people with body dysmorphic disorder include various parts of the face and head (e.g., hair, nose, eyes, lips), as well as other body parts (e.g., waist, legs, breasts, buttocks, penis). Most people with this problem feel as if more than one area of their body is defective, and some individuals are dissatisfied with their entire body. Although many people with this disorder seek cosmetic surgery to correct the imagined defect, they are often unhappy with the results of the surgery.

Treatment of Body Dysmorphic Disorder

Researchers have only recently begun to examine medicinal treatments for body dysmorphic disorder. Preliminary findings from several studies suggest that the SSRI antidepressants are effective for treating this condition. The SSRIs include fluoxetine (Prozac), fluvoxamine (Luvox), sertraline (Zoloft), and paroxetine (Paxil). These medications are discussed in more detail in earlier chapters on depression (chapter 9) and obsessive-compulsive behavior (chapter 13).

Several initial studies suggest that cognitive behavioral therapy may also be helpful for people suffering from body dysmorphic disorder. Cognitive strategies are used to teach the individual to identify unrealistic and distorted beliefs about the perceived defect and learn to replace distorted beliefs with a more realistic view. Behavioral strategies such as exposure and ritual prevention encourage the person to confront anxiety-provoking situations (e.g., socializing with other people) without engaging in various behaviors to hide the perceived physical defect. The patient is also encouraged to stop other compulsive rituals such as checking mirrors, asking for reassurance, and making comparisons to other people.

Overcoming Perfectionistic Thinking and Behavior in Body Image Problems

Chapters 7 and 8 describe a number of strategies that are helpful for changing perfectionistic beliefs and behaviors. In this section, we highlight several of these techniques, as well as a few other ideas for dealing with perfectionism in the context of problems related to being overly concerned with your physical appearance.

Education

Education is an important tool for combating distorted beliefs about dieting, body image, and related topics. Unfortunately, there is a lot of bad information out there. The media constantly presents a distorted view of the ideal body shape. Magazines, television, and movies often suggest new diet and exercise plans, show off underweight models and celebrities, and generally send out the message that it is extremely important to be thin and attractive. To combat this potentially harmful message, it is important that you check out the facts regarding diet, exercise, weight, and health.

For example, there is growing evidence that, to a large extent, body weight is determined by genetics. With healthy eating and moderate physical activity, your body will naturally find it's genetically preferred weight. Research increasingly suggests that a healthy lifestyle (especially fitness), rather than body weight, is one of the best predictors of health.

Challenging Perfectionistic Beliefs

Rather than assuming that your perfectionistic beliefs are true, it is important to test the validity of your beliefs by examining the evidence. The following therapy vignette illustrates some of the questions that you might ask yourself in order to become more accepting of your physical appearance. In this example, the client is taught to challenge his perfectionistic beliefs about what it means to be balding.

Therapist   How much time do you spend thinking about that fact that you are balding?

Client   It's on my mind all the time. I haven't dated in about three years, mostly because I'm afraid of having someone discover my bald head. I wear a toupee, but I still worry that it might fall off sometime. I even went as far as to phone the Hair Club for Men about a month ago. If I could afford a hair transplant, I would do it in a second.

Therapist   Do you recall how you came to be so unhappy about being bald?

Client	I've always hated it. I'm only thirty-five! I should have more hair than I do. I think baldness is unattractive. I think other people find it unattractive as well.
Therapist	Do you have any evidence that other people find baldness unattractive?
Client	Before I started wearing the toupee, a few people made comments about my thinning hair. Also, I constantly hear jokes about bald people. For example, on *Seinfeld*, people are always making fun of the fact that the "George Costanza" character is bald.
Therapist	Have you ever teased someone about some physical characteristic?
Client	I used to make fun of my brother because he's shorter than me. But now that I've lost my hair, I don't make fun of anyone about anything.
Therapist	Did the fact that you teased your brother mean that shorter people are unattractive?
Client	I know that some women prefer men who are taller, but I think there are lots of people who couldn't care less.
Therapist	Turning our attention back to *Seinfeld*, is George's balding head the only thing that was ever made fun of on the show?
Client	No. In fact, that show makes fun of everything and everyone.
Therapist	So, it is possible to be teased about almost any physical feature. What does that say about your earlier statement that you knew that your baldness was unattractive because you were teased?
Client	I guess that just because I was teased doesn't mean that it's ugly.
Therapist	Can you think of any evidence that baldness is attractive?
Client	Well, there are a number of bald celebrities that I know many people find attractive. People like Sean Connery and Patrick Stewart. Also, some people shave their heads. I guess that means that they find baldness attractive.

Therapist	What if someone did find you unattractive because you were bald? Would that mean that everyone would find you unattractive?
Client	I suppose not. Different people like different things.

Changing Social Comparison Habits

Perfectionism often leads to the habit of comparing oneself to other people who are seen as better in particular dimensions. For example, if you are overly concerned about being overweight (even though you are at a healthy weight), you may tend to compare yourself to people who are underweight. Or, you may compare your current weight to your weight in the past, at a time when you were strictly dieting and therefore likely below your natural, healthy weight. These types of comparisons serve to maintain your perfectionistic thoughts. If you are overly concerned about your weight, you need only consider the body type you may have inherited from your family (collect information about your parents and extended family—what did they weigh at your age, and what were their eating and exercise habits at the time?). You might also try to determine what your own adult weight has been at times in your life when you were eating a healthy diet and exercising moderately.

Finally, instead of focusing on people whose body type is different than yours (although perhaps what you consider to be more ideal), try to see what is attractive in people whose body type is closer to your own. Comparisons with extremely thin people (e.g., models) is what leads many women to try dieting. For most women, this means fighting your natural body type. Not surprisingly, 95 to 98 percent of dieters regain the weight they lose within five years. In the meantime, many struggle with binge eating and feelings of failure. Learning to evaluate your lifestyle rather than your weight and learning to compare yourself to those of your body type are extremely important steps in changing unrealistic, perfectionistic thoughts and attitudes about your body.

Similarly, if you are dissatisfied with the size of your nose, it is not helpful to compare yourself to people with smaller noses. If your nose is larger than average, you will find that most people have smaller noses, but that will tell you very little about your physical attractiveness. Remember, half of the people you encounter each day also have noses that are bigger than average. It doesn't necessarily mean that you are unattractive. In fact, most people are different than the average person on one feature or another. If you must compare yourself to other people, don't just make comparisons based on your physical features that bother you.

Hypothesis Testing and Exposure

One of the most powerful ways of testing perfectionistic thoughts about your physical appearance is to create small experiments that are likely to disprove your beliefs. For example, if you are fearful that other people won't be attracted to you if you are wearing shorts, try wearing shorts when you are out with other people and see what happens. Chances are that people will treat you no differently than when you are wearing long pants.

If the thought of having other people see some aspect of your physical appearance is terrifying, exposure practices may be helpful. Exposure (described fully in chapter 8) involves entering a feared situation repeatedly for an extended period, until the situation no longer produces anxiety. To deal with distorted perceptions regarding some aspect of your body, practices may include allowing people to see the "defective" feature. For example, practices may involve taking off your hat to expose your bald head or not wearing makeup in order to expose a mole or scar. You may want to start by making a list of avoided situations, rank ordering them, and trying them out gradually.

Ritual Prevention

Ritual prevention involves stopping the compulsions that you rely on to reduce your anxiety about your physical appearance. Following are examples of how ritual prevention can be used for various problems related to distorted body image:

- Avoid weighing yourself more than once per month.
- Do not look in the mirror except when getting ready for work in the morning.
- Comb your hair no more than twice per day.
- Do not wear sunglasses to cover your eyes.
- Stop all dieting and purging.
- Stop going to tanning salons.

Further Readings

Perfectionism

Self-Help Readings

Burns, D. D. 1980. The perfectionist's script for self-defeat. *Psychology Today* November, 34–57.

Mallinger, A. E., and J. Dewyze. 1992. *Too Perfect: When Being in Control Gets Out of Control.* New York: Fawcett Columbine.

Readings for Professionals

Blatt, S. J. 1995. The destructiveness of perfectionism: Implications for the treatment of depression. *American Psychologist* 50:1003–1020.

Cognitive Behavioral Therapy

Self-Help Readings

Burns, D. D. 1989. *The Feeling Good Handbook.* New York: Plume.

Butler, G., and T. Hope. 1995. *Managing Your Mind: The Mental Fitness Guide.* New York: Oxford University Press.

Ellis, A., and R. Harper. 1975. *A New Guide to Rational Living.* Englewood Cliffs, N.J.: Prentice Hall.

Greenberger, D., and C. A. Padesky. 1995. *Mind Over Mood: A Cognitive Therapy Treatment Manual for Clients.* New York: Guilford Publications.

McKay, M., M. Davis, and P. Fanning. 1997. *Thoughts and Feelings: Taking Control of Your Moods and Your Life,* 2d. ed. Oakland, Calif.: New Harbinger Publications.

Readings for Professionals

Barlow, D. H., ed. 1993. *Clinical Handbook of Psychological Disorders*. 2d ed. New York: Guilford Publications.

Beck, J. S. 1995. *Cognitive Therapy: Basics and Beyond*. New York: Guilford Publications.

Clark, D. M., and C. G. Fairburn, eds. 1997. *Science and Practice of Cognitive Behavior Therapy*. New York: Oxford University Press.

Ellis, A. 1962. *Reason and Emotion in Psychotherapy*. New York: Lyle Stuart.

Freeman, A., K. M. Simon, L. E. Beutler, and H. Arkowitz, eds. 1989. *Comprehensive Handbook of Cognitive Therapy*. New York: Plenum Press.

Hawton, K., P. M. Salkovskis, J. Kirk, and D. M. Clark, eds. 1989. *Cognitive Behavior Therapy for Psychiatric Problems: A Practical Guide*. New York: Oxford University Press.

Leahy, R., ed. 1997. *Practicing Cognitive Therapy: A Guide to Interventions*. Northvale, N.J.: Jason Aronson, Inc.

Persons, J. B. 1990. *Cognitive Therapy in Practice: A Case Formulation Approach*. New York: Norton.

Salkovskis, P. M., ed. 1996. *Frontiers of Cognitive Therapy*. New York: Guilford Publications.

Van Hasselt, V. B., and M. Hersen, eds. 1996. *Sourcebook of Psychological Treatment Manuals for Adult Disorders*. New York: Plenum Press.

Communication Training

Self-Help Readings

McKay, M., M. Davis, and P. Fanning. 1995. *Messages: The Communications Skills Book*, 2d ed. Oakland, Calif.: New Harbinger Publications.

Readings for Professionals

Bedell, J. R., and S. S. Lennox. 1997. *Handbook for Communication and Problem-Solving Skills Training: A Cognitive-Behavioral Approach*. New York: John Wiley and Sons.

Procrastination

Self-Help Readings

Burka, J. B., and L. M. Yuen. 1983. *Procrastination: Why You Do It and What to Do about It*. Reading, Mass.: Addison-Wesley.

Roberts, M. S. 1995. *Living Without Procrastination: How to Stop Postponing Your Life*. Oakland, Calif.: New Harbinger Publications.

Depression
Self-Help Readings

Burns, D. D. 1980. *Feeling Good: The New Mood Therapy*. New York: Signet.

Copeland, M. E. 1992. *The Depression Workbook: A Guide for Living with Depression and Manic Depression*. Oakland, Calif.: New Harbinger Publications.

Ellis, A. 1988. *How to Stubbornly Refuse to Make Yourself Miserable about Anything. Yes, Anything!* New York: Carol Publishing.

Gilbert, P. 1997. *Overcoming Depression: A Self-Help Guide Using Cognitive Behavioral Techniques*. London: Robinson Publishing.

Readings for Professionals

Beck, A. T., A. J. Rush, B. F. Shaw, and G. Emery. 1979. *Cognitive Therapy of Depression*. New York: Guilford Publications.

Beckman, E. E., and W. R. Leber, eds. 1995. *Handbook of Depression*, 2d ed. New York: Guilford Publications.

Klerman, G. L., M. M. Weissman, B. J. Rounsaville, and E. S. Chevron. 1984. *Interpersonal Psychotherapy of Depression*. New York: Basic Books.

Anger
Self-Help Readings

McKay, M., P. D. Rogers, and J. McKay. 1989. *When Anger Hurts: Quieting the Storm Within*. Oakland, Calif.: New Harbinger Publications.

Social and Performance Anxiety
Self-Help Readings

Desberg, P. 1996. *No More Butterflies: Overcoming Shyness, Stagefright, Interview Anxiety, and Fear of Public Speaking*. Oakland, Calif.: New Harbinger Publications.

Johnson, S. 1997. *Taking the Anxiety out of Tests: A Step-by-Step Guide*. Oakland, Calif.: New Harbinger Publications.

Markway, B. G., C. N. Carmin, C. A. Pollard, and T. Flynn. 1992. *Dying of Embarrassment: Help for Social Anxiety and Phobia*. Oakland, Calif.: New Harbinger Publications.

Marshall, J. R. 1994. *Social Phobia: From Shyness to Stage Fright*. New York: Basic Books.

Robin, M. W., and R. Balter. 1995. *Performance Anxiety*. Holbrook, Mass.: Adams Publishing.

Schneier, F., and L. Welkowitz. 1996. *The Hidden Face of Shyness: Understanding and Overcoming Social Anxiety*. New York: Avon Books.

Readings for Professionals

Antony, M. M. 1997. Assessment and treatment of social phobia. *Canadian Journal of Psychiatry* 42:826–834.

Antony, M. M., and D. H. Barlow. 1997. Social and specific phobias. In *Psychiatry*, edited by A. Tasman, J. Kay, and J. A. Lieberman. Philadelphia, Pa.: W. B. Saunders Company.

Beidel, D. C., and S. M. Turner. 1998. *Shy Children, Phobic Adults: Nature and Treatment of Social Phobia*. Washington, D.C.: American Psychological Association.

Chambless, D. L., and D. A. Hope. 1996. Cognitive approaches to the psychopathology and treatment of social phobia. In *Frontiers of Cognitive Therapy*, edited by P. M. Salkovskis. New York: Guilford Publications.

Heimberg, R. G., M. R. Liebowitz, D. A. Hope, and F. R. Schneier, eds. 1995. *Social Phobia: Diagnosis, Assessment and Treatment*. New York: Guilford Publications.

Hope, D. A., and R. G. Heimberg. 1993. Social phobia and social anxiety. In *Clinical Handbook of Psychological Disorders*, 2d ed., edited by D. H. Barlow. New York: Guilford Publications.

Scholing, A., P. M. G. Emmelkamp, and P. Van Oppen. 1996. Cognitive-behavioral treatment of social phobia. In *Sourcebook of Psychological Treatment Manuals for Adult Disorders*, edited by V. B. Van Hasselt and M. Hersen. New York: Plenum Press.

Stein, M. B., ed. 1995. *Social Phobia: Clinical and Research Perspectives*. Washington, D.C.: American Psychiatric Press.

Turner, S. M., M. R. Cooley-Quille, and D. C. Beidel. 1996. Behavioral and pharmacological treatment for social phobia. In *Long-Term Treatments of Anxiety Disorders*, edited by M. R. Mavissakalian and R. F. Prien. Washington, D.C.: American Psychiatric Press.

Generalized Anxiety and Worry

Self-Help Readings

Davis, M., E. R. Eshelman, and M. McKay. 1995. *The Relaxation and Stress Reduction Workbook*, 4th ed. Oakland, Calif.: New Harbinger Publications.

Copeland, M. E. 1998. *The Worry Workbook*. Oakland, Calif.: New Harbinger Publications.

Readings for Professionals

Borkovec, T. D., and M. A. Whisman. 1996. Psychosocial treatment for generalized anxiety disorder. In *Long-Term Treatments of Anxiety Disorders*, edited by M. R. Mavissakalian and R. F. Prien. Washington, D.C.: American Psychiatric Press.

Brawman-Mintzer, O., and R. B. Lydiard. 1997. Generalized anxiety disorder. In *Psychiatry*, edited by A. Tasman, J. Kay, and J. A. Lieberman. Philadelphia, Pa.: W. B. Saunders Company.

Brown, T. A., T. A. O'Leary, and D. H. Barlow. 1993. Generalized anxiety disorder. In *Clinical Handbook of Psychological Disorders*, 2d ed., edited by D. H. Barlow. New York: Guilford Publications.

Davey, G. C. L., and F. Tallis, eds. 1994. *Worrying: Perspectives on Theory, Assessment and Research*. New York: John Wiley and Sons.

Rapee, R. M., and D. H. Barlow, eds. 1991. *Chronic Anxiety: Generalized Anxiety Disorder and Mixed Anxiety-Depression*. New York: Guilford Publications.

Schweizer, E., and K. Rickels. 1996. Pharmacological treatment for generalized anxiety disorder. In *Long-Term Treatments of Anxiety Disorders*, edited by M. R. Mavissakalian and R. F. Prien. Washington, D.C.: American Psychiatric Press.

Wells, A., and G. Butler. 1997. Generalized anxiety disorder. In *Science and Practice of Cognitive Behavior Therapy*, edited by D. M. Clark and C. G. Fairburn. New York: Oxford University Press.

Obsessive-Compulsive Disorder

Self-Help Readings

Baer, L. 1991. *Getting Control: Overcoming Your Obsessions and Compulsions*. Boston, Mass.: Little, Brown.

Foa, E. B., and M. J. Kozak. 1997. *Mastery of Your Obsessive Compulsive Disorder: Client Workbook*. San Antonio, Tex.: The Psychological Corporation.

Foa, E. B. and R. Wilson. 1991. *Stop Obsessing! How to Overcome Your Obsessions and Compulsions*. New York: Bantam Books

Kozak, M. J., and E. B. Foa. 1997. *Mastery of Your Obsessive Compulsive Disorder*. San Antonio, Tex.: The Psychological Corporation.

Neziroglu, F. and J. A. Yaryura-Tobias. 1991. *Over and Over Again*. Lexington, Mass.: D. C. Heath and Company.

Schwartz, J. M. 1996. *Brainlock: Free Yourself from Obsessive-Compulsive Behavior*. New York: Regan Books.

Steketee, G., and K. White. 1990. *When Once Is Not Enough: Help for Obsessive Compulsives*. Oakland, Calif.: New Harbinger Publications.

Readings for Professionals

Foa, E. B., and M. J. Kozak. 1996. Psychological treatment for obsessive-compulsive disorder. In *Long-term Treatments of Anxiety Disorders*, edited by M. R. Mavissakalian and R. F. Prien. Washington, D.C.: American Psychiatric Press.

Franklin, M. E., and E. B. Foa. 1998. Cognitive-behavioral treatments for obsessive compulsive disorder. In *A Guide to Treatments That Work*, edited by P. E. Nathan and J. M. Gorman. New York: Oxford University Press.

Kozak, M. J., and E. B. Foa. 1996. Obsessive-compulsive disorder. In *Sourcebook of Psychological Treatment Manuals for Adult Disorders*, edited by V. B. Van Hasselt and M. Hersen. New York: Plenum Press.

Kozak, M. J., and E. B. Foa. 1997. *Therapist Guide for Mastery of Your Obsessive Compulsive Disorder*. San Antonio, Tex.: The Psychological Corporation.

Pato, M. T., J. L. Eisen, and K. A. Phillips. 1997. Obsessive-compulsive disorder. In *Psychiatry*, edited by A. Tasman, J. Kay, and J. A. Lieberman. Philadelphia, Pa.: W. B. Saunders Company.

Pigott, T. A., B. Dubbert, F. L'Heureux, S. Canter, and D. L. Murphy. 1996. Pharmacological treatment for obsessive-compulsive disorder. In *Long-Term Treatments of Anxiety Disorders*, edited by M. R. Mavissakalian and R. F. Prien. Washington, D.C.: American Psychiatric Press.

Riggs, D. S., and E. B. Foa. 1993. Obsessive compulsive disorder. In *Clinical Handbook of Psychological Disorders*, 2d ed., edited by D. H. Barlow. New York: Guilford Publications.

Salkovskis, P. M., and J. Kirk. 1997. Obsessive-compulsive disorder. In *Science and Practice of Cognitive Behavior Therapy*, edited by D. M. Clark and C. G. Fairburn. New York: Oxford University Press.

Steketee, G. S. 1993. *Treatment of Obsessive Compulsive Disorder*. New York: Guilford Publications.

Swinson, R. P., M. M. Antony, S. Rachman, and M. A. Richter, eds. 1998. *Obsessive Compulsive Disorder: Theory, Research, and Treatment*. New York: Guilford Publications.

Body Image and Eating Disorders

Self-Help Readings

Cash. T. F. 1997. *The Body Image Workbook: An 8-Step Program for Learning to Like Your Looks*. Oakland, Calif.: New Harbinger Publications.

Cooper, P. J. 1995. *Bulimia Nervosa and Binge Eating: A Guide to Recovery*. London: Robinson.

Fairburn, C. G. 1995. *Overcoming Binge Eating*. New York: Guilford Publications.

Kano, S. 1989. *Making Peace with Food: Freeing Yourself from the Diet/Weight Obsession*. New York: Harper & Row.

Phillips, K. A. 1996. *The Broken Mirror: Understanding and Treating Body Dysmorphic Disorder*. New York: Oxford University Press.

Readings for Professionals

Fairburn, C. G., and G. T. Wilson. 1996. *Binge Eating: Nature, Assessment, and Treatment*. New York: Guilford Publications.

Garner, D. M., and P. E. Garfinkel, eds. 1997. *Handbook of Treatment for Eating Disorders*. New York: Guilford Publications.

References

American Psychiatric Association. 1994. *Diagnostic and Statistical Manual of Mental Disorders* 4th ed. Washington, D.C.:American Psychiatric Association.

Antony, M. M. 1997. Assessment and treatment of social phobia. *Canadian Journal of Psychiatry* 42: 826–834.

Antony, M. M., and D. H. Barlow. 1997. Social and specific phobias. *Psychiatry*, edited by A. Tasman, J. Kay, and J. A. Lieberman. Philadelphia, Pa.: W. B. Saunders Company.

Antony, M. M., C. L. Purdon, V. Huta, and R. P. Swinson. 1998. Dimensions of perfectionism across the anxiety disorders. *Behavioral Research and Therapy* 36:1143–1154.

Barlow, D. H. 1988. *Anxiety and Its Disorders: The Nature and Treatment of Anxiety and Panic.* New York: Guilford Publications.

Barlow, D. H., B. F. Chorpita, and J. Turovsky. 1996. Fear, panic, anxiety, and disorders of emotion. In *Perspectives on Anxiety, Panic, and Fear*, edited by D. A. Hope. The Nebraska Symposium on Motivation 43: 251–328. Lincoln, Nebr.: University of Nebraska Press.

Beck, A. T., A. J. Rush, B. F. Shaw, and G. Emery. 1979. *Cognitive Theory of Depression.* New York: Guilford Publications.

Blatt, S. J., J. P. D'Afflitti, and D. M. Quinlan. 1976. Experiences of depression in normal young adults. *Journal of Abnormal Psychology* 85:383–389.

Bouchard, T. J., D. T. Lykken, M. McGue, N. L. Segal, and A. Tellegen. 1990. Sources of human psychological differences: The Minnesota study of twins reared apart. *Science,* 250:223–228.

Brownell, K. D., and J. Rodin. 1994. The dieting maelstrom: Is it possible and advisable to lose weight? *American Psychologist* 49:781–791.

Burns, D. D. 1980a. *Feeling Good: The New Mood Therapy.* New York: Signet.

Burns, D. D. 1980b. The perfectionist's script for self-defeat. *Psychology Today,* November, 34–57.

Clark, D. A., and C. L. Purdon. 1993. New perspectives of a cognitive theory of obsessions. *Australian Psychologist* 28:161–167.

Crockenberg, S. 1985. Toddler's reactions to maternal anger. *Merrill-Palmer Quarterly* 31:361–373.

Di Nardo, P. A., L. T. Guzy, J. A. Jenkins, R. M. Bak, S. F. Tomasi, and M. Copland. 1988. Etiology and maintenance of dog fears. *Behavior Research and Therapy* 26:241–244.

Dwyer, J. T., J. J. Feldman, C. C. Seltzer, and J. Mayer. 1969. Body image in adolescents: Attitudes toward weight and perception of appearance. *American Journal of Clinical Nutrition* 20:1045–1056.

Ellis, A. 1962. *Reason and Emotion in Psychotherapy*. New York: Lyle Stuart.

———. 1993. Changing rational-emotive therapy (RET) to rational-emotive behavior therapy (REBT). *The Behavior Therapist* 16:257–258.

Ellis, A., and W. Dryden. 1987. *The Practice of Rational-Emotive Therapy*. New York: Springer.

Friedrich-Cofer, L., and A. C. Huston. 1986. Television violence and aggression: The debate continues. *Psychological Bulletin* 100:346–371.

Frost, R. O., and P. Marten. 1990. Perfectionism and evaluative threat. *Cognitive Therapy and Research* 14:559–572

Frost, R. O., P. Marten, C. Lahart, and R. Rosenblate. 1990. The dimensions of perfectionism. *Cognitive Therapy and Research* 14:449–468.

Garner, D. M., P. E. Garfinkel, D. Schwartz, and M. Thompson. 1980. Cultural expectation of thinness in women. *Psychological Reports* 47:483–491.

Heimberg, R. G., H. R. Juster, E. J. Brown, C. Holle, G. S. Makris, A. W. Leung, F. R. Schneier, A. Gitow, and M. R. Liebowitz. 1994. Cognitive-behavioral versus pharmacological treatment of social phobia: Post treatment and follow-up effects. Paper presented at the meeting of the Association for Advancement of Behavior Therapy, San Diego, Calif. November.

Herman, C. P., and J. Polivy. 1984. A boundary model for the regulation of eating. In *Eating and its Disorders*, edited by A. J. Stunkard and E. Stellar. New York: Raven Press.

Hewitt, P. L., and G. L. Flett. 1990. Perfectionism and depression: a multidimensional analysis. *Journal of Social Behavior and Personality* 5:423–438.

———. 1991a. Perfectionism in the self and social contexts: conceptualization, assessment, and association with psychopathology. *Journal of Personality and Social Psychology* 60:456–470.

———. 1991b. Dimensions of perfectionism in unipolar depression. *Journal of Abnormal Psychology* 100:98–101.

———. 1993. Dimensions of perfectionism, daily stress, and depression: A test of a specific vulnerability hypothesis. *Journal of Abnormal Psychology* 102:58–65.

Izard, C. E. 1991. *The Psychology of Emotions*. New York: Plenum Press.

Juster, H. R., R. G. Heimberg, R. O. Frost, C. S. Holt, J. I. Mattia, and K. Faccenda. 1996. Social phobia and perfectionism. *Personality and Individual Differences* 21:403–410.

Kain, K., S. Godfrey, and P. R. Doob. 1994. *Movement Never Lies: An Autobiography*. Toronto, Ontario: McClelland and Stewart.

Kandel, E. R. 1983. From metapsychology to molecular biology: Explorations into the nature of anxiety. *American Journal of Psychiatry* 140:1277–1293.

Kendler, K. S., M. C. Neale, R. C. Kessler, A. C. Heath, and L. J. Eaves. 1992. The genetic epidemiology of phobias in women: The interrelationship of agoraphobia, social phobia, situational phobia, and simple phobia. *Archives of General Psychiatry* 49:273–281.

Kessler R. C., K. A. McGonagle, S. Zhao, C. B. Nelson, M. Hughes, S. Eshleman, H. U. Wittchen, and K. S. Kendler. 1994. Lifetime and 12-month prevalence of DSM-III-R psychiatric disorders in the United States: Results from the National Comorbidity Survey. *Archives of General Psychiatry* 51:8–19.

Keys, A., J. Brozek, A. Henschel, O. Michelson, and H. L. Taylor. 1950. *The Biology of Human Starvation*, Vol. 1. Minneapolis: University of Minnesota Press.

Killen, J. D., C. B. Taylor, M. J. Telch, K. E. Saylor, D. J. Maron, and T. N. Robinson. 1986. Self-induced vomiting and laxative and diuretic use among teenagers: Precursors of the binge-purge syndrome. *Journal of the American Medical Association* 25:1447–1449.

Klerman, G. L., M. M. Weissman, B. J. Rounsaville, and E. S. Chevron. 1984. *Interpersonal Psychotherapy of Depression*. New York: Basic Books.

Lemerise, E. A. and K. A. Dodge. 1993. The development of anger and hostile interactions. In *Handbook of Emotions*, edited by M. Lewis and J. M. Haviland. New York: Guilford Publications.

McCrae, R. R., and P. T. Costa. 1986. Clinical assessment can benefit from recent advances in personality psychology. *American Psychologist* 41:1001–1003.

———. 1990. *Personality in Adulthood*. New York: Guilford Publications.

McKay, M., M. Davis, and P. Fanning. 1995. *Messages: The Communications Skills Book*, 2d ed. Oakland, Calif.: New Harbinger Publications.

Merriam-Webster, Inc. 1993. *Merriam Webster's Collegiate Dictionary*, 10th ed. Springfield, Mass.: Merriam-Webster, Inc.

Nasser, M. 1986. Comparative study of the prevalence of abnormal eating attitudes among Arab female students of both London and Cairo universities. *Psychological Medicine* 16:621–625.

Nurnberger, J. I., and Z. Cooper. 1992. Genetics. In *Handbook of Affective Disorders*, 2d ed, edited by E. S. Paykel. New York: Guilford Publications.

Öst, L. G. 1989. One-session treatment for specific phobias. *Behavior Research and Therapy* 27:1–7.

Plomin, R., H. M. Chipuer, and J. C. Loehlin. 1990. Behavior genetics and personality. In *Handbook of Personality: Theory and Research*, edited by L. A. Pervin. New York: Guilford Publications.

Polivy, J., and C. P. Herman. 1993. Etiology of binge eating: Psychological mechanisms. In *Binge Eating: Nature, Assessment, and Treatment*, edited by C. G. Fairburn and G. T. Wilson. New York: Guilford Publications.

252   *When Perfect Isn't Good Enough*

Rachman, S. 1976. The passing of the two-stage theory of fear and avoidance: fresh possibilities. *Behavior Research and Therapy* 14:125–131.

———. 1977. The conditioning theory of fear-acquisition: a critical examination. *Behavior Research and Therapy* 15:375–387.

———. 1997. A cognitive theory of obsessions. *Behavior Research and Therapy* 35:793–802.

Radke-Yarrow, M. and G. Kochanska. 1990. Anger in young children. In *Psychological and Biological Approaches to Emotion*, edited by N. L. Stein, B. Levinthal, and T. Trabasso. Hillsdale, N.J.:Erlbaum.

Salkovskis, P. 1998. Psychological models of obsessive compulsive disorder. In *Obsessive Compulsive Disorder: Theory, Research, and Treatment*, edited by R. P. Swinson, M. M. Antony, S. Rachman, and M. A. Richter. New York: Guilford Publications.

Salkovskis, P. M., and P. Campbell. 1994. Thought suppression induces intrusion in naturally occurring negative intrusive thoughts. *Behavior Research and Therapy* 32:1–8.

Skre, I., S. Onstad, S. Torgerson, S. Lygren, and E. A. Kriglen. 1993. A twin study of DSM III-R anxiety disorders. *Acta Psychiatrica Scandinavica* 88:85–92.

Stunkard, A., T. Sorensen, and F. Schulsinger. 1980. Use of the Danish adoption register for the study of obesity and thinness. In *The Genetics of Neurological and Psychiatric Disorders*, edited by S. Kety. New York: Raven Press.

Tellegen, A., D. T. Lykken, T. J. Bouchard, K. J. Wilcox, N. L. Segal, and S. Rich. 1988. Personality similarity in twins reared apart and together. *Journal of Personality and Social Psychology* 54:1031–1039.

Trebbe, A. 1979. "Ideal Is Body Beautiful and Clean Cut." *USA Today*, September 15, 1–2.

Trinder, H., and P. M. Salkovskis. 1994. Personally relevant intrusions outside the laboratory: Long-term suppression increases intrusion. *Behavior Research and Therapy* 32:833–842.

Wells, A. 1997. *Cognitive Therapy of Anxiety Disorders: A Practice Manual and Conceptual Guide*. New York: John Wiley and Sons.

Wilson, G. T., C. G. Fairburn, and W. S. Agras. 1997. Cognitive-behavioral therapy for bulimia nervosa. In *Handbook of Treatment for Eating Disorders*, 2d ed., edited by D. M. Garner and P. E. Garfinkel. New York: Guilford Publications.

Wiseman, C. V., J. J. Gray, J. E. Mosimann, and A. H. Ahrens. 1992. Cultural expectations of thinness in women: an update. *International Journal of Eating Disorders* 11:85–89.

Wolpe, J. 1958. *Psychotherapy by Reciprocal Inhibition*. Stanford, Calif.: Stanford University Press.

Wood, W., F. Y. Wong, and J. G. Chachere. 19910 Effects of media violence on viewer's aggression in unconstrained social interaction. *Psychological Bulletin* 109:371–383.

About the Authors

Martin M. Antony, Ph.D., C. Psych., is Associate Professor in the Department of Psychiatry and Behavioural Neurosciences at McMaster University. He is also Chief Psychologist at St. Joseph's Hospital in Hamilton, Ontario. He is actively involved in clinical research in the area of anxiety disorders, teaching and education, and maintains a clinical practice. He received his Ph.D. in clinical psychology from the University at Albany, State University of New York in 1994 and completed his pre-doctoral internship training at the University of Mississippi Medical Center in Jackson, MS. Previously, Dr. Antony was Assistant Professor in the Department of Psychiatry, University of Toronto and staff psychologist in the Anxiety Disorders Clinic, Clarke Institute of Psychiatry. He has published several books, including *Obsessive-Compulsive Disorder: Theory, Research and Treatment*, with Drs. R. Swinson, S. Rachman, and M. Richter, as well as *Mastery of Your Specific Phobia* (patient and therapist manuals) with Drs. Michelle G. Craske and David H. Barlow. He has also published numerous research papers and book chapters in the areas of cognitive behavior therapy, obsessive compulsive disorder, panic disorder, social phobia, and specific phobias. He is actively involved in clinical research in the area of anxiety disorders, teaching and education, and maintains a clinical practice.

Richard P. Swinson, M.D., is Professor and Morgan Firestone Chair of the Department of Psychiatry and Behavioural Neurosciences, Faculty of Health Sciences, McMaster University. He is also Professor in the Department of Psychiatry at the University of Toronto and Psychiatrist in Chief at St. Joseph's Hospital and Hamilton Psychiatric Hospital in Hamilton, Ontario. Previously, he held several appointments at the Clarke Institute of Psychiatry, including Vice President of Medical Affairs, Chief of Medical Staff, and Head of the Anxiety Disorders Clinic. Dr. Swinson is currently chair of the examination board in Psychiatry for the Royal College of Physicians and Surgeons of Canada. He has published approximately 200 scientific papers, book chapters, and reports, mostly on behavior therapy, anxiety disorders, and related topics. In addition, he was a member of the DSM-IV subcommittees for obsessive compulsive disorder and for panic disorder and agoraphobia.

More New Harbinger
Self-Help Titles

HEALING FEAR
New Approaches to Overcoming Anxiety
Therapist Edmund Bourne shares the hard-won wisdom and the healing techniques that helped him overcome his own struggle with anxiety.
Item HFR Paperback, $16.95

WORKING ANGER
Preventing and Resolving Conflict on the Job
A step-by-step program designed to help anyone who has trouble dealing with their own anger or other people's anger at work.
Item WA Paperback, $12.95

BETTER BOUNDARIES
Owning and Treasuring Your Life
If you feel like you have trouble saying no to others, this book can help you establish more effective boundaries.
Item BB Paperback, $15.95

THE DAILY RELAXER
Distills the best of the best to bring together the most effective and popular techniques for learning how to relax.
Item DALY Paperback, $12.95

DON'T TAKE IT PERSONALLY
The Art of Dealing with Rejection
Reveals the power of negative childhood messages and shows how to depersonalize responses and develop a new sense of self-acceptance and self-confidence.
Item DOTA Paperback, $15.95

THOUGHTS & FEELINGS
Taking Control of Your Moods and Your Life
Now in its second edition, the most complete and useful guide to cognitive-behavioral techniques ever written is better than ever.
Item TF2 Paperback, $19.95

Call **toll-free 1-800-748-6273** to order. Have your Visa or Mastercard number ready. Or send a check for the titles you want to New Harbinger Publications, 5674 Shattuck Avenue, Oakland, CA 94609. Include $4.50 for the first book and 75¢ for each additional book to cover shipping and handling. (California residents please include appropriate sales tax.) Allow four to six weeks for delivery.

Prices subject to change without notice.

Some Other
New Harbinger Titles

Surviving Your Borderline Parent, Item 3287 $14.95

When Anger Hurts, second edition, Item 3449 $16.95

Calming Your Anxious Mind, Item 3384 $12.95

Ending the Depression Cycle, Item 3333 $17.95

Your Surviving Spirit, Item 3570 $18.95

Coping with Anxiety, Item 3201 $10.95

The Agoraphobia Workbook, Item 3236 $19.95

Loving the Self-Absorbed, Item 3546 $14.95

Transforming Anger, Item 352X $10.95

Don't Let Your Emotions Run Your Life, Item 3090 $17.95

Why Can't I Ever Be Good Enough, Item 3147 $13.95

Your Depression Map, Item 3007 $19.95

Successful Problem Solving, Item 3023 $17.95

Working with the Self-Absorbed, Item 2922 $14.95

The Procrastination Workbook, Item 2957 $17.95

Coping with Uncertainty, Item 2965 $11.95

The BDD Workbook, Item 2930 $18.95

You, Your Relationship, and Your ADD, Item 299X $17.95

The Stop Walking on Eggshells Workbook, Item 2760 $18.95

Conquer Your Critical Inner Voice, Item 2876 $15.95

The PTSD Workbook, Item 2825 $17.95

Hypnotize Yourself Out of Pain Now!, Item 2809 $14.95

The Depression Workbook, 2nd edition, Item 268X $19.95

Beating the Senior Blues, Item 2728 $17.95

Call **toll free, 1-800-748-6273,** or log on to our online bookstore at **www.newharbinger.com** to order. Have your Visa or Mastercard number ready. Or send a check for the titles you want to New Harbinger Publications, Inc., 5674 Shattuck Ave., Oakland, CA 94609. Include $4.50 for the first book and 75¢ for each additional book, to cover shipping and handling. (California residents please include appropriate sales tax.) Allow two to five weeks for delivery.

Prices subject to change without notice.